■   ■   ■

B O O K

The Philip E. Lilienthal imprint
honors special books
in commemoration of a man whose work
at University of California Press from 1954 to 1979
was marked by dedication to young authors
and to high standards in the field of Asian Studies.
Friends, family, authors, and foundations have together
endowed the Lilienthal Fund, which enables UC Press
to publish under this imprint selected books
in a way that reflects the taste and judgment
of a great and beloved editor.

The publisher gratefully acknowledges the generous support of the Philip E. Lilienthal Asian Studies Endowment Fund of the University of California Press Foundation, which was established by a major gift from Sally Lilienthal.

Tokyo Vernacular

Tokyo Vernacular

Common Spaces, Local Histories, Found Objects

Jordan Sand

UNIVERSITY OF CALIFORNIA PRESS
Berkeley · Los Angeles · London

University of California Press, one of the most
distinguished university presses in the United States,
enriches lives around the world by advancing scholarship
in the humanities, social sciences, and natural sciences. Its
activities are supported by the UC Press Foundation and
by philanthropic contributions from individuals and
institutions. For more information, visit www.ucpress.edu.

University of California Press
Berkeley and Los Angeles, California

University of California Press, Ltd.
London, England

Library of Congress Cataloging-in-Publication Data

Sand, Jordan, 1960–.
  Tokyo vernacular : common spaces, local histories,
found objects / Jordan Sand.
    pages cm
  Includes bibliographical references and index.
  ISBN 978-0-520-27566-9 (cloth : alk. paper)—
  ISBN 978-0-520-28037-3 (pbk. : alk. paper)
    1. Tokyo (Japan)—History—1945–   2. Historic
  preservation—Japan—Tokyo—History—20th
  century.   3. Historic buildings—Conservation and
  restoration—Japan—Tokyo—History—20th
  century.   4. Architecture—Government policy—
  Japan—Tokyo—History—20th century.   I. Title.
  DS896.66.S26   2013
  952'.13504—dc23
                                    2013013266

Manufactured in the United States of America

22 21 20 19 18 17 16 15 14 13
10 9 8 7 6 5 4 3 2 1

In keeping with a commitment to support
environmentally responsible and sustainable printing
practices, UC Press has printed this book on Rolland
Enviro100, a 100% post-consumer fiber paper that is
FSC certified, deinked, processed chlorine-free, and
manufactured with renewable biogas energy. It is
acid-free and EcoLogo certified.

For M, O, and Y

Friendship would seem to hold cities together.

—Aristotle, *Nicomachean Ethics*

Contents

Illustrations

Acknowledgments

This short book took a long time to write. Along the way, it changed from autobiography to anthropology to history.

While I was studying architecture history at Tokyo University in the mid-1980s, I rented a house in Yanaka, not far from the Hongo campus, and became involved in a local preservation movement that had just started in the neighborhood. At the time, I envisioned writing a personal account of life in Yanaka that would describe an old neighborhood confronting redevelopment and my own place in it. My greatest debt from these years is to the editors of the magazine *Yanesen*, who enriched my experience of Tokyo in more ways than I can enumerate, and to whom I dedicate this book. I also benefited from the guidance of Suzuki Hiroyuki at Tokyo University, and from contact with other members of the architecture history programs at Tokyo University and Tokyo University for the Arts.

I left Yanaka and moved to New York in 1988 without writing that book. The idea of an anthropology of public memory in Tokyo took shape after the opening of the Edo-Tokyo Museum in 1993. This led me to write the essay "Monumentalizing the Everyday," which was published in *Critical Asian Studies* in 2001 after going through numerous reviews and iterations. Some reviewers of drafts commented that I seemed to have a chip on my shoulder about the museum. They were right: I had held on to the sentiments of the local preservationist, for whom the past was still alive, and the museum seemed to me to entomb it. Writing and revising that essay required an exorcism of my former self in order to assess the reawakening and reinventing of the city's past from an objective distance. My thanks to Ted Bestor and Alan Tansman, who both encouraged me to write a book on this subject, and to the members of the Edo-Tokyo Forum, staff of the Tokyo Metropolitan Government's Bureau of Citizens and Cultural Affairs, and researchers and curators at the Edo-Tokyo Museum, who listened to my criticisms of that institution and generously opened its archives to me. I also benefited from conversations with Fujimori Terunobu, Jinnai Hidenobu, and Mori Mayumi. In the United States, a series of workshops organized by Annabel Wharton of Duke University and a conference organized by Janell Watson at Virginia Tech gave me the chance to try out ideas on colleagues in a variety of disciplines.

The frame became more explicitly historical after 2005, when I was in residence at Princeton University's Shelby Cullom Davis Center, participating in weekly seminars on the city. These seminars, under the deft and imaginative leadership of Gyan Prakash, together with conversations with other Princeton faculty, Davis fellows, and colleagues at the Institute for Advanced Study, greatly stimulated my thinking on how to place Tokyo's case in global context.

A paper presented at the conference "Contested Spatialities," organized at Harvard by Raja Adal and Ellie Choi in 2008, became the basis for chapter 1.

My research was generously supported by a grant from the National Endowment for the Humanities in 2006 and a Fulbright Fellowship in 2008–2009. I am indebted to Yoshimi Shun'ya for hosting me at Tokyo University in 2008–2009.

Interviews with Takahashi Hiroshi of Total Media, Abe Yukihiro and Yoneyama Isamu at the Edo-Tokyo Museum, Aoki Toshiya at the Matsudo City Museum, Kaneko Atsushi at Parthenon Tama, Ichihashi Yoshinori at the Shōwa Everyday Museum in Kita-Nagoya, and Saotome Katsumoto at the Tokyo Air Raids and War Damage Center deepened my understanding of the contemporary situation of history museums in Japan.

Many people read and responded to versions of the chapters in this book and a yet larger number gave me useful ideas in the context of public forums. I learned from them all. I can now only list the colleagues whose comments remain noted somewhere in my laptop, although I am sure there were others: Noriko Aso, Mark Auslander, Ted Bestor, Kim Brandt, Álex Bueno, Alan Christy, Gregory Clancey,

Sheila Crane, Christian Dimmer, Ted Fowler, Eli Friedlander, Sheldon Garon, Carol Gluck, Peter Gluck, Laura Hein, Andreas Huyssen, Philip Kafalas, Christine Kim, Hoyt Long, Patricia Maclachlan, Tobie Meyer-Fong, Morinobu Shigeki, Narita Ryūichi, Christopher Reed, Wesley Sasaki-Uemura, Satō Kenji, Ellen Schattschneider, Henry Smith, Ravi Sundaram, Ken Surin, Alan Tansman, Gavin Whitelaw, and Winnie Wong.

Sabine Frühstück, Ian Miller, and Julia Adeney Thomas provided incisive readings of the whole manuscript at its final stage.

Reed Malcolm at University of California Press encouraged me, bore with me, and shepherded this project through. Jacqueline Volin and Emily Park improved my prose.

Niikawa Shihoko kept me company.

Jordan Sand
Tokyo, May 2013

Note: Japanese names in this book appear in Japanese order, family name first.

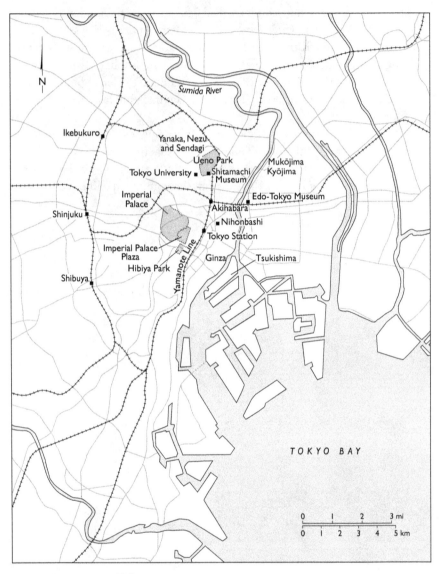

MAP. Contemporary Tokyo.

Introduction

Rediscovering Tokyo's Vernacular

It is usually the detached spectator of the city—the planner or urban geographer or sociologist—who sees it primarily in terms of flux and change: these similes of multiplying cells, of encircling tentacles, of increasing communication loads, of floods and erosion correspond to his notion of the essential urban landscape—a landscape of movement and perpetual aimless growth. But does the city dweller himself understand the city in these terms? Does he want to understand it in these terms? We have our doubts.

—John Brinkerhoff Jackson, "Images of the City" (1961)

THE VERNACULAR AND MONUMENTALITY

The last decades of the twentieth century saw a worldwide efflorescence of public history and preservation. In what Andreas Huyssen has called a "voracious museal culture," vast numbers of new sites and objects came to be identified as historically significant and were set apart for commemoration.[1] The range of meanings sought in the vestiges of the past expanded, too. Politically, preservation took a populist turn, while commercially, heritage became part of a global industry.

Tokyo came late to this trend, ostensibly with little material to preserve. Destroyed and rebuilt repeatedly since its founding, the city by the 1970s retained little in the way of building stock that was more than a generation old. Tokyo had been built of wood and other perishable materials, and U.S. firebombs razed the majority of it in 1945. Well after historic preservation had become a commonplace feature of the culture and economy of major cities in other wealthy countries, Tokyo lacked preservation districts, adaptive reuse projects, preservation architects, or suppliers of recycled or replicated period fittings and materials for old buildings. Physical evidence of the past in the streets of Tokyo was fragmentary and largely unmarked. It rarely possessed market value. Without prized buildings and streetscapes to display the city's past, it seems reasonable to suppose, Tokyo could not be expected to celebrate its history in the way cities elsewhere were doing.

Nevertheless, despite what appeared to be unpromising terrain for historic preservation, in the 1970s and 1980s neighborhood activists, scholars, architects, artists, and writers set about recording and preserving the traces of Tokyo's past, and large audiences responded by searching for the same places and things or consuming them vicariously through books, magazines, museum exhibits, and television programs. In the 1990s, new theme parks, malls, and restaurants capitalized on Tokyo's past. The Tokyo Metropolitan Government began to treat the city's history as one of its greatest assets. A new subway line that opened in 1999 was named the "Great Edo Line," taking the city's former name. Riding a wave of nostalgia for the old city, the film *Always*, which depicted life in an ordinary working-class Tokyo neighborhood in 1958, swept the Japanese Academy Awards in 2006. Thus, by the early years of the new millennium, Tokyo's past, including its quite recent past, had been transformed into a valuable—indeed highly marketable—cultural heritage.

Why and how did this happen? The awakening of heritage consciousness in Tokyo involved no iconic preservation battle around a famous district or building and no significant change in the legal status of landmarks. Municipal and national government came late to the reevaluation of the city's past and provided little protection to historic features of the cityscape. The preservationist turn in Tokyo thus fits poorly into a story of activists persuading authorities to institute legislation and save historic buildings from the wrecking ball. On the other hand, the critical view of heritage as late capitalism's deft co-optation of consumers' sense of deracination and longing for a simpler world fails to explain the motivations of ordinary Tokyo citizens engaged in recovering pieces of the past around them. Something caused Tokyoites to view their city through a new lens and mobilized some of them to research, preserve, and celebrate what they found. This process of the city's historicization needs itself to be historicized, and its movements, actors, audiences, and contexts examined in their specific forms, which, despite the global nature of the phenomenon, are inevitably particular, since every city has its own cultural and political traits.[2]

Every city also has its own vernacular: a language of form, space, and sensation shaped by the local history of habitation. Newcomers encounter a city's vernacular in a torrent of signals demanding interpretation. Occupants, by contrast, apprehend the city's vernacular intuitively, navigating it without needing to bring it to consciousness. The landscape of the vernacular city is a fabric continually being woven. Threads of the past cross with new ones. The individual threads tend to be invisible, except at the margins or in the interstices of the larger pattern. As a generative grammar rather than a fixed tradition, the vernacular incorporates modern buildings and products of mass culture.[3] Yet enduring patterns of land tenure, construction, housing, and commerce developed over generations sustain a readable local idiom. The enduring features of Tokyo's vernacular in the latter half of the twentieth century included small lots, local street grids but no uniform overall street plan, construction in wood, low-rise buildings, dense shopkeeping and petty manufacturing neighborhoods downtown and an uptown originally comprising walled estates with large gardens (most of which were converted to public institutions or subdivided for single-family houses), and a highly developed rail network that limited the need for private automobiles.[4]

As more amateurs and ordinary citizens became engaged in preservation, the objects of their interest were frequently parts of this vernacular city, since the vernacular city connected directly to their lives in a way public monuments did not. In embracing Tokyo's vernacular, preservationists and their audiences rejected the grand scale and abstract symbolism of monuments. Monumental conceptions of nationhood, expressed in architecture, large public spaces, and pageantry that asserted a unity of citizenry and state, were widely viewed with suspicion in non-Communist countries after World War II, particularly in the defeated former Axis powers.[5] Yet it would be hasty to assume that the turn from the monumental to the vernacular that began in Tokyo in the 1970s was a reaction against Japan's fascist past. By this time, the war predated the memories of young Japanese. If anything, the ethic of vernacular urbanism emerged in Japan from a questioning of the *postwar* nation-state. The 1964 Olympics in Tokyo and the 1970 World Exposition in Osaka (both of which were firsts in East Asia), carried forward prewar plans and mobilized citizens for the monumental expression of a supposedly reborn Japan. In mass demonstrations throughout the 1950s, culminating in Anpo 1960, opposition politics took monumental form as well. Although born under an undemocratic regime, the monumental nation thus enjoyed a robust life within postwar democracy.

Preservation in the form it took in late twentieth-century Tokyo belonged to an era in which mass society had rendered the symbolic language of the monumental national public meaningless. In place of symbolism, vernacular preservationists fixed upon basic materiality and what art historian Alois Riegl, in a classic essay, called "age value": the palpable presence of the past's remains.[6] If, as J. B. Jackson suggests, the "detached spectator" is inclined to read the city in terms of abstractions, the engaged inhabitant seeks markers of human presence that can be confirmed at the level of the body and the senses. At this level, the remnants of the vernacular city seemed to speak directly, without recourse to either state symbolism or official expertise.

For many involved in recovering and using Tokyo's past, participation was not explicitly a political gesture. Yet running through all the interpretations of vernacular heritage in the late twentieth century was the ideal of a city constructed and inhabited according to terms other than those dictated by capitalism and state-led development. A spectrum of activities, ranging from writing local histories and preserving buildings to documenting sites in photographs and exhibiting artifacts, championed a vision of Tokyo at variance with developmental agendas for both the city and the nation-state. In place of the politics of the national public, this new vision idealized a commons claimed by urban citizens without official sanction. Uncovering common memories and reappraising familiar landscapes offered a new set of values concerning the space of the city and the rights residents had in it. The local and familiar, the small, the ephemeral, and even the seemingly trivial became values in themselves, placed above any universal political conception. This antimonumentalism reconceived the city around the everyday.

Yet the paradox of cultural heritage is that although it is rooted in the familiar (as indeed the word *heritage* itself gestures toward family inheritance), it acquires significance only when it has begun to appear exotic. In what sociologist Ogino Masaharu has called a "doubling of the world," treating something as heritage opens a gap between the everyday life of the observer and another everyday life, framed as the object of "museological desire"—which Ogino provocatively describes as "the bourgeois desire for the belongings of others."[7] The gap between the familiar and the exotic need not represent an unbridgeable distance. Amid the globalization of culture and the popular valorization of heritage, it has become common for people to experience their own local environments and traditions through the eyes of others. In a media-saturated society, some form of mediation always enters between the everyday as lived time and the everyday as valued heritage. This "doubling of the world" engenders tension between the ideal of common property and the pervasive commodification of that property to gratify "bourgeois desire." But if we recognize late twentieth-century museal culture as encompassing both the aspiration to commonality and the dilemma of culture's commercial exploitation—as part of a vision of urban citizenship outside the frameworks of formal politics and, at the same time, part of a mass mediation of local experience—we may come closer to understanding it in its historical context.

PUBLIC AND PRIVATE IN TOKYO'S SOCIAL TRANSFORMATION

The chapters that follow look at particular historical forms and lineages in the rediscovery of Tokyo's vernacular landscape. This introduction sketches three post-1960s sociopolitical developments that created the conditions for this rediscovery: the fading in Japan of the twin ideals of the democratic national public and nuclear-family privacy; the country's economic growth and the growth of international tourism; and, after 1971, the global dematerialization of wealth. Each of these broad changes altered the physical experience of Tokyo and the politics of property in the city. Together they signaled the end of a modern property regime that had established not only rights in land, but who built the city, how it was regulated, how it was occupied, and what features of the landscape were given cultural and mnemonic value. The more volatile, speculative regime that gradually came to displace the modern regime removed the last vestiges of secure foundation in any notion of tradition, but it offered a fertile environment for making use of the past.

As migrants flowed into Tokyo and other cities in the late 1950s and 1960s to provide the labor for Japan's economic miracle, the national population shifted from a predominantly rural to a predominantly urban one.[8] Most of the urban newcomers sought to climb what housing scholar Hirayama Yōsuke calls the "housing ladder," a standard trajectory from a rented lodging in an old wooden building, to a rented unit in a reinforced concrete residential block on a state-planned suburban estate (*danchi*), and finally to a privately owned single-family suburban home. This trajectory, with several intervening steps, is represented graphically in the imaginary *sugoroku* (a kind of snakes-and-ladders) game board in figure 1, which was printed in the New Year's edition of the newspaper *Asahi shinbun* in 1973.[9] In suburban housing estates and

FIGURE I. The housing ladder depicted as a board game. Illustration by Hisatani Masaki. *Asahi shinbun,* January 1973.

detached houses, a large cohort of middle-class nuclear families characterized by strong social and economic homogeneity accumulated the same appliances in the same years, fulfilling a national ideal of prosperity and contributing to the growth of domestic industries.[10]

Nuclear-household formation, private homeownership, and the accumulation of new consumer durables marked successful middle-class life in urban Japan during the years of high economic growth. They also constituted the private half of the modern property regime, sanctioned and promoted by the state through housing and urban policy, and built and financed by corporate capital. The regime demanded a large, stable, and "domesticated" pool of white-collar labor. Its stereotypical citizen, presumed male, laid claim to a private space theoretically sequestered from the market and from the demands of communities beyond that of the nuclear family. There, in a scenario seen in the centers of twentieth-century capitalism around the world, he stored the wife and children who guaranteed his "reproduction"—the reproduction both of his labor in a daily cycle and of his social status projected forward into the next generation.

The public and private components of the modern property regime were integral to each other.[11] With the memory still fresh of an emperor-centered wartime state that exhorted Japanese subjects to "sacrifice the private" and devote themselves to the nation (*messhi hōkō*), participants in postwar democratic movements fought to protect their private rights as much as to have a voice in national policy.[12] Suburbanization mapped this political ethos spatially. Writing in 1960, at the time of the protests against the U.S.-Japan security treaty that marked the zenith of mass citizen activism, philosopher Kuno Osamu observed that the modern "citizen" (*shimin,* a term that was new in common parlance at the time) was born of the separation of home and workplace. As historian Yasumaru Yoshio notes, the *seikatsusha*—the occupant or protagonist of everyday life—was born of this same separation.[13] The adult male, protected and rejuvenated in the privacy of the nuclear-family home, went into the city not only as a worker for capitalist enterprise but as a national citizen, sharing the public space of a politics that guaranteed the sanctity of the private sphere.[14] Throughout the 1950s, 1960s, and 1970s, the state poured money in the form of low-interest loans into making a nation of homeowners. Meanwhile, as Ueno Chizuko and others have pointed out, "everyday life conservatism" (*seikatsu hogoshugi*)—a position on national political issues based on the determination to keep state police power and the military demands of the U.S. alliance from infringing on the sovereignty of the private sphere—formed a strong basis for citizen activism from the late 1950s onward.[15] Thus, the normalization of the nuclear-family household and private homeownership shored up both the state, in its cultivation of a compliant labor force for economic development, and the forces of national democratic protest against the state's military and diplomatic policy.

Some journalists and intellectuals in the 1960s took a cynical view of what they called "my-homeism," by which they meant the salaried male worker's petit bourgeois attachment to his suburban home at the cost of homosocial bonds built around the office and the pub.[16] Marxist feminists subsequently articulated a sharp critique of this bourgeois regime founded on the segregation of two gendered spheres. Yet, in spite of these negative representations, large numbers of new households climbed the housing ladder and followed the urban-suburban trajectory, showing the powerful attraction of the private space guaranteed by a suburban home in the quarter century after World War II.

By the mid-1970s, the "my-home" ideal had lost its luster. Prosperity brought rising expectations, and urban sprawl brought falling returns. The national housing authority began reducing the number of rental *danchi* units it built in 1971, as this intermediate step on the ladder ceased to hold the aura of the modern that it had possessed in the decades before.[17] The housing market was glutted by 1975.[18] The volume of housing loans continued to expand exponentially through the 1970s, as mortgages replaced cash payments.[19] Yet what people acquired was farther away from center city, resulting in longer commutes and placing most suburbanites in districts where they had no social ties.[20] Thus, as ever-growing numbers of urban Japanese sought private homeownership into the 1980s, the frustrations and inadequacies of this model of urban living came to be felt more keenly.

Meanwhile, the architectural avant-garde had offered a different model of urban living as early as 1960, when the Metabolists, a group made up mostly of students trained by Tange Kenzō at Tokyo University, published their manifesto, "Metabolism: Proposals for a New Urbanism," which was distributed on the occasion of the World Design Conference held in Tokyo. The Metabolists' sketches of futuristic cities circulated widely overseas and were republished in Japan repeatedly throughout the 1960s. Metabolist architects were given the opportunity to demonstrate their concept at Expo '70, with pavilions designed under Tange's direction. They envisioned urbanites of the future living in high-rise megastructures into which each occupant would plug a dwelling capsule or cluster of capsules. Metabolist architect Kurokawa Noriaki called the hypothetical occupant of the Metabolist city *Homo movens*. Reflecting the increasing rootlessness of contemporary society, the capsule dweller was autonomous and itinerant.[21] This individualist—and implicitly masculinist—image of the future citizen, unbound by family or local community, conformed readily to the self-image of the male youth who dominated the campuses and the political protest movements of the 1960s. In high modernist manner, Metabolist plans assumed the city could be rebuilt from a tabula rasa condition and that the architect would play the role of master planner. Unlike the urbanism of European modernists, however, the Metabolist conception of the city assumed continual, organic, and irregular growth. Metabolism thus took the chaotic mutability of the Tokyo built environment, which had been seen as a deficit, and turned it into an asset. At the same time, it modeled a society of atomized individuals or households and a mono-lithic state (in the guise of the invisible builder), in which private and public were mutually constitutive but sharply delineated, without medi-ating spaces or institutions.[22]

According to geographer Matsubara Hiroshi, the aggregate trend in Tokyo construction shifted around 1974 from horizontal sprawl of single-family housing on the periphery to vertical growth of office build-ings and apartments in the central districts. The vast migration to the capital that had accompanied high economic growth had ended by this time, new nuclear-household formation had peaked, and the dream of private homeownership had become a reality for the majority of those new households.[23] Beginning in the mid-1970s, speculative construction replaced building to order in suburban housing, and large real estate corporations began spending more on advertising in order to market suburban neighborhoods by image.[24] Meanwhile, concrete apartment buildings of single-room units (known as *wan-rūmu manshon,* "one-room mansions") began to appear in the central wards of the city. By 1983, single rooms constituted a quarter of the new units built.[25] Devel-opment of the city had raced ahead, driven increasingly by corporate capital and leaving the visionary urban designs of elite architects to live on only in paper form.

The early 1970s also saw the failure of radical politics and dwindling participation in mass rallies.[26] One of the symbolic marks of this political watershed in Tokyo was a physical evacuation of public space in 1969: the police removal of anti–Vietnam War activists from the Shinjuku Sta-tion West Exit Plaza, described in chapter 1. It is common to claim that since the 1970s, cities in advanced capitalist countries have ceased to be sites of political struggle.[27] Japanese journalists and intellectuals often speak of the 1960s in Japan as the "season of politics" (*seiji no kisetsu*), rendering the subsequent decades apolitical by implication. This inter-pretation depends, however, on a narrow definition of politics in terms of national issues and universalist political doctrines. If politics is under-stood generally as the collective mobilization of interest, it is clear that political activism continued to flourish and evolve in Japan in the years after 1969, albeit in different spaces and less radical forms.[28]

After the collapse of the utopian visions of radical politics and the failure of the mass mobilizations of the 1960s, new types of claims emerged beyond the claim of national citizens to public space. Japanese citizen mobilizations shifted from the politics of the nation-state in the 1960s to local quality-of-life issues in the 1970s, and from organized politics based on stable locality in the 1970s to formal and informal networks of people with personal claims of a more diffuse, affective nature in the 1980s.[29] These changes all expressed themselves in spatial and physical terms. The antitreaty protests of 1960 took the form of well-organized marches and "snake dancing" around the National Diet Building, site and symbol of Japan's parliamentary democracy. Student movement leaders in 1968 tried to keep alive the tactic of appropriating public space by creating "liberated zones" (kaihōku) at strategic locations such as the gates of universities. The police crackdown on the student movements and the forced evacuation of Shinjuku West Exit Plaza cleared the campuses and streets of these occupations of public space. In the 1970s, the most conspicuous urban mobilizations were led by groups at the municipal or local level (often started by housewives) against U.S. military bases, polluting factories, and high-rise buildings that damaged the quality of life in residential neighborhoods.

The preservationism that came to flourish in the 1980s in the wake of these environmental battles was part of a struggle over both objects of local meaning and representations of locality. More Japanese in the 1980s were assembling around physical places than around political ideals, preferring to speak out as patrons of a favorite shop or as admirers of a vista rather than as national citizens, and asserting themselves through aesthetic choices rather than through claims of universal rights. Claims made for particular places and objects of memory were more personal—yet at the same time, in contrast to single-issue residents' movements, they were tied to propositions about the city as a whole, situated in larger national or global cultural contexts.

The closure of the national public sphere and the nuclear-family private sphere as spaces of utopian hope thus permitted new spaces to open in between. The mass politics of the public and the intimate phenomenology of the private were brought together in mobilizations for the small common spaces of local community. Organized claims to the streets in the name of direct enfranchisement gave way to exploration of new ways of claiming the streets on aesthetic as much as social and political grounds. And the pursuit of a standardized, modern material life (seikatsu) embodied in new consumer durables—together with the suspicion of materialism that had always shadowed this pursuit—found sublimation in the revival of vestiges from the everyday past. Eventually, postindustrial mass society's insatiable mining for auratic artifacts and sites of memory led the culture of preservationism back to the very same houses and consumer durables that barely a generation earlier had embodied a bright future—now conceived instead as evocations of a fond past.[30]

WEALTH AND URBAN COMPARISON

As jet travel became a mass phenomenon, global competition among cities as destinations engendered efforts to promote local cultural distinctiveness.[31] Architectural preservation played a role in this. Yet the growth of a historicist aesthetic was entwined with how residents saw their own cities as well with the tastes of tourists. In Tokyo's case, as elsewhere, wealth and leisure provided the conditions for preservation activism. Just as the luxury of choice and comparison encourages tourists to seek out local difference, the historicization of everyday life depended on local audiences with the luxury to see the urban spaces and objects around them aesthetically, detached from the question of their practical necessity.

The national economy had moved into a new phase in the late 1970s, with conspicuous results for the landscape of the capital region. In the period from 1976 to 1980, Japanese manufacturing firms showed a net internal surplus, holding more funds than they had invested, for the first time in postwar history. This encouraged them to invest overseas, spend more on research and development, and speculate in land and stocks. Pressure from the United States to curtail exports provided another push for Japanese manufacturers to move operations offshore. Meanwhile, the weight of manufacturing within Japan was shifting toward microtechnology. By 1982, Japan boasted two of the top five semiconductor makers in the world. By 1986, Japanese firms held the top three positions.[32] As manufacturers moved production overseas, heavy industry became a less visible part of the domestic urban landscape. More Tokyoites donned suits and "office-lady" uniforms, commuted to bright new office blocks, and went out at night in commercial districts like the western Tokyo hubs of Shinjuku and Shibuya, where high-rise buildings housing restaurant and boutique complexes were covered with electronic signage and moving-image billboards. As tourism, film, and photography spread images of these spectacular consumption centers to the rest of the world, Tokyo, whose name had been synonymous with urban industrial pollution in 1970, became an archetype of the postindustrial city.[33]

Rise in the value of the yen precipitated by the floating of the dollar in the early 1970s made it easier for Japanese to visit the United States and Europe, effectively launching Japan's postwar overseas tourism industry. The number of Japanese going abroad annually more than doubled between 1972 and 1979 (from 1,392,000 to 4,038,000) and more than doubled again between 1979 and 1988 (from 4,038,000 to 8,427,000).[34] Concurrently, as heavy industry moved away from Tokyo and the city became cleaner in the late 1970s and early 1980s, it also became a popular destination for foreign tourists. Tokyo residents in the 1980s thus lived in a city that was culturally located on the map of global leisure in a way it had not been before, and that was positioned as much in relation to other cities in the world as to other places in Japan. While some Japanese pundits continued to hold up the standard of Paris or New York for comparisons unfavorable to their own capital, what was now called the "Asianness" of Tokyo—meaning its crowds, its lack of monumentality, and its profusion of irregular and unplanned spaces—became a popular theme in writing on the city, and was seen now as part of its appeal.[35]

THE DEMATERIALIZATION OF WEALTH

The floating of world currencies after 1971 opened the way for private investors to gamble on them at precisely the time that digitization and the growth of electronic communications were erasing the distances among markets. In the early 1970s, computer networks, new financial instruments, and new methods of calculation began transforming finance into a world-enveloping instantaneous betting machine. The financial system that emerged operated not only across national borders but divorced from any necessary relation to specific material commodities or sites of production.[36]

The consequences of this for the landscapes of cities were manifold yet indirect. Dematerialization of wealth accelerated the already visible departure of industry from certain core cities in the world economy, streamlining the urban hierarchy around financial centers.[37] By 1990, New York's largest export was wastepaper.[38] Trade in abstractions (the masses of ephemeral data presumably printed on that wastepaper), rather than in material commodities, was what now made New York a core city in the world economy. New building construction in the core "global cities" served an international class of businesspeople and tourists demanding high-tech offices, condominiums, and mega-hotels.

Industrial-era buildings, particularly in ports rendered functionless by the technology of shipping containers, were demolished or converted into leisure facilities.

In Tokyo, these changes in the world economy were not felt fully until the real estate bubble that followed deregulation in the early 1980s and the forced revaluation of the yen in the Plaza Accords of 1985. Having experienced rapid in-migration, continued growth of light industry, and low-rise construction throughout the 1950s and 1960s and into the 1970s, Tokyo as a whole entered the period of deindustrialization and speculation in a different condition from cities like New York. The high-tech transformation that began in the 1970s and accelerated in the 1980s took place in only certain parts of the city. The city's old downtown persisted in Shitamachi, a loosely defined area of commercial and industrial neighborhoods that retained traces of the traditional social and physical geography, in which the front streets were dominated by owner-occupied retail shops and workshops and the back streets were lined with wood-built rental housing. Although most of Shitamachi had been destroyed in the firebombing of 1945, the rows of tightly packed houses had been rebuilt in much the same form, and pockets of prewar shops and housing had survived. By late in the twentieth century, many streets in Shitamachi looked mildly dilapidated, but they were occupied by a stable—albeit aging—population, and they retained some of their industrial-era functions. Statistics on the city's employment structure reflected this. In 1986, more than one-fifth of employed Tokyo residents worked in manufacturing. Nearly half (46 percent) of the factories where they worked employed only one to three people.[39]

Like major cities in other capitalist countries, Tokyo was what Harvey Molotch has called a "growth machine": all elites involved in the city's planning agreed that its primary function was to generate wealth.[40] But in Tokyo's case, a national government whose mission was to manage and sustain the country's economic development played the central role in this growth coalition. Tokyo thus served as both corporate-bureaucratic headquarters for Japanese capitalism and showpiece of state-led modernization. The stark opposition between this national status and the small scale and fragility of surviving industrial and preindustrial streetscapes set the contrast between the new city and the vestiges of the old in sharper relief.

In 1983, under pressure from the United States to increase imports, Prime Minister Nakasone Yasuhiro initiated a series of measures to privatize public assets, deregulate private-sector investment in urban redevelopment, and increase the national capacity to consume new goods (the policy term of the time was *naiju kakudai,* "expanding domestic demand"). Collectively, these measures were called *minkatsu,* an abbreviation meaning "stimulating the private sector." *Minkatsu* policy began to affect Tokyo when Nakasone proposed in July 1983 that building-volume limits be raised throughout the city to permit high-rise growth. Since zoning was under municipal rather than national authority, this did not go directly into effect, but the prime minister's statements spurred real estate speculation by encouraging projections of wholesale redevelopment of districts zoned for low-rise residences and small shops into districts of mid- and high-rise apartments and commercial buildings. Real estate speculation itself functioned as a powerful dematerializing force, since it severed the tangible and visible ties that had existed between residence, wealth in land, and social status within local society. Other urban development measures under the name of *minkatsu* included ending rent control on houses built before 1946, a move that targeted both old houses and the old people who usually occupied them.[41] In early 1984, Nakasone announced plans to sell large tracts of public land as part of the privatization of the Japan National Railroads (JNR), along with other public monopolies. The JNR was eventually dissolved at the beginning of 1987. In the interim, speculation had raised the value of lots around old JNR sites severalfold.[42]

The fourth Comprehensive National Development Plan (or Zensō), drafted in 1986 and issued in 1987, projected—and thereby helped promote—increased concentration of economic functions in the Tokyo region. It also emphasized the need to rebuild the capital to better accommodate the international financial elite. This position was echoed in the long-term plan issued by the Tokyo Metropolitan Government (TMG) in 1986.[43] By creating an environment for large-scale urban redevelopment in Tokyo, the Nakasone administration and allies in the TMG hoped to simultaneously assuage the United States and solve the apparent space problem created by the demand of foreign companies for offices in Tokyo, with the triumphant outcome that Tokyo would become the next global financial center.

Increasing domestic demand, the other ingredient of this program, was a problem of changing not just consumption habits but lifestyles, which in turn would influence property in land, buildings, and their contents. The goals of postwar economic growth policies having been achieved by the early 1970s, most urban Japanese already possessed all the consumer durables they had room for. Further consumption growth, an economic white paper stated in 1983, could come only from increasing the capacity of Japanese houses. In this state- and capital-driven argument, houses were containers for commodities, and international politics required that the country import more commodities; therefore, houses would have to be rebuilt.[44] Naturally this militated against placing value in either old houses or old belongings, which had to make way for the new in order to cope with overproduction on both sides of the Pacific and keep the strategic relationship afloat.

Like the dollar shock of 1971, the critical phase of the economic bubble that followed *minkatsu* was triggered by U.S. financial strategy. On September 22, 1985, at the Plaza Hotel in New York, representatives of the so-called G5 nations reached agreement on a series of measures to push up the value of the yen against the dollar in order to reduce American trade deficits. This meeting precipitated a crisis from which Japan's economy would still be struggling to recover more than twenty years later. The manipulations of the Ministry of Finance had sheltered Japan from the effects of international financial markets for a decade and a half; the Plaza Accords compelled the country now to enter global exchange on American terms.

Markets reacted dramatically to the announcement from New York. The dollar went into a free fall against the yen that would continue until late 1987, when it settled at slightly over half its 1985 value. Tokyo shops filled with imported luxury goods that had suddenly been rendered cheap by the high yen. Fearing the impact on domestic manufacturers, the Bank of Japan reduced interest rates steadily in 1986 and 1987 until they reached 2.5 percent; then, under U.S. pressure, the bank held them there for the next two years. Companies and individuals took advantage of the easy credit by going on a speculating spree that sent the stock and real estate markets soaring.[45]

Central Tokyo land values had already been rising by double-digit percentages annually since 1983. They nearly tripled from 1986 to 1987.[46] With the exception of a brief downturn during the oil crisis of 1975, Japanese urban land values had increased every year since World War II, which gave Tokyo real estate the appearance of the perfect no-risk investment.[47] Now foreign firms were clamoring for office space, and the government was moving to eliminate land-use restrictions and height limits. But not deep beneath the surface of market calculation lay the most fundamental of many myths of native uniqueness prevalent at the time: that the turf of the archipelago itself was somehow different from elsewhere, so beyond rational calculation that it did not obey market rules. Just as imperialist promoters of Manchurian lebensraum in the 1930s had believed that Japan was in crisis because the archipelago could not accommodate its population, many Japanese investors in the 1980s believed that land would always appreciate simply because Japan was—to use the common phrase—a "small island nation."

The terms "efficient use" (*yūkō riyō*) and "high use" (*kōdo riyō*) provided a powerful rhetoric for urban land policy during the economic bubble. As Reiko Evans and Ōno Teruyuki have noted, these terms signified a vaguely defined aspiration rather than a clear policy, despite their wide use by national bureaucrats, business leaders, and journalists. The Ministry of Construction had disseminated the term "high use" in a 1983 land policy document. The Mitsubishi Corporation, which held a large portion of the commercial lots around Tokyo Station, proposed a sixty-tower redevelopment plan for the area called the "Manhattan Plan" in 1988, touting it as a realization of the directive for "efficient use." In the overheated market environment of the time, Mitsubishi's plan plainly sought to make a public virtue of the company's ambitions to profit on potential future demand for office space, masking a speculative venture as a form of urban rationalization.[48] Beginning in 1986, the same language also began to surface in the courtroom, where for the first time the economic merits of an owner's plans for a plot of land were considered as legitimate cause to warrant termination of a lease against the wishes of the lessee. Legal experts criticized this decision as confusing public and private law, but "efficient use" was nevertheless recognized as deserving deference in several legal cases during the late 1980s.[49]

From 1983 to 1986, the first three years of Nakasone's *minkatsu* policy, 30 percent of central Tokyo land passed from the hands of individuals to corporations. In the same period, the majority of new construction in Tokyo as a whole shifted from wood to concrete and steel, making the dominant aspect of the city increasingly one of inorganic materials. Tokyo housing shifted from single-family dwellings to multiunit apartment buildings in precisely the same years (see graphs in figure 2).

Suzuki Shun'ichi, Tokyo's governor from 1979 to 1994, was the consummate manager for the capital city as "growth machine" of a developmental state. A loyal politician of the ruling Liberal Democratic Party, Suzuki had begun his career during the war years in the Home

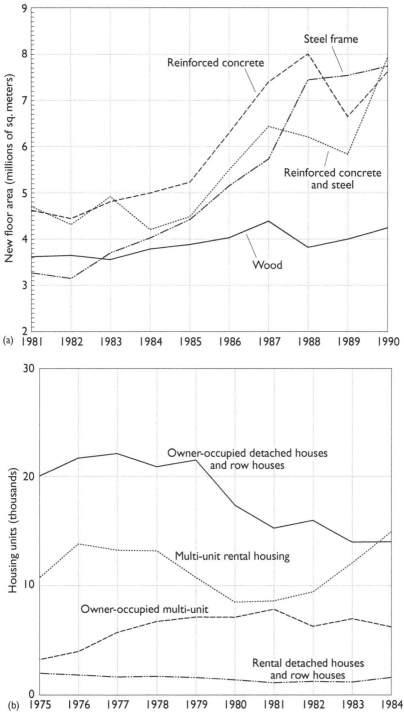

FIGURE 2. (a, *above*) Tokyo building starts by building material, 1981–1990; (b, *below*) new housing construction in the Tokyo metropolitan region, 1975–1984. Adapted from *Tōkyōto kenchiku tōkei nenpyō.*

Ministry. He came to the governor's office on a promise to balance the city budget after the tumultuous era of reformist governor Minobe Ryōkichi. In addition to financial acumen, Suzuki had a long track record in the business of staging state spectacles. He was lieutenant governor during the Tokyo Olympics, which he was largely responsible for overseeing. From 1967 to 1970, he served as secretary general in charge of Expo '70.[50] His administration as Tokyo governor continued in the pattern of these earlier roles, characterized by slogans for broad, vaguely defined campaigns ("My Town Tokyo," "Tokyo Renaissance," "World City Tokyo," and "Tokyo Frontier") and by construction projects that sought to produce architectural icons for national and global consumption (what critics called *hakomono gyōsei,* or "box-building government"). The Tokyo City Hall building, completed in 1991, the Edo-Tokyo Museum, completed in 1993, and the sprawling new business and leisure developments on landfill in Tokyo Bay (planned originally in conjunction with a World Cities Exposition that was canceled after Suzuki lost reelection in 1994) represented the crowning accomplishments in a career of spectacles and monuments. When local identity emerged as a cultural value in the 1980s, it was recognized within Suzuki's political vision only as it served the marketability of the national capital.

THE PRODUCTION OF LOCALITY

Around 1986, the Suzuki administration's favored slogan shifted from "My Town Tokyo" to "World City Tokyo." Although Tokyo's politicians did not know it at the time, the real estate bubble was inflating rapidly around them. Prices seemed justified by the high demand from foreign firms for office space. Suzuki's new slogan reflected the national government's gamble and the governor's own faith that this demand would continue to expand indefinitely, while what was widely believed to be a superior native form of capitalism brought about the transfer of global hegemony to Japan. Thus the promise of "My Town Tokyo"—evoking a city that, despite its size, could be the object of citizens' affections—was supplanted by a promise that Tokyo would now be a global magnet for visitors and investors, physical proof of Japan's new status as superpower.[51]

For all the superficiality of this language of municipal boosterism, the tension between the phrases "my town" and "world city" reflected a real dilemma for late twentieth-century Tokyo culture. Was it possible for locality to be asserted in ways that were not subsumable to the nation or configured by a global market in cultural goods? Just as the municipal agenda for Tokyo remained inseparable from national politics, local discourses and sites would repeatedly be swallowed into the nation by mass media, state institutions, and the market—sometimes as a result of the naïve or conscious rhetoric of the champions of locality themselves.[52]

As Frederic Jameson has observed, in postindustrial society the spheres of culture and economy fused. Global financial speculation and the burgeoning of tourism into the world's largest industry brought about a condition in which culture, high or low, no longer existed as an autonomous sphere. Local culture became the raw material of capitalism and of national political agendas. In Japan, public investment in producing locality began first in regional government offices outside Tokyo, where under the rubric of "cultural administration" (*bunka gyōsei*) a new branch of government developed in the 1970s, concerned with creating or enhancing local identity in order to attract tourists, heighten native-place pride, and make the public face of government appear more friendly to residents.

The local articulated tightly with the national in this trend. Intellectuals advocating a rebalance of relations between the central government and the prefectures and municipalities supported what was popularly called the "Era of Regionalism" (Chihō no jidai). The same rhetoric was adopted by Prime Minister Ōhira Masayoshi in a campaign called the Garden Cities Plan, which promised to promote the individuality of each region (*chiiki no kosei*). Ōhira's plan was in turn absorbed into the national vision of an "Era of Culture" (Bunka no jidai), laid out in detail by an advisory group to the prime minister in a report published in 1980. Ōhira's brain trust proclaimed that Japan's modernization was complete and called for the forging of a new "comprehensive Japanese culture" no longer dependent on Western models.[53] Local initiatives were thus seamlessly incorporated into the promotion of national culture.

Although the new focus on local culture could thus appear artificially manufactured by the state, it is unlikely that it felt that way to many of those involved at the local level. More individuals in Japan's postindustrial economy after 1970 were engaged in what Michael Hardt and Antonio Negri call "affective labor"—jobs in services and professions that shape consumers' emotional experience—relating them more closely to cultural production than in the industrial era, when the majority of workers manufactured material goods.[54] For the growing population working in some connection to the production of consumer experience, the idea of local character, like corporate identity, made natural sense, even if it followed common formulae diffused nationwide. Moreover, cultural administration drew on long intellectual traditions in Japan built around folklore and folk craft, both of which privileged the everyday and the local while absorbing them into discourses of the Japanese nation.[55]

In 1980, the Tokyo Metropolitan Government created a new office called the Bureau of Everyday Life Culture (Seikatsu Bunkakyoku).[56] The subsequent growth of cultural administration in Tokyo moved in close parallel to the expansion of the bubble economy. The TMG had limited resources to cope with the crisis engendered by real estate speculation combined with national government policies that concentrated capital and administrative functions in the Tokyo region. Unable to change national policy and with little desire to reverse economic trends, TMG bureaucrats turned instead to the convivial rhetoric of fostering the "warmth" and "humanity" in local culture.[57]

Shitamachi by the 1980s had become the site of frequent evocations of the city's vernacular past and local character. Tokyo's new suburbs—made up of bedroom towns serviced by highway-side supermarkets, chain restaurants, and convenience stores—provided a sharp contrast to Shitamachi's streets of owner-occupied shops and back alleys of wooden tenements, which embodied the coherence of stable habitation, architecture, and community.[58] For adult residents of the new suburbs, Shitamachi had the appeal of a more authentic, indigenous urbanism.[59] For young people who had grown up in the suburbs, it was also simply exotic. Yet thanks to national media, the nostalgic perception of Shitamachi was readily shared by nonresidents and residents alike, irrespective of age. Popular films and television programs in a lineage reaching back to the prewar "theater of commoners" (shomingeki) idealized the everyday lives of working-class and petit bourgeois households, and were often set in Shitamachi. The long-running film series It's Tough Being a Man (Otoko wa tsurai yo, 1969–1995), which starred Atsumi Kiyoshi as "Tora-san," showed intimate neighborly relations around a Shitamachi dumpling shop. By the time the series came to an end in 1995, Tora-san had become a revered national institution. As Richard Torrance has shown, the films' clever plots and dialogue are better read as subtle social satire than as nostalgia, but their popularity nevertheless built on nostalgia for the setting and the kind of family and neighborhood life they portrayed.[60] The location of the series in Shibamata, on Tokyo's eastern periphery, made the district into a new archetype of Shitamachi for the national audience.

This shared reinvention of Shitamachi generated new projects and enterprises within particular districts and at the level of the city as a whole. Although few buildings were given official protection, municipal government, merchants' associations, and popular magazines nurtured neighborhood revivals and a tourist industry built around literary landmarks, surviving shops selling traditional products, and anything that could be used to evoke the atmosphere of the old downtown.[61]

Preservation in this milieu undergirded and defined locality, a value particularly difficult to sustain in the bubble years, and one that advocates were involved in both creating and consuming. This was true regardless of whether their investments had the character of resistance to or collaboration with national agendas and the commodification of the past. In its new uses in Tokyo and elsewhere, the past existed to generate difference, producing the exoticism upon which local identities and the local appeal of cities depended. It was to be preserved neither as a record of progress nor as a tragic memento mori of the world's irreversible decay, but as a heterotopia, an otherness in the midst of the contemporary world.[62]

USES OF THE PAST AND USABLE PASTS

A robust frame already existed for Tokyo's historical past, even though it had left few visible signs in the streetscape. This was the modern city's precursor, Edo: castle town and capital of the Tokugawa shogunate from 1600 to 1868. Edo had become a site of nostalgic return as early as the 1880s, when a group of former Tokugawa officials formed the Edokai (Edo Society) and began publishing a journal of reminiscences and chronicles of the old regime's last years. Nostalgic writers in the early twentieth century retreated to the culture and literature of Edo, which they idealized as the antithesis to a deracinated and aesthetically vulgar modernity. This corpus of antiquarian historiography and literary nostalgia provided inspiration to the populist cultural history that emerged in the 1970s as Edo studies (*Edogaku*).[63] By this time, however, students of Edo no longer had a personal link to members of the official and literary circles of the old capital, whose writing had become exotic to them.[64]

This exoticism, together with the democratic populist sensibilities of the postwar generation, led Edo studies toward a stronger interest in the scenes and habits of everyday life in the old city, which, unlike literary traditions, were immediately accessible through material things. As Edo studies became Edo-Tokyo studies in the 1980s by incorporating study of the modern period, Edo came to be conceived increasingly as the space of an alternative everyday life. As Augustin Berque writes, Edo-Tokyo studies emphasized two ideas: first, that "the space of Tokyo has remained in some way irreducible to what modern Westernization has foisted upon it," and second, that "far from being merely premodern, even before the Meiji era that space possessed, and still possesses, qualities proper to postmodernity."[65] The reinvented Edo of the 1980s served as a utopian antithesis to a frenetic and globalized contemporary Tokyo, but ironically it also appeared sometimes as a mirror of the postindustrial consumption capital that Tokyo had become.

Because mass-mediated modernity and constant traffic between the capital and other regions of Japan assured that much of the imagery of the local past could readily be felt as part of a common national past, Edo-Tokyo revivals always stood at risk of being exploited in support of redemptive narratives of the nation. However, the legacy of the older personal and belletristic nostalgia—sometimes referred to as "fair-weather clog" (hiyorigeta) nostalgia, after the title of Nagai Kafū's classic 1915 work in the genre—persisted in an attitude toward the city's past characterized by a determined localism. The very specificity of recalling a particular neighborhood, alleyway, or old shop that some literary figure of the past had once frequented positioned the author and the work outside narratives of the nation. These local nostalgias, tied to particular places rather than to the ideological fusion of blood and soil, were thus free from the demand to find redemption in the past, free to dwell in reflection—and, it should be said, free also to be cultivated in idle uselessness.[66]

For the literary imagination, the city could be an accumulation of memories, in Walter Benjamin's sense, but the material frame of Tokyo's architecture militated against this sensibility in everyday life. Even before destruction in 1923 and 1945, frequent fires had prevented the city from accumulating a stock of buildings that might transmit intergenerational memory. Front-street shops were built more sturdily starting in the nineteenth century, but it was not until these began to be replaced by reinforced concrete and steel structures that they came to be regarded as a significant heritage—and even then, few were preserved, since land values greatly exceeded the value of the buildings. Many of the buildings that had survived firebombing were destroyed during redevelopment in preparation for the 1964 Olympics.[67] National building codes and successive municipal administrations promoted Tokyo's reconstruction from a city of two- and three-story wooden structures to one of multistory reinforced concrete structures in the 1970s and 1980s, leaving only scattered pieces of the old streetscape intact. Because of the fragmentary nature of what remained, expansion of the range of Tokyo's usable pasts and their modes of use from the realms of textual history and literature to the study and celebration of material traces depended no less on work of the imagination. Vernacular preservationism signified the concrete mobilization of historical imagination in the cultural politics of the city.

This book looks at four sites for the mobilization of the vernacular past in Tokyo since the 1960s: the public square, the neighborhood, the street, and the museum. Each of these also represents a field of activity and a set of propositions about the city. Chapter 1 tells a story about the national public and the public square that serves as a kind of myth of origin for the everyday city. The expulsion of protesters from Shinjuku Station's West Exit Plaza in 1969 symbolically marks the end of monumental public space as a useful site of urban citizenship in Tokyo and begins a period of wandering in search of new sites of resistance. Chapter 2 moves down in scale from the citywide question of public and commons to the subject of local community. I look at the growth of historical consciousness and preservation activism in old downtown neighborhoods, focusing specifically on a district where local community was invented anew from the material of the past. This invention of local community illustrates how the crisis of the real estate bubble catalyzed new thinking about city living. At the same time, it shows the extent to which the identity of a place is spoken and written into existence. The protagonists in chapter 3 are an eclectic group of scholars, artists, and popular writers who called themselves the Street Observation Studies Society (Rojō Kansatsu Gakkai). The street observationists scoured Tokyo and other cities for marks of the past at a yet-smaller scale, documenting traces that revealed the imprint of people's hands and of nature in making the urban streetscape, often in subtle and quixotic ways. Among Tokyo preservationists, the Street Observation Studies Society had the greatest investment in the palimpsestic character of the everyday city. The street observationists' aesthetic vision recalls the writing of Walter Benjamin and other theorists of the urban fragment, and the objects they selected invite comparison to found art, but they put their energy into a praxis of walking, photographing, and labeling rather than the creation of a theoretical or artistic oeuvre. Their method was easily imitated, giving street observation, despite its eccentric surrealist style, the character of a popular movement. In chapter 4, I turn to historical exhibits of everyday life in museums, including the Edo-Tokyo Museum, an icon of bubble-era architecture and Tokyo's newfound historicism. Here I trace the trajectories of surviving fragments taken out of circulation and used to narrate the past, together with reconstructions of the city's past as a lifeworld counterposed to the city of the present. The Edo-Tokyo Museum and other everyday life museums and exhibits designed in the 1980s proved to be the starting point of a sweeping transformation in the function of museums as sites of memory in Japan. The shape of the new museology, one more tied to personal experience and nostalgia, became clearer in public museum projects and commercial theme parks in the 1990s. Its full political implications only began to emerge in the first decade of the twenty-first century.

Each of these four sites connects to issues of urban property and the basis of claims that residents make to it. The history of ideals of the public square and the commons reveals city residents testing the spatial and legal boundaries of the modern property regime; the continuity of local community, physically embodied in the neighborhood and the alley, raises the issue of collectively held property (a limited commons); bricolage construction and appropriation, embodied in the fragment or found object in the street, articulate a notion of property defined by material making and marking; and museum-based preservation creates repositories of property removed from commercial circulation and made into a collective inheritance (while the museum itself is simultaneously an act of commemoration and an iconic form of public property). Together the four constitute a matrix of forms of property in places and material things: belonging to all, belonging to certain people by virtue of shared habitation, belonging to those who have wrought it from nature, and belonging to an officially defined patrimony.

CHAPTER I

Hiroba

*The Public Square and the Boundaries of the
Commons*

POLITICS AND THE PIAZZA

In 1939, as the war in Asia escalated and Japanese authorities increasingly repressed dissent at home, Marxist historian Hani Gorō published a small paperback about Michelangelo. The book opened with a photo and description of Michelangelo's "David." Hani portrayed the artist himself as an underdog fighter for justice like the subject of his sculpture. He described Florence's central Piazza della Signoria, where the "David" stands, in the following way:

> This was the *piazza* [*hiroba*] where several thousand representatives of the citizen masses [*shimin minshū*] of the free city and independent state of Florence gathered in an atmosphere filled with energy to debate and pass resolutions and translate them to action, in order for the people of the nation [*karera kokumin*] to manage the politics of their beloved country [*karera no ai suru kokka*] themselves, and in order to protect and develop their autonomous politics, creating no gap for autocrats to arise from within and protecting themselves from invaders from without.[1]

These words express in a nutshell the ideal that Hani propounded of the *piazza,* public square, or—in the modern Japanese translation term— *hiroba.* This term, which literally means simply "broad open space," here represented a universal ideal. In *Toshi* (The city), a work published a decade later, Hani would call this ideal *jiyū naru kōtsū*—a free traffic or intercourse among citizens.[2] Although Hani's *Michelangelo* was not censored, the author was later lionized for speaking out against militarism during the war, and the book came to be revered as a classic. As postwar Japanese rejected what they called their "feudal" past, along with the emperor worship and militarism of the war years, and pursued the language and action of a democratic polity, Hani's portrait of a self-governing urban citizenry acquired a utopian appeal.

Postwar intellectuals feared, however, that Japan lacked not only a tradition of democratic citizen politics but also a tradition of urban spaces suited to such politics. Writing in the journal *Toshi mondai* in 1956, urban geographer Sugimura Nobuji surveyed plaza types in the cities of European countries and their colonies, noting that plazas marked these cities apart, because Japan—and indeed all of the Orient with the exception of countries that had been European colonies—lacked them. He theorized that plazas had been built in the West in part because when large numbers of people gathered, a sense of citizenship formed.[3] Sugimura thus understood plazas as instruments of citizen making. Without them, civic participation in Japan was naturally hindered.

The absence of plazas was felt particularly acutely by architects. In the urban studies volume of *Kenchikugaku taikei* (Compendium of architectural studies), a standard multivolume architectural reference work published in 1960, architects Yoshizaka Takamasa and Tonuma Kōichi contrasted the cities of ancient Greece, where the agora revealed "a healthy interpretation of humanity within the community of citizens, however limited," with Japan's ancient capitals, whose urban form expressed "Oriental despotic rule lacking communal solidarity." This trait, they wrote, became yet more pronounced in the feudal cities that emerged in Japan during the subsequent medieval and Tokugawa periods.[4]

To compensate, postwar architects designed "citizens' plazas" (*shimin hiroba*), most often adjacent to new municipal and prefectural office buildings. Later architects observed critically that these plazas were seldom used by ordinary citizens.[5] Meanwhile, civic aspirations invested in the *hiroba* were reflected in the term's popularity in journalism and policy circles, along with the term "citizen" (*shimin*). Newspapers sometimes printed readers' contributions in columns called "readers' plazas." The long-term plan for Tokyo published by the progressive Minobe administration in 1971 was called "Plan for a Tokyo of Plazas and Blue Skies," although it did not in fact propose the construction of new plazas. Like the blue skies—a metonym for antipollution policy—the plaza here was notional, pointing toward a democratic civil society.

Yet as Hani's characterization of Florence's Piazza della Signoria reveals in its promiscuity of terms for the urban citizenry and the national citizenry, popular sovereignty and public authority, the citizens who gathered in the public square were conceived as much in the terms of modern nation-state citizenship as in the frame of an urban public sphere. And although Hani spoke of "free intercourse," suggesting the interaction of multiple subjects and opinions, Japanese advocates of the urban plaza in the 1950s and 1960s were as likely to emphasize its importance as a site of solidarity and of the expression of a unified national voice.

A conception of the plaza or public square as an open commons—the site of a public formed through spontaneous and unorchestrated interaction, where universal access but not universal consensus is guaranteed—thus stood in tension with a conception of the plaza as the instrument of citizen solidarity, the site of a public formed through unified mass action. This tension between different ways of figuring the public politically had its architectural counterpart in the problem of monumentality. In addition to providing space for citizens to gather, trade, and exchange opinions, public squares and plazas have historically been built to enhance vistas of buildings and sculptures, making them monuments bearing symbolic or commemorative meaning. Monumental space symbolically aggrandizes the power of the people who occupy it, too. Much like the excess beyond mere function that a monumental setting imparts to a structure, the space of unified mass action acquires a significance beyond the mere capacity to hold large numbers of people. As a space of politics writ large, the *hiroba* becomes a monumental site, where the collective will exceeds the will of the individual.[6] The public square in Japan's early postwar decades embodied in unresolved form both the grand political idea of popular sovereignty and an emergent space for the traffic of ideas, the unified voice of the people and a cacophony of people's voices, the monumental and the everyday.

OPEN SPACES IN THE CITY'S HISTORY

Japanese cities had possessed open spaces, and crowds had gathered in them, for centuries. After Edo was destroyed by fire in 1657, the Tokugawa shogunate created broad avenues and open spaces around bridges to serve as fire breaks. Over time, these spaces were transformed into informal markets and entertainment districts.[7] In addition, some Buddhist temples opened their precincts to the general public, making them popular sites for commercial and leisure activities. What the

Tokugawa city lacked, from the standpoint of modern democratic ideals, was a space explicitly granted to the citizenry for the purpose of gathering. Nor did the Meiji government consider the provision of monumental open spaces essential to the city's modernization. German architects Hermann Ende and Wilhelm Beckmann, commissioned in 1886 to redesign the central districts of the capital, proposed a baroque city plan that would have had large public squares, but the Meiji government chose instead to focus on regularizing the street pattern and providing basic infrastructure for commercial development. As the transport network developed, it became common practice to create open spaces—mainly traffic rotaries—in front of train stations. Apart from these, the Meiji city did not have planned spaces called *hiroba,* plaza, or square. For the modernizing state in the 1880s, traffic flow thus took priority over monumentality.[8] After the Great Kanto Earthquake of 1923, there were once again plans for a new city that would include public squares, but these plans were largely thwarted, this time not by government but by the organized interests of landowners.[9]

Hibiya Park, the country's first planned public park, was one of the capital's first open spaces to acquire political significance as a site of mass gathering.[10] Created in 1903 on grounds just south of the Imperial Palace, the park became a frequent site of mass demonstrations beginning with the protests against the Portsmouth Treaty of 1905. Political rallies continued in Hibiya through the 1910s. May Day demonstrations were held at Ueno Park and other parks in Tokyo from 1920 until 1936, when they were banned. In accordance with the Public Order and Police Law instated in 1900, all gatherings in parks and other outdoor public spaces required permits from the police. The use of public space in these mass political events was thus premised on state sanction. Violence erupted in a few cases when permits were not granted or when the demonstrators transgressed the boundaries of the state-sanctioned public by marching out of the park—as when demonstrators attempted to bring their protest from Hibiya to the gates of the palace in 1905. Two competing models of national sovereignty clashed in this incident: one in which the people amassed in public might appeal to their emperor directly and one in which public parks provided space for pacification of the masses, with police present to maintain order and buffer the emperor and his ministers.[11]

Events tied to a public that was unambiguously coeval with the Japanese monarch, since all sovereignty resided in him, took place in the front plaza of the Imperial Palace beginning in the late nineteenth century. Here, crowds witnessed military parades and displays of captured arms and celebrated national holidays in the presence of the emperor. In November 1940, fifty thousand people sang and shouted *banzai* together following the reading of a rescript by the Shōwa emperor in this plaza to celebrate twenty-six hundred years of imperial rule.[12] The land was imperial household property, and the events were carefully orchestrated around the presence of the emperor, under whose gaze they took place.[13]

In 1945, under the Allied occupation, the front plaza of the Imperial Palace was declared a public park. For five years, it became the site of May Day demonstrations, spearheaded by the resuscitated Communist Party, which referred to the site as the People's Plaza (Jinmin Hiroba). Like earlier political assemblies in parks, these events were sanctioned by permits from the police. As Hara Takeshi has noted, in their focus on a charismatic leader standing on a podium, Communist Party rallies in front of the palace bore a structural similarity to the military reviews and imperial celebrations that had taken place in the plaza before the end of the war.[14] The Left's appropriation of this public space so closely tied to the imperial state came to an end in the violence of May Day 1952, just three days after Japan had regained independence. Two demonstrators died and hundreds of demonstrators and police were injured. On this occasion, the demonstrators had applied for a permit to use the plaza, been denied, and marched toward the palace anyway. The clash between police and demonstrators was thus sparked by the same contest seen in Hibiya in 1905, between police and representatives of the political opposition, over claims to the central symbolic site of national sovereignty.

In the same fashion, claims to space on the part of large groups of politically mobilized Tokyoites in the first two postwar decades were driven by the vision of a unified national public. Citizens protested in places they understood as public property, either because it had been granted to them by the state or because they treated it as their own by right as the citizens of a democratic polity. This meant that generally they gathered in structured and directed assemblies that expressed unitary political objectives rather than engaging in debate, discussion, and the "free traffic" of ideas. When Kuno Osamu claimed that Japan's first citizens were born in the Anpo antitreaty revision protests of 1960, he meant that at these mass protests—the largest Japan had ever seen—Japanese expressed their individual wills in concert, aware of their responsibility as the bearers of sovereignty in a democracy. This enormous mobilization of

ordinary people unquestionably signified a watershed in political consciousness. Yet as monumental spaces of a unified public and sites of
mass assembly, the proverbial *hiroba* of postwar democracy did not fundamentally differ from either the *hiroba* of wartime fascism or the *hiroba*
of Communist May Day protests.

The Anpo protests of 1960 took place on the grounds of the National
Diet Building, where the nation's elected representatives were gathered,
and in the surrounding streets. Here, citizens representing numerous
groups and political positions, not directed by a single party, assembled
to express themselves freely. Different groups approached national politics and the theater of protest in conflicting ways. Members of the student Communist bund, Zengakuren, defied the established parties of
the Left by protesting without their sanction and breaking into the Diet
grounds. Newly created independent citizens' groups sought to dissolve
the boundary between the demonstrations and the everyday city by
encouraging passersby to join them spontaneously.

Yet because of the nature of the cause, citizenship in the Anpo protests still ultimately manifested itself in the display of national solidarity. Protesters understood their presence around the Diet Building as a
temporary occupation for a single purpose. Most of the protest took the
form of organized and choreographed marches. As George Packard
notes, demonstration marches were conducted with permission from
the Tokyo Public Safety Commission until May 20, 1960, after which
the marches were held without permits, but remained focused on the
Diet Building and unified in their demands. Although the students'
effort to enter the building by force resulted in violent clashes with the
police, Packard reports that protesters adhered to police restrictions by
not carrying placards when they protested on the Diet grounds without
permits.[15]

Conservative politicians in the Diet, meanwhile, referred to the building grounds as "sacred space" (*seichi*) and sought to pass a bill forbid-
ding protest there altogether. Anpo thus shared with the Hibiya protests
of 1905 and the May Day protests in the palace plaza the character of
a battle between politically mobilized national subjects and the government over a space of national sovereignty. Despite the horizontal organization among protesters from many walks of life that suggested a
widely held new sense of the meaningfulness and obligation of civic
participation, then, Anpo as it played out in the streets had as much in
common with earlier forms of mass politics as it did with the continu-
ous "free intercourse" among urban citizens idealized by Hani or the

face-to-face communication that Jürgen Habermas considered the foundation of the democratic public sphere.[16]

ANTIMONUMENTAL SPACES AND PUBLICS

As Wesley Sasaki-Uemura has noted, the failure of the Anpo protests to prevent the renewal of the U.S.-Japan security treaty signaled "the end of united-front mass movements on the national scale," yet the groups that had gathered around the Diet in 1960 continued as a multiplicity of "micro-publics" pursuing local and national political issues in print. This new political activism flourished particularly in the medium of *minikomishi*—privately printed newsletters and journals, often written in a personal, epistolary style.[17] Anpo thus contributed to the development of an increasingly diverse democratic public sphere. Grassroots groups born in the context of the 1960 demonstrations, like the Voiceless Voices (Koe Naki Koe No Kai), valued spontaneity and horizontal ties while resisting institutionalization.[18] These traits would persist in other movements as part of a citizen politics that kept parties and universal political philosophies at arm's length, seeking instead to engage other citizens in everyday places and on issues of everyday life.

A related constellation of ideas emerged in writing about urban space after the 1960 protests. In 1961 and 1962, Itō Teiji, Isozaki Arata, and others collaborated on a group of studies and essays that would become "Urban Space in Japan" (Nihon no toshi kūkan), a special issue of the journal *Architecture Culture* (Kenchiku bunka), published in December 1963. The issue elaborated a series of conceptual keywords for understanding Japanese space, beginning with the term *kaiwai,* a colloquialism for "vicinity" or "district," which was translated to English in the journal as "activity space." While taking examples from contemporary vernacular streetscapes as well as from famous Buddhist temple complexes and other historical sites, the spatial theory of *kaiwai* (on which Itō and others would elaborate further in later writing) fused an organicist reading of Japanese space as an integrated order with an emphasis on spontaneity and irregularity.[19]

In contrast to earlier writers, who had lamented Japan's lack of a tradition of civic monumentality to match that of the West, which they believed had left the nation mired in feudalism, this new approach championed historical and contemporary uses of common space in Japan as evidence of an antimonumental countertradition. Trends in Anglo-American urban writing helped validate the shift in perspective.

The Image of the City, Kevin Lynch's classic microstudy of urban residents' perceptions of the cityscape, was translated by students of Tange Kenzō in 1958. Jane Jacobs's *Death and Life of Great American Cities,* first published in 1961, was widely read by Japanese students of architecture and planning.[20] As the intimate and accidental came to challenge the monumental and symbolic in urban design thought, Japan seemed to have something unique that distinguished it favorably from the West.

Kaiwai, Itō explained, was constituted by "the set of individual activities of people, or the accumulation of devices [*shisetsu*] that trigger a set of activities." He conceived *kaiwai* as a distinctively Japanese pattern that was spatial yet undelineated, a kind of "mist," or atmosphere, generated by what happened there rather than by the drawing of boundaries.[21] This definition left a broad spectrum of spatial forms, or experiences, open for inclusion. A photograph of nighttime crowds in the Shinjuku Kabukichō entertainment district and an illustration of a market street scene from an Edo-period guidebook (*meisho zue*) provided the special issue's first visual examples. Itō and his colleagues had chosen *kaiwai* in their pursuit of a uniquely Japanese kind of space, but in fleshing out the idea, they had arrived at a phenomenon that was more social than spatial. Examples showed spaces defined not by formal design features but by the spontaneous uses of occupants. The authors described *kaiwai* as a Japanese spatial essence characterized by subjectivity, indeterminacy, and "assemblage of individual experiences." The spatial components of *kaiwai* were then analyzed into parts, the first of which, tellingly, was what they called *arare,* or scattered composition (translated in the journal as the "by-chance system").[22]

Like Kevin Lynch and Gordon Cullen, whose urban design guide *Townscape* they also referenced, Itō and his colleagues worked from existing places or depictions of places. The idea that there existed a set of essential Japanese spatial forms was a given at the outset of the project, which followed a special issue on the essential forms of urban space in the West. But for the editors, and for Itō in particular, the attempt to frame general principles of Japanese urban space created an opportunity to consider the contemporary vernacular of Tokyo, together with already iconic spaces like Ise Shrine and the pilgrimage site of Konpira, in relation to recent international trends in urban design thought. The result was a collection of images and interpretations that would make native streetscapes an appealing starting point for subsequent urban and architectural theory. The authors gave their interpretation double appeal by finding that the techniques of the Japanese urban vernacular produced an in-between space (*ma*) defined by the distribution of signs in a manner "strangely linked to the present era dominated by the language of computer-generated signs [*denki keisanki no kigō*]."[23] In a move that had served modernism and would soon serve postmodernism, Japanese tradition was thus revitalized as peculiarly contemporary.[24]

Because the significance of *kaiwai* lay in spontaneity, the concept accorded with the ideal of a space of free intercourse that had been envisioned by Hani and pursued in post-Anpo citizen movements. At the same time, speaking of appropriation and interaction shifted attention from the conditions for mass mobilization and solidarity toward an anarchic model. Although Itō and his colleagues concerned themselves only with form, *kaiwai* implicitly raised the social and legal problem of access: to what degree were urban open spaces available for appropriation, by whom, and within what limitations? Talk of *kaiwai* thus made visible a distinction that Hani and other democratic theorists had not made: between public property, which was held by the state and granted to citizens under particular conditions, and commons, which was beyond the control of the state or granted passively to the citizens who appropriated it. Commons, the necessary foundation of *kaiwai*'s "activity space," implied a right not to be excluded, rather than a right to participate based on sovereignty. The new appeal to the spontaneous, anarchic, and nonmonumental undoubtedly signified a retreat from the ideals of the public, but not a retreat from politics itself.[25] In *kaiwai*, Itō offered an idea that would be cited and adapted repeatedly in subsequent decades: that the unique character of Japanese urbanism lay in the ways in which ordinary people appropriated space spontaneously and in the kinds of places that accommodated and lent themselves to this spontaneous appropriation. *Kaiwai* thus supplemented citizen politics with an aesthetics of the everyday.

SHINJUKU WEST EXIT UNDERGROUND PLAZA, 1969

In the spring of 1969, protests against the Vietnam War began drawing large crowds to Shinjuku Station, a commuter hub that had grown to become the city's largest in the years since the war.[26] Here, in the Shinjuku West Exit Underground Plaza (Nishiguchi Chika Hiroba), a crowd of protesters, other activists, and onlookers, gathering without a demonstration plan or permit, injected politics into an everyday space of transit. The form of protest that they engaged in was politically readable as

FIGURE 3. Demonstrators in Shinjuku West Exit Underground Plaza pour out into the roadway, summer 1969. Photograph by Yamada Shūji. *Asahi jaanaru*, March 30, 1973. © Yamada Shūji.

a mass mobilization for a national cause, yet in its structure and behavior it was closer to Hani's original ideal of free intercourse. The protesters' ultimate expulsion from the station by metropolitan police revealed the degree to which advanced capitalism demanded a rationalization of public space for unimpeded movement. This defeat contributed to an intellectual turn among urban writers and activists toward other forms of common space (see figure 3).[27]

The Shinjuku district had already been the site of several turf battles by this time. In 1967, groups of youth popularly referred to as *fūten-zoku* (drifters), who were considered the Japanese counterpart to hippies, were forcibly removed by police from the area in front of the east exit. Antiwar demonstrators clashed with riot police outside the station on October 21, 1968, Peace Day, with student radicals flooding onto the tracks and stopping rail traffic until late at night.[28] In January 1969, riot police shut down a performance by avant-gardist Kara Jurō's Situation Theater and arrested members after the group set up its tent in a park outside the west exit of the station without a permit.

Elsewhere in Tokyo, riot police had recently crushed an extended occupation of campus buildings at Tokyo University and Nihon University by radical students associated with Zenkyōtō, the Student Joint Struggle Committee. Police removed the barricades students had built in January 1969. In contrast with 1960 Anpo, none of these activists sought to claim public space as a right of national citizens. The student radicals targeted the very same liberal political theorists who had provided intellectual foundations for the 1960 protests, accusing them of being bourgeois elitists.[29]

Hani, in contrast, managed to be urban theorist of the moment a second time, for a new postwar generation. In December 1968, he published *The Logic of Cities* (Toshi no ronri), which was immediately embraced by campus protesters, making it another bestseller. Here Hani himself was critical of all the earlier talk of *hiroba,* and he blamed liberal political thinkers like Maruyama Masao for using the term in what he considered a "completely untheoretical" and "utopian" manner. The real issue, Hani now averred, was the city's autonomy from the state. Self-government, he claimed, was what the Greek agora, the Roman forum, and the Renaissance piazza had guaranteed.[30] Within their barricades, the students created what they called "liberated zones" (*kaihōku*), a term with echoes of the Chinese Communist revolution as well as of the Paris Commune. Hani's ideal of urban autonomy also took the Paris Commune as a model, regarding it as a modern struggle to revive the principles of the Renaissance-era free city. For Hani, the freedom that the city made possible challenged not only the despotic state but the conservative forces of the family and rural village, institutions that many intellectuals regarded as feudal remnants. This view of urban liberation had natural appeal to Tokyo youth, most of whom had recently left rural homes to come to the city for education and work.

Henri LeFebvre's urban critique was also influential among activists in Tokyo's "liberated zones." LeFebvre's history of the Paris Commune was translated into Japanese and published in two volumes in 1967 and 1968. One aspect of LeFebvre's work in particular struck a chord for student activists in Tokyo, as it had for students in Paris: the idea that the Commune had in its essence been a "grandiose fête," in which class barriers were broken down by spontaneous action in the streets.[31] As in Paris, the student movement in 1968 Tokyo combined concrete demands for university self-government with a romantic rejection of bureaucracy and rationalism.

The antiwar organization Beheiren (Citizens' Federation for Peace in Vietnam) championed the festive element of protest while eschewing the violent tactics that student radicals espoused. Drawing from the

methods of the citizens' groups that had emerged in 1960 Anpo, Beheiren worked through a horizontal and "rhizomatic"—rather than
hierarchical—structure, allowing anyone with common goals to use the
name and rejecting alignment with political parties.[32] Writer Oda
Makoto, the most visible Beheiren spokesman, described the group's
demonstrations as foremost about mutual acknowledgment and communication.[33] A "spirit of play," Oda asserted, should predominate in
the movement over moralism and "politicization in the bad sense." He
proposed ideas like protesting American military bases by flying kites
and sending up fireworks.[34] In intellectual historian Yumiko Iida's reading, Beheiren's playfulness reflected the group's acceptance of mass consumer society. Beheiren provided space for individual self-expression
with a lower level of political commitment than the student movement.
Group leaders understood that mass media made any organized public
activity into a spectacle, and they sought to turn that spectacle to their
own advantage. Additionally, unlike the radical, diffuse, and sometimes
opaque messages of the campus protests, the single issue of opposition
to the Vietnam War enjoyed the sympathy of the majority of Japanese.

The new Shinjuku West Exit Plaza, legally property of the Tokyo
Metropolitan Government and the suburban rail companies, was the
pride of city planners when it was completed in 1965. It was seen as the
first step toward developing west Shinjuku into a new central business
district. The design received the Japan Society of Architects Prize (Nihon
Kenchiku Gakkai Shō) for that year. Photographs at the front of commemorative books published in 1968 for the hundredth anniversary of
the Meiji Restoration displayed the recently completed West Exit
Plaza's two-story structure, designed to link rail, bus, and foot traffic
with maximum efficiency. Because of this layered structure, the designers touted it as the world's first "three-dimensional plaza" (*rittai
hiroba*). By 1969, an estimated one million people passed through the
west exit of Shinjuku Station each weekday, making it one of the most
heavily trafficked points on the planet.[35]

Early that year, members of the student groups pushed off the campuses began to gather in the roofed lower-level portion of the West Exit
Plaza, leafleting, soliciting donations, and debating with one another.
On Saturday evenings beginning in late February, they were joined by
guitarists and singers affiliated with Beheiren who called themselves
"folk guerrillas" and led sing-alongs. Listeners stood or sat on the floor
in circles around them. Passersby stopped and stood on the periphery of
the circles. After the sing-alongs, the circles would break up into smaller

groups for what participants described as discussion or debating sessions (*tōronkai*). By May, hundreds were participating in the Saturday night gatherings. Other groups came nightly to collect signatures and donations for a variety of causes, including an organization dedicated to preserving the Lucky Dragon, a boat affected by nuclear fallout in 1954 that had become the symbol of the antinuclear movement, and a group of architects opposed to Expo '70, which was scheduled to be held the following year in Osaka.[36] Still others came to lecture anyone who would listen, or brought mimeographed collections of their own poetry and laid them out on the floor for sale. According to journalist and activist Konaka Yōtarō, who visited several times in May, discussion groups formed around issues such as Okinawa's return to Japanese sovereignty, the political party system, the limits of the concept of "citizen," and whether bureaucratic institutions were inherently evil.[37]

The folk guerrillas maintained a routine. Two or three arrived with guitars around 6:00 P.M., sang a standard repertoire of antiwar songs (including, for example, "We Shall Overcome") and parodies like "The Riot Cop Blues" (Kidōtai burūsu) and "Let's Join the Self-Defense Force" (Jieitai ni hairō), passed around the microphone, and invited others to address the crowd or lead a song. They closed around 8:00 P.M. with "The Internationale" and quickly departed. Some passengers complained that they couldn't use the public telephones in the plaza because of the noise. A few businesses facing the plaza also complained that the crowds hurt sales. This provided sufficient grounds for the police to declare that the gatherings violated the traffic law (*dōro kōtsūhō*) and railway commerce law (*tetsudō eigyō hō*) and attempt to clear the plaza. Riot police were deployed beginning May 14.[38] Joined by representatives of Zenkyōtō, the crowd swelled to three thousand on the Saturday of the following week. The police held back. The *Asahi* reported that riot police trying to clear the plaza had had "the reverse effect of creating PR."[39] After the folk guerrillas had left, a "scrum" (*sukuramu*) of students stayed on, protesting the upcoming renewal of the U.S.-Japan security treaty (1970 Anpo) with the snake-dancing demonstrations customary from 1960 Anpo and other mass street mobilizations. The same pattern continued through June. On June 28, hearing news of a postal strike nearby and eight hundred riot police positioned around the periphery of the station, Zenkyōtō students decided to march out of the plaza toward the post office. This time, police responded with tear gas, evacuating the plaza.[40] Nevertheless, sing-alongs continued for two more weeks. Finally, on July 19, protesters arrived to find all the signs in the plaza area changed from "Shinjuku West Exit Underground Plaza" to "Shinjuku West Exit Underground Concourse" (Shinjuku Nishiguchi Chika Tsūro), and the entire area filled with riot police, who shooed along everyone who arrived, preventing them from sitting or standing still. Twelve people were arrested, including one of the folk guerrillas. Later that night, radical students fought with police outside the east exit, but the crowds were effectively dispersed in the West Exit Plaza. In August, some of the folk guerrillas got a permit from the public safety commission and held a rally in Hibiya Park, but many present apparently judged it pointless and tried to return to Shinjuku, where they were repelled again by riot police.[41] This brought an end to the gatherings, discussions, and sing-alongs in the Shinjuku West Exit Underground Plaza.

The animating issue for Beheiren and for most of the people gathered in the plaza was an international one, and both ethnic nationalist and pan-Asian nationalist rhetoric were evident in the statements of Behei-ren leaders, as Simon Avenell has shown in his study of postwar concepts of the citizen in Japan.[42] Yet these gatherings differed from earlier political events in the streets of Tokyo because they were built around interaction among strangers. The folk guerrillas' sing-alongs were choreographed in the sense that they began at a fixed time announced by flyers, and many passing commuters doubtless viewed them as an obstruction rather than a welcome presence, but the gatherings still seemed to those participating to represent a moment of unplanned communal solidarity. It was this solidarity that attracted the attention of reporters and was particularly mourned by participants and journalists after the plaza was evacuated. Whether they were there intentionally or by accident, participants claimed something like what LeFebvre called the "right to the city" (in his book of that title, the Japanese translation of which was published in July 1969): the common right of access to open space by virtue of being an inhabitant of the city, rather than the right of a politically enfranchised national public.[43]

In spatial terms, the Shinjuku West Exit Underground Plaza in early 1969 was characterized by three features that distinguished it from the sites of earlier political assemblies: (1) it was not a publicly *sanctioned* space, like a park; (2) it was a place that people were compelled to pass through continually for everyday purposes, such as commuting and shopping; and (3) the crowds that formed there were multifocal, taking the shape of seated groups and milling pedestrians, rather than marching demonstrators, and coalescing only briefly for demonstrations, debates, or sing-alongs. The events combined some of the ideals of a Habermasian public sphere based on rational debate of questions of justice with an element of the carnivalesque, as the very name of the central players—the folk guerrillas—makes clear.

A reporter from the *Asahi* newspaper, which followed the Shinjuku gatherings enthusiastically, described the scene on a Saturday in late June in theatrical terms, calling it a "spiritual liberated zone" (*seishin no kaihōku*). The reporter's sketch began with two anonymous observers on the mezzanine noticing young people gathering in midafternoon. One observer remarks to the other, "Look, it's starting again." Around 4:00 P.M. a troop of sixty girls from Tokyo Girls Junior College arrive and sing "The Internationale," after which one of them, holding a microphone, delivers a speech. They begin a snake-dancing demonstration in the taxi waiting area, moving rhythmically with their staves (standard equipage of the radical student movement), "dipping their hips deeply in the *gewalt* style" (*gebaruto;* the German word *gewalt,* meaning force or violence, was used in the Japanese student movement to refer to violent protest or resistance), then linking hands across the street in a "French demo" (*Furansu demo*). Students from another private girls' college argue with Zenkyōtō boys collecting donations, asking why they advocate violence. Discussion groups form. "If you identify yourself," the reporter writes, "anyone can become the lead player [*shuyaku*]." When the folk guerrillas arrive, all the small groups form into a single mass. There are songs, appeals, and jokes, then "The Internationale" again. Several hundred students stay after the folk guerrillas depart—some still singing, others going to the east exit to demonstrate.[44] The style of this report not only emphasized the spectacle-like nature of the event and its choreography, but presented it in language that assumed readers' familiarity with the show and its participants.

To what extent national debate about the war was advanced by means of protests, songs, and encounters with commuters and police in Shinjuku is difficult to judge, but from the perspective of sympathizers, this was not the point. As Ken Hirschkop writes of Mikhail Bakhtin's conception of the public square, "Unlike the public sphere, the public square does not encourage discourse in order to produce a rational outcome, freed from local prejudice, but in order to produce a 'historical becoming,'" in which dialogue itself has greater significance than decision making.[45] The students and Beheiren activists who participated, together with the journalists who drew larger messages from these gatherings, saw a "community of encounter" (in the phrase of Konaka

Yōtarō) signifying the potential realization of an autonomous urban civil society.[46] This itself was the "historical becoming," a new kind of social behavior and consciousness facilitated by the space of the plaza but brought about by the willingness of people passing through it to stop and sing and talk with strangers.[47]

The innovations for which the design of the Shinjuku West Exit Plaza was praised at the time of its completion in 1964 represented a conception of the plaza's function precisely opposite that championed by the Beheiren activists and other occupiers in 1969. The operative concept in the design was unimpeded motion.[48] The Society of Architects' report described it as a "flow plaza" (ryūdō hiroba) and emphasized the effectiveness of the two-story spiral structure in dealing with an anticipated peak traffic of 100,000 pedestrians and 2,500 vehicles at one time by directing the flow in three-dimensional space.[49] Planners from the Tokyo Metropolitan Government and the rail companies had collaborated on the design with architects from the office of Le Corbusier disciple Sakakura Junzō and representatives of the Odakyū department store (whose building stood atop the west exit). Odakyū had wanted to maximize the amount of space for commercial use, but designers insisted on opening the spiral traffic ramp to the sky, which reduced the total floor area in order to bring light and air from one side into the roofed underground plaza.[50] Discussing the design in the journal Shin kenchiku (New architecture) in 1968, the architects expressed their frustration that the master plan had already been set before they were brought into the project, thus limiting their role, and that the plaza was conceived primarily for vehicle traffic, with no consideration given to pedestrian-level vistas of the building façade. Still, neither the judgment accompanying the Society of Architects' award nor the designers' own disgruntled reflections on the design process made reference to the plaza's potential as a gathering place. Sasaki Takafumi, who interviewed the designers in Shin kenchiku, remarked that "the fundamental spatial problem of how people will move and act [within the new west exit area] remains unresolved." Perhaps thinking of the recent street demonstrations in Shinjuku and elsewhere, he added, "Human beings are acting more spontaneously, in ways architects cannot predict."[51]

In this space designed for optimal flow, the occupiers created swirls and eddies. Generally, they didn't dam the flow: blocking traffic was a tactic of student radicals but not part of the folk guerrillas' approach. Allowing passage while encouraging participation involved a delicate balance of conflicting aims, however, as comments made by Beheiren members after the plaza's evacuation reveal: "The police say that it interferes with traffic," one told the *Asahi*. "Certainly, it does pose an impediment, but that doesn't mean it's impossible to pass through. We've tried to handle traffic management ourselves, too. Some people have said if we want to sing and hold debates, we should do it in a park, but we just want to do it with as many people as possible."[52] In a later reflection, participant Yoshioka Shinobu wrote, "The folk singing wasn't to make people listen to the song but a device to make people walking through turn toward one another and talk. Admittedly, it was a fragile device."[53] This is why the move to Hibiya Park failed: the occupiers didn't seek open space; they sought interaction with other Tokyo citizens. Although everyone, including the designers themselves, acknowledged that the plaza was not a particularly inviting or socially conducive space, it enjoyed a greater volume of passersby to encounter than anywhere else.[54]

Following the evacuation and renaming, discussion in the *Asahi* turned to the question of whether the West Exit Plaza was a plaza (*hiroba*) or a passageway (*tsūro*). Participants in the protests viewed the change of signage as no more than a sleight of hand on the part of the police and station managers. Some plaza advocates asserted that they didn't care what the place was called, because people ought to be able to gather wherever they pleased. Yet the figure of the *hiroba* and the ideals of citizenship that had been invested in it over the preceding decades lent moral weight to the sense that this incident had tested a fundamental condition of democratic institutions. The name *hiroba*, when combined with the spontaneous emergence of demonstrations and debate there, made the area adjacent to the station exit a potential "community of encounter" rather than merely an open space or the space of transit that it was clearly designed to be. For their part, the police, too, saw the power in a name, as evidenced by their going to the trouble of changing forty-five signs in the station overnight.[55] Labeling the site a passage or concourse rather than a plaza asserted ex post facto the legitimacy of the charges of violating traffic law for which two members of the folk guerrillas had been arrested prior to the final crackdown.[56] It was difficult to charge the singers with the usual "demonstration without permit" as long as they held no placards and didn't march. Police claimed that the change of signs represented a clarification by the city planning office that the plaza was legally a "municipal road," and that since it was a municipal road, they had charged the singers with performing and seeking to attract an audience in the street without a license.[57] Impromptu performance in a public open space like a park would presumably have dictated more lenient treatment, allowing police to intervene only if it could be shown that the performers were causing serious inconvenience to others. Although the term *hiroba,* which appeared in a range of planning laws, did not define an explicit set of use rights, the public discourse in planning and politics endowed it with greater citizen sovereignty than a road.

It was clear that the designers had chosen the name *hiroba* mainly for its "feel-good" quality—precisely the tendency that Hani had criticized—and not in order to announce its suitability for spontaneous civic activism, let alone mass demonstrations. Writer and participant Sekine Hiroshi put it pithily in an article published less than a year later, under a title that declared the incident already entirely a thing of the past, "The History of Shinjuku West Exit Plaza": "In short, all that had happened is that an imitation *hiroba* became a real *hiroba,* so the establishment used its power to suppress the *hiroba,* and confessed anew that this *hiroba* was an imitation." Citing architect Miyauchi Yasushi, Sekine acknowledged at the same time that the west exit had never been a particularly good space for a public square.[58]

In a letter published in the *Asahi,* Sekine called on Minobe Ryōkichi, Tokyo's progressive governor, to answer the charge that the metropolitan government had deceived Tokyo citizens by labeling the space a plaza. Minobe did not reply. Nor did he mention the incident in the memoir of his time in office that he published a decade later.[59] Reflecting the priority of state interests in the national capital, the Tokyo Metropolitan Police Department was under the direction of the National Public Safety Commission, not the metropolitan governor.[60] If urban autonomy was measured by the degree to which the city's highest elected official could intervene publicly in a confrontation between citizens and police, this was a clear indication of the limits of Tokyo's autonomy.

Yet, more than showing the limits of urban autonomy, the evacuation of the plaza showed the limits of urban commons. It therefore also distinguished public property rights from common property rights, both of which had been part of the conceptual investment in the idea of *hiroba* and the theory of *kaiwai.* In representations prior to 1969, the plaza as an officially sanctioned monumental space had been easily confounded with the plaza as an everyday space of unrestricted access. As long as political subjecthood was conceived as residing in a unified nation—"the people" rather than just "people"—monumental public spaces manifestly held as property of the state, like Hibiya Park, the Imperial Palace Plaza, and the grounds of the Diet, were the natural sites of contest, and European plazas and squares could be imagined in a broad and undifferentiated way as embodying both individual freedom and collective politics. Shinjuku West Exit Plaza, by contrast, bore neither the juridical status of state property nor its monumental symbolism. It was simply a space of transit. Nor did the activists from Beheiren and other groups who took over a portion of the plaza on Saturday nights claim to do so on behalf of the nation. Their claim was instead to common rights: the right to gather, sing, debate, and distribute leaflets; the right not to be excluded from use of a space that did not bear the exclusionary marks of private property. The fact that this space had been labeled *hiroba* seemed to gesture toward hallowed democratic civic ideals. By the same token, the authorities' handling of that civic idealism by the facile device of changing the plaza's name revealed that the combination of public right and common access that believers had imagined a *hiroba* inherently guaranteed had never actually existed.

Because the term *hiroba* had been made to signify much more than simply an open space, the attempt to manifest the *hiroba* ideal in this misnamed place, together with the eventual failure of that attempt, turned advocates' attention to articulating the conditions for *hiroba*-like events and behaviors. A week after the final evacuation, the *Asahi* published a group of readers' opinions under the headline "We Want a 'Plaza'" ("Hiroba" ga hoshii). The newspaper reported having received ninety-seven letters, the overwhelming majority supporting the gatherings in Shinjuku. "It is true," the reporter observed, "that Tokyo has no place for free debate out of doors like New York's Washington Square or London's Hyde Park." The pro-Beheiren letters the article quoted dwelled more on the importance of free discussion and the atmosphere of the gatherings than on the plaza as a space or the question of rights of access.[61] *Hiroba* as the figure of a political aspiration to communality, spontaneity, and free appropriation of space could manifest itself in different places and times, and advocates were beginning to detach it from earlier conceptions of public open space. Some participants, for example, regarded the Zenkyōtō students' mode of appropriation in Shinjuku, which monopolized the space and courted confrontation with the police while following the formal logic of the mass action, as inimical to their conception of commons. Anarchist Takenaka Tsutomu wrote in the newsletter *Folk Report* that "foolish" radicals had ruined the seeds of a "festival-style commune" of the kind LeFebvre had described.[62]

If the failure of the 1960 Anpo protests to stop renewal of the security treaty with the United States revealed that the postwar state would not accommodate direct citizen democracy, the evacuation of Shinjuku West Exit Underground Plaza revealed that the corporate-dominated mass society Japan had become in the intervening decade would not accommodate an uncircumscribed right of commons in central Tokyo. Peaceful citizen protests against the Vietnam War, although inconvenient, posed no direct threat to the government. The problem from the perspective of the authorities was location. The designers of Shinjuku's west exit had put particular emphasis on the idea of the "flow plaza" and the three-dimensional traffic pattern because the new station exit served as the gateway to a rapidly growing business district in which several of the country's first high-rise office blocks were then being constructed. Assembled initially without plan, simply an accident of the available space and the convenience of Shinjuku as a meeting place, the antiwar sing-alongs and discussion groups had occupied the busiest commuter hub in the world—an unsurpassed example of the bureaucratically managed society (*kanri shakai*) that student activists and intellectuals of Japan's New Left, like their counterparts in Paris, saw as the enemy of democracy. Whatever other political factors underlay it, the police action announced vividly that civic gatherings would not be allowed to impede the smooth flow of office workers that sustained Japanese corporate capitalism. West Shinjuku, the emergent business center soon to become a new city government center as well, was not a place to linger, sing, or turn and talk to strangers.

URBAN THEORY IN THE AFTERMATH OF THE SHINJUKU INCIDENT

The eviction of protesters from Shinjuku West Exit Plaza in 1969 had little direct impact on the politics of either the antiwar movement or the student movement. Beheiren moved on to other venues and strategies. Student radicals had already suffered a major defeat on the campuses and had never treated the West Exit Plaza as a symbolic space of decisive importance anyway. The real significance of the Shinjuku occupation lay in its role as the historical marker of a turn in perceptions of urban space and what citizens could do with it. The 1970s would see an outpouring of literary, semiotic, and historical readings of Japanese cities. Maeda Ai, perhaps the most important urban cultural theorist to emerge to prominence in the 1970s, later noted that the events in Shinjuku helped shape a new era of urban theory. Even though the Shinjuku gatherings had been suppressed, they had offered a utopian image of a spontaneous public appropriating common space.[63] At the same time, the incident's disappointing denouement, in which civic ideals lost to the dictates of urban rationalization, effected the final separation of the public and the commons. As a result, urban theorists and activists turned toward exploring the possibilities in common, everyday spaces divorced from the monumentality of the public square and national politics. After 1969, new writing on Tokyo reinvented the city, building upon the earlier work of Itō Teiji and his colleagues to champion an urbanism focused on the everyday and the local. In place of the city as modern metropolis and site of mass politics, urban theorists reconceived Tokyo as a palimpsest of historical traces—some buried, some on the surface but overlooked, and some requiring the work of the imagination.

The idea of unplanned native gathering places, captured in the term *kaiwai* by Itō Teiji in 1963, was revived in August 1971 in the journal *Architecture Culture,* which had earlier published the special issue "Urban Space in Japan." This issue, again under the editorship of Itō, was called "The Japanese Hiroba" (Nihon no hiroba).[64] Itō opened the issue with the perennial question of whether Japan had *hiroba* and admitted that the answer must be "no" if, by *hiroba,* one meant a place like the Greek agora or the Italian piazza. However, he proposed that if one defined *hiroba* as "a device for creating relations among people, whether social, economic, or political," then indeed Japan had a tradition to draw upon.[65] The concept of *kaiwai,* which had provided the axis for Itō's construction of a general typology of distinctive native spatial forms in the earlier publication, here became the key to a theory of Japanese analogues to the European public square. Itō asserted that, historically, the *hiroba* in Japan had "existed by virtue of being made a *hiroba*" (*hirobaka suru koto ni yotte sonzai shite kita*) through the spontaneous action of citizens, in contrast to Western *hiroba,* which were planned and formally recognized spaces.[66] This encompassing and tautological formulation, with the unusual term *hirobaka suru* (meaning to make, or to become, a *hiroba*) liberated Itō and his collaborators to find *hiroba* in Buddhist temples, riverbanks, bridges, and street corners, among other places not normally referred to as *hiroba.*[67]

Itō's expanded reading of *hiroba* accorded well with the ethos of Beheiren's festival-like protests.[68] And indeed, festivals were among the spatiotemporal appropriations highlighted in the "The Japanese

Hiroba." Other articles provided historical examples and evaluated contemporary urban spaces for their *hiroba* character, focusing particularly on the potential for spontaneous use. The authors observed that the "owners and managers" of these spaces had historically tended to stand in opposition to the people who made them *hiroba*.[69] This model of urban space as founded in conflicting interests contrasted with the stress on natural symbiosis and harmony in the group's earlier study.

Studies of a variety of unplanned and antimonumental spaces followed. "The Japanese Hiroba" retained the concern with public access that the recent incidents had raised, but other writing moved away from universal questions of public access and common rights in central places. Sociological and spatial studies of the city turned to the *sakariba,* or "flourishing place," as a key feature of Japanese urban culture. *Sakariba,* a native term in use since the Tokugawa period, referred to entertainment districts and marketplaces, and was thus defined by consumption as well as by the tendency of people to gather. This line of urban study responded to the rapid growth of youth-oriented consumption centers in Tokyo and elsewhere, exemplified by Shinjuku in the 1960s and Shibuya in the 1970s and 1980s. It thus departed from the explicitly political issues of urban autonomy and rights of access and congregation, taking an oblique approach to the value of commons. The battle for a more encompassing citizen control of central space in Tokyo had been lost to the police and, by extension, to the invisible hegemony of capitalist mass society.[70]

Other new readings of Tokyo chose to focus not on large gathering places, but on the margins and interstices of the city: back alleys, waterways, and open lots. Already in late 1969, philosopher Yoshimoto Takaaki, whose ideas played a central role in the campus debates, had written an essay eulogizing the Tokyo alley as a locus of organic community. Yoshimoto condemned Maruyama Masao and other leading liberal thinkers who had seen the 1960 demonstrations as a fight for democracy, arguing that they were deluded by their bourgeois faith in representative institutions and in their own role as intellectual leaders enlightening and guiding the mass public. Ordinary people, he maintained, had nothing to do with this enlightenment faith.[71] Yoshimoto's interpretation of the social meaning of Tokyo's back alleys appeared at the head of the first issue of *Toshi* (The city), a journal of poetry, photography, and essays under his own editorship. For Yoshimoto, the continuity of the streetscape and habits of life in the alleys of Yanaka, the Tokyo neighborhood where he lived at the time, provided the evidence that most urban residents had no use for the enlightenment ideals of liberal thinkers. Here, in narrow cul-de-sacs, he found a common space shared by tenants, which he read as the last vestige of ancient rights that had protected householders from "despotic rule." In contrast to earlier theories of the city's past, however, in Yoshimoto's interpretation, the "despotism" of the premodern state was augmented by an equally despotic modernity. For Yoshimoto, the ordinary folk had taken a stance of continued passive resistance across the centuries. "I have affection for these old houses surviving almost forgotten in the mammoth city," he wrote, "not from antiquarianism . . . but because they provide proof that both the good and the evil of modernity have passed right over their inhabitants without leaving a scratch. There is something that matches the foundations of my thought there . . . showing that existing has value even if you yourself have no meaning." This view led him to call for the eradication of every hint of planning and construction that bore the marks of what he termed "the conceptual public."[72]

In 1971, literature scholar Okuno Takeo combined examples from fiction with personal recollections in a nostalgically tinged study of the urban empty lot (*harappa*) as an ur-public space where the dramas of childhood were played out. The world of children's play in empty lots, Okuno asserted, was not only spontaneous but classless.[73] He referred to the alley and the empty lot as "originary landscapes" (*genfūkei*), using a neologism that came into use at this time and was popularized by Okuno's work. The idea fused personal and collective memory. "Originary landscape" became a central concept in subsequent writing on the city, a means of anchoring spatial analyses in memory and the phenomenology of individual experience.[74] In reality, the empty lots Okuno recalled had disappeared because they were transitory by nature. Far from being the unclaimed commons that Okuno's memory made them, the many empty lots of early and mid twentieth-century Yamanote (Tokyo's western suburbs) were actually sites awaiting development, part of a twentieth-century frontier in the process of being converted to housing for Tokyo's growing population. Nevertheless, Okuno's writing helped canonize the empty lot together with the alley as part of a constellation of utopian topoi of the urban commons.

Kawazoe Noboru, former editor of *Shin kenchiku* and leading theorist for Metabolism in the 1960s, turned from championing the urban megaplans of the Metabolists toward microstudies of everyday life in the early 1970s. In 1979 he published a history of gardens and decorative plant cultivation in the city titled *Tokyo's Originary Landscape* (Tōkyō no genfūkei). Kawazoe's vision of a green Edo reflected the environmental concerns of the 1970s and contrasted sharply with the preference for high-tech solutions among architects in the developmentalist 1960s.[75] Taken as a program for the city, however, it was in its way more radical than the futurism of the Metabolist movement, which projected continued urban development based on contemporary master plans. In a concluding chapter, Kawazoe wrote, like Okuno, of his own memories of playing in open lots and in an old, untended garden next to his childhood home on what was at the time the urban periphery, which he called a "world of freedom" for children. He recalled the cul-de-sac in front of his house as a *hiroba* for the three houses on either side.[76] Spaces like these had become rare by the 1970s, but they could still be found scattered throughout Tokyo. Conjured as "originary landscapes" by writers like Okuno and Kawazoe, they took on political significance, forming an alternative Tokyo unrepresented and unrepresentable on public maps.

Water was soon added to the canon of marginal spaces where traces of the urban commons survived from a utopian past. Architecture critic Hasegawa Takashi traced a long tradition of antimodernist (in Hasegawa's term, "medievalist") urban writing and aesthetics in Tokyo in his 1975 book *Urban Corridors* (Toshi kairō), an extended historical essay whose cornerstone was that westernizing Meiji "civilization" had brutally destroyed the premodern capital's waterways. The beauty of the old Edo-Tokyo, Hasegawa wrote, had prompted nineteenth-century visitors to compare the city to Venice. Like Yoshimoto, Hasegawa adopted a tone of critique rather than of wistful nostalgia, taking the city of the past as a site of resistance. Here, the waterways, as liminal spaces, furnished the sign of a commons that had been neglected and paved over by the modern state, which reoriented the city toward the streets. The old city of waterways was not lost but hidden, Hasegawa argued, and Nihonbashi, the bridge at Edo-Tokyo's center, was "the glorious gateway to an intricately constructed secret city," whose vestiges might still be found.[77] He interpreted the "medievalists" as engaged in subtle and often willfully self-marginalizing acts of sabotage against the post-Meiji state's modernization project. Hasegawa's imaginative recasting of nineteenth-century Tokyo would influence subsequent writers. In the early 1980s, urban historian Jinnai Hidenobu fused this reading of waterways as the lost map of an alternative city with the focus on unplanned market spaces in *sakariba* studies by showing that bridges and riverbanks had been the great sites of spontaneous gathering in Edo, foci of "the people's energy," he claimed, equivalent to the *hiroba* of Europe. Reinvented in native terms, the figure of the *hiroba* thus lived on in urban writing as a node of political meaning.

As this literature of urban history and memory began to mesh with both municipal policy and municipal activism in the 1980s, new forms of spatial appropriation thus depended on uses of the city's past, rediscovered and reinvented. History had played a crucial role in the activism of the 1960s, but as Hani's writings reveal, the history on which activists drew was a universal history—physically rooted in European sites and forms like the piazza, and theoretically rooted in the developmental schemata of Marxism or of other strains of post-enlightenment European thought. The spatial politics of Tokyo after Shinjuku turned from this universal history toward local histories, subjective experiences, and sensory connections between history and memory to counter the experience of a mass-mediated urban life that appeared increasingly homogeneous.

All the sites excavated by urban writers after 1969—alleys, empty lots, waterways, and unplanned markets—shared two key features: they were vaguely defined in property terms, and they were marginal spaces. In turning toward these other spaces of encounter and gathering, urbanists set aside the issue of sovereignty; the question was no longer whose domain a place was when push came to shove—as it had been in the writing of Hani Gorō, in the campus protests, and in the gatherings in Shinjuku in 1969—but what people did with it, what possibilities it offered up for creative use. Closure of the carnivalesque political moment of Shinjuku had put the mass politics of the center that had preceded it into a distant past. Both the state pageantry and the May Day violence of the Imperial Palace Plaza were forgotten.[78]

CODA

Although in itself, the Shinjuku incident had no significant political consequences and did not enter the postwar political narrative as a national watershed in the manner of 1960 Anpo, retrospectively it has come to mark a watershed in the history of urban space and culture in Tokyo. Indeed, Maeda's observation that the campus protests and the Shinjuku incident affected subsequent urban theory can be extended further. The new urbanism of margins and interstices that emerged after the incident influenced district-level planning in Tokyo, such as in the revival beginning in the mid-1970s of small waterways in the city as recreation spaces, some of which were converted into what were called "intimate water parks" (*shinsui kōen*).[79] Its ramifications were evident in the 1980s in the myriad local municipal events and museum exhibits celebrating Tokyo's old downtown, Shitamachi, as a city of alleyways—along with the commercial exploitation of this identity.

Shinjuku marked both an end to hopes invested in direct democracy in the public square and the beginning of an era in which the relations between media, activism, and urban public space were more complex. As revealed by the *Asahi shinbun*'s close tracking of the Shinjuku occupation—including reportage in a style that read almost like theater commentary—in a city as saturated with media as Tokyo, there was no longer a way to separate "true" democratic communication from the scoop, the human-interest piece, or the spectacle. Beheiren activists, like activists around the world in 1969, recognized that politics was now intensely mass-mediated. Habermas and critical sociologists after him have stressed the decisive role of modern mass-media technologies in the undoing of the democratic public sphere. From a Habermasian perspective, the Beheiren protesters and their supporters or interlocutors in Shinjuku must be said to have come late to the square, historically speaking. In the decade between Anpo and Shinjuku, television had entered practically every household in Japan, extending deep into private life the reach of a different kind of public space built by the state-run broadcasting company NHK and a handful of commercial networks, a vast new space of national experience shared entirely passively.[80] Gathering to sing and debate in public was the antithesis to participating in society by watching television at home. In subsequent years, the Shinjuku protests acquired the appearance of a last stand for politics based on direct public interaction, since much of everyday life in the course of the high-growth years had been transformed, particularly for white-collar workers, into the blindered, arduous commute through anonymous crowds to homogenous offices, and the return home to a private sphere whose sole connection to the outside world was the television set.

Many commentators after the incident perceived its meaning in ironic terms. Some found symbolic meaning, for example, in the creation of new *hiroba* and *hiroba*-like leisure spaces in the following year. Expo '70 opened its gates, despite protests that had been held against it in Shinjuku and elsewhere. The centerpiece of this monumental expression of the developmental state was the "Festival Plaza" (Matsuri hiroba) designed by architect Tange Kenzō (see figure 4). More significant than

FIGURE 4. Festival Plaza at the 1970 World Exposition in Osaka. Photograph courtesy Nihon bankoku hakurankai kinen kikō.

this particular *hiroba* in the longer subsequent history of urban public space was the introduction in summer 1970 of what were called "pedestrian paradises" (*hokōsha tengoku*): major shopping streets in Tokyo and other Japanese cities closed off to vehicular traffic for several hours on Sunday afternoons to create temporary public leisure zones. One of the first of these was in Shinjuku.[81] An essay in the progressive weekly *Asahi jaanaru* in 1973 took the Shinjuku incident and the "pedestrian paradise" phenomenon as opposing examples of spaces being redefined by those who claimed them: in Shinjuku, the space had been transformed by citizens, the writer observed, whereas the pedestrian paradise presented the new guise of power, appearing to offer a *hiroba* to the citizenry, then ripping off its mask and revealing the reality of the police state at the moment that citizens sought to "exercise true spontaneity."[82] Architecture critic Funo Shūji later wrote that the Shinjuku incident exposed the structures of control in the city and the naïve humanism of architects who had imagined they could create spaces of communication. He went on to explain the "pedestrian paradise" as an adroit recasting of the radical students' "liberated zone" that demonstrated the system's power of co-optation. Both of them were in formal terms, after all, the same thing: a street blocked to vehicular traffic.[83]

The potential of a "pedestrian paradise" to function as an urban commons was put to the test in 1972, when publishers of small journals and pamphlets tried to hold a "mini-communications" (*minikomi*) market to encourage free exchange of information in the Sunday pedestrian zone in Shinjuku. Police forced the vendors to leave, on the grounds that they had no permit. The police action suggested a decision to nip in the bud the kind of spontaneous interaction among strangers implied by this unlicensed market before political groups moved in.[84] Since the *minikomi* market had been designed to skirt standard publishing and distribution, which limited dissemination of information, the pedestrian paradise was thus revealed to be a new kind of openly policed public space built around limited free intercourse and controlled communication.

Yet, as tidy a narrative as it offered critics, the end of the Shinjuku occupation and the beginning of police-regulated pedestrian paradises did not constitute a direct causal sequence. Linking the suppressed occupations of public space in 1968 and 1969 to the new managed public leisure spaces that appeared beginning in 1970 depended on an argument that assumed the omnipotence of state bureaucratic management and the inevitable acquiescence of individuals in mass consumer society. In fact, pedestrian paradises had begun in response to citizens' initiatives in cities outside Tokyo. With smog and traffic problems frequently at the top of the news in 1970, pedestrian paradises were welcomed throughout the country as a first step toward more livable cities.[85] Nor, conversely, did politics leave the streets of Tokyo after the evacuation of Shinjuku West Exit Plaza or the closing of pedestrian paradises to pamphleteers, although no subsequent incident would present the terms of public space and common access with quite the same combination of vividness and broad appeal as the Shinjuku incident had. Street demonstrations and illegal occupations for a range of political causes were seen in later years. Homeless people built a shantytown of cardboard houses in the corridors of Shinjuku west exit in the 1990s, and their supporters fought with police in an effort to prevent their removal.[86] In the first decade of the twenty-first century, youthful protesters against Liberal Democratic Party leadership and Tokyo's conservative governor Ishihara Shintarō used the rave as a demonstration tactic, dancing through the streets of Shibuya, the new commercial center that had risen following Shinjuku's decline as a youth mecca in the 1970s.[87] Members of the supposedly introverted and apolitical *otaku* subculture tested the boundaries of permitted public behavior in the Akihabara electronics district with music and dance performances in the streets beginning in 2006 and continuing until a deranged slasher killed seven passersby among the youthful crowd in June 2008, which provided the police an excuse to suspend the weekly "pedestrian paradise" there. In the year following the meltdown at Fukushima Daiichi Nuclear Plant in March 2011, Japanese from many walks of life joined demonstrations in downtown Tokyo against the national government and Tokyo Electric. The latent potential of the streets of the capital for mass politics remained to resurface in such moments.

Whether one hears the story of the Shinjuku incident as tragedy, comedy, or farce depends on one's view of postwar Japanese politics, of the global moment of 1968, and of postmodernity. Abstracting and universalizing the problem in this way, however, risks returning discussion to the old, ideologically charged question of whether Japan ever created "citizens." Rather than testing events in Tokyo against universal definitions of civil society and democracy, in the chapters that follow I will maintain the focus at ground level, on the city as a place where people cohabit, a spatial frame for human action and sensibility. From this perspective, this is a story about shifting appropriations. There are many ways to occupy and claim urban space, including marching (making it a space of mass politics), selling and buying goods or services (making it a marketplace), gathering to interact with friends and strangers (making it a public square in the Bakhtinian sense), foraging (treating it as commons in the pre-urban sense), and clearing and building upon it (claiming a piece of it as frontier to be exploited). An era of organized mass gatherings in Tokyo had its spaces and contests over space—in Hibiya and other parks, the palace plaza, and the grounds of the Diet Building. The struggles and the failure of Anpo 1960 ushered in a decade of spontaneous, focused gatherings, which ultimately found, appropriated, and fought for Shinjuku West Exit Underground Plaza. When this moment had passed, an era began of more diverse and disparate gatherings of people, initiating contests around local community, marginal spaces, and the vestiges of the city's past.

CHAPTER 2

Yanesen

Writing Local Community

All community is a question of degree. . . . The one extreme is
the whole world of men, one great but vague and incoherent
common life. The other extreme is the small intense
community within which the life of an ordinary individual is
lived, a tiny nucleus of common life with a sometimes larger,
sometimes smaller, and always varying fringe. Yet even the
poorest in social relationships is a member in a chain of social
contacts which stretches to the world's end.

—Robert MacIver, *Community: A Sociological Study, Being an
Attempt to Set Out the Nature and Fundamental Laws of Social Life*
(1917)

The Shitamachi townspeople, who were mostly merchants
and craftsmen, didn't care a whit about political goings-on
either in the shogun's capital or the emperor's capital. We
didn't know anything about the human race. In fact, we
didn't know a thing about the Yamanote district across town.
You might even go so far as to say we didn't know the place
we lived in was called "Shitamachi."

—Kaburaki Kiyokata (1944), translated by Edward Fowler in Maeda
Ai, *Text and the City: Essays on Japanese Modernity*

Perhaps no large city in the twentieth century was rebuilt as frequently
and on as sweeping a scale as Tokyo. Yet piecemeal development
changed the cityscape as profoundly as the catastrophic effects of the
Great Kanto Earthquake in September 1923 and the firebombing in
March 1945. It took the form seen in many other market-dominated

urban economies, transforming rows of houses into apartment blocks and mom-and-pop shops into commercial high-rises, proceeding unevenly and leaving pockets of older streets and building stock behind. The two contiguous Tokyo neighborhoods of Yanaka and Nezu, located on either side of the boundary between Bunkyō and Taitō Wards, survived much of the century in this way, by dint of chance and neglect rather than intent. The fires in 1923 and 1945, both of which engulfed nearby areas, met the open land of Ueno Park and the Tokyo University campus and left Yanaka and Nezu, to their northwest, largely unscathed. Construction booms in the 1960s concentrated elsewhere, and Yanaka and Nezu remained backwaters. Gradually in the 1970s and accelerating in the 1980s, these neighborhoods became objects of historical study and preservation activism.

This chapter focuses on this process of discovery and reinvention. Although other parts of the city underwent similar transformations, Yanaka and Nezu—together with a third contiguous neighborhood named Sendagi—stand out because they were literally invented as a place with a single identity. This place was invented primarily through the labor of three residents, editors of the quarterly magazine of local news and oral history, *Chiiki zasshi: Yanaka, Nezu, Sendagi* (Neighborhood magazine: Yanaka, Nezu, Sendagi), commonly abbreviated *Yanesen,* which began publication in 1984. Yanaka, Nezu, and Sendagi were equally striking for the degree to which they developed a historical identity without the aid of municipal institutions. Since they occupied separate wards, nothing bound the three neighborhoods together in the eyes of authorities. Nor was local history or preservation a significant concern of either ward government at the time that the magazine was founded. The story is thus about how *Yanesen,* the magazine, created "Yanesen," the place.

Yanesen magazine stood in a long lineage of nostalgic writing about Tokyo neighborhoods, local customs, and the homes and haunts of past literati and illustrious people. Unlike previous recollections of old Tokyo, however, which tended to be the reflections of individual writers, it was a collective effort, and the editors were not motivated by personal nostalgia. *Yanesen* also became the organ of a neighborhood preservation movement, yet it was not born in a surge of local pride or preservation consciousness. Instead, *Yanesen*'s editors and activists discovered their mission and invented their locale in the same process.

Yanaka, Nezu, and Sendagi are all administrative designations within modern Tokyo, each one a cluster of *chō*—Yanaka in Taitō Ward and Nezu and Sendagi in adjacent Bunkyō Ward.[1] All three district names have existed in official documents and on published maps for centuries, although the territory they designate has changed over time. By 1984, when the first issue of *Yanesen* was published, all three were quiet, largely residential neighborhoods a few minutes by subway from the central business district in Marunouchi. Yanaka was known particularly as the site of one of the city's two original municipal cemeteries (brought under public authority in 1874). It had little industry or trade, containing a mix of Buddhist temples and the small range of businesses that catered to them, together with residential blocks, some quite well-to-do. Nezu had a few streets of small shops, restaurants, and bars, and was more working-class, but its industry was modest compared to the factory districts to the east and it had nothing approaching the commercial power of the old downtown centered in Nihonbashi. Sendagi shared a main street with Nezu but was otherwise mostly white-collar residential in character, made up of single-family houses. Although contiguous, and compact enough that one could pass from one end of the "Yanesen" area to another in a half hour's stroll, the three had always had distinct identities. At earlier stages in their lives, before becoming the comparatively marginal places they were when the magazine was founded, both Yanaka and Nezu had seen more flamboyant epochs in which they attracted numerous visitors.

Throughout the seventeenth century, particularly following the Meireki Fire of 1657, Buddhist temples that had originally established themselves in the center of the city moved to the safety and open land of Yanaka. By the end of the century, the village of Yanaka housed over sixty temples. This brought large numbers of parishioners, who came on visits to family tombs. The pleasant suburban location and the presence of the temples attracted urbanites on day outings generally, encouraging the development that commonly occurs in such places of what are known as "temple towns" (*monzenchō*), with streets of shops and teahouses. In the 1740s, Yanaka came under the jurisdiction of the town magistrate (*machi bugyō*), indicating the shogunate's recognition that it had become part of the city. Yanaka in the latter half of the Tokugawa period was thus a flourishing suburban location, both a religious center and a popular destination for tourists.[2] Teahouses lured passersby with attractive young women, one of whom was made a citywide celebrity through her depiction in wood-block prints, spawning a second level of tourism that continues to the present day, focused on places associated with her and with the artist who depicted her.[3] Tennōji (originally called Kannōji), Yanaka's largest temple, ran a lottery, which was one of the area's major draws from the time it was officially sanctioned by the shogunate in

Genroku 13 (1701) until it was banned in Tenpō 13 (1843). The area was at its peak of popularity in the beginning of the nineteenth century.[4] The persecution of Buddhism in the first years of the Meiji regime (1868–1873) preceded expropriation in 1874 of most of the land of Tennōji for the municipal cemetery. A large tract held by Kan'eiji, a temple in the adjacent Ueno district, was converted into a public park in 1873 and subsequently housed the national museum and zoo, making it the capital's officially sanctioned site of modern, public leisure and leaving Yanaka in the shadows as a destination for outings.

Nezu similarly attracted traffic from elsewhere until the late nineteenth century and declined afterward. The magnet in Nezu was a prostitution quarter, established in 1706. One of a number of quarters without official sanction, the Nezu quarter went through several forced closings and reopenings through the course of the Edo period. Like other prostitution quarters, Nezu was also frequently visited by fire, and the buildings reportedly grew more opulent with each reconstruction. The new government of Tokyo prefecture (*Tōkyō-fu*) granted the brothels authorization in 1869, and as the city recovered its population and grew in the 1870s and early 1880s, Nezu reached the height of its prosperity. By 1885, it was the largest of Tokyo's newly licensed prostitution districts, with 106 brothels (*kashi zashiki*) and 943 prostitutes, second in population only to the official quarter in Shin Yoshiwara.[5] Nezu had a reputation as a plebeian alternative to the more elite official prostitution quarter. Its clientele were predominantly carpenters and craftsmen—the working classes of the eighteenth- and nineteenth-century city. Establishment of the Imperial University in nearby Hongō after the Restoration, however, compelled a change in the character of the area. Driven by concern over the dissipation of the nation's elite youth, in June 1888, the Ministry of Education forced the brothels to move to newly built landfill in Suzaki, on the far side of the Sumida River. Carpenters and craftsmen remained a substantial part of the resident population in the Nezu area, along with shopkeepers and households in a mix of cottage industries. But Nezu ceased to be a place for outsiders to visit. Nor did it become a significant part of the modern working-class city, since its industries remained small and specialized. Lacking modern industry, dominated by wooden row houses and tenements on lots too subdivided to be converted to appealing residential real estate, Nezu had become a relic by the 1960s.[6] The neighborhood retained one material vestige of the old quarter: an ornamental *karahafu* entry attached to a former teahouse that had been converted to a newspaper delivery center and employees' dormitory. This historical marker of Nezu's gaudier past was so well hidden that by the time it was rediscovered in the 1980s, no one besides the owner of the building was aware of it.[7]

When they founded the magazine, the editors of *Yanesen* were all young mothers living in the neighborhood. Mori Mayumi and her sister, Ōgi Hiromi, had grown up the daughters of two dentists in Dōzaka, on the edge of the neighborhood whose boundaries their magazine created. They had known the neighborhood since childhood, but because their family background was white-collar professional, they were outsiders to the social worlds of the shopkeepers, small manufacturers, Buddhist temples, and proletarian backstreet inhabitants around whom the popular image of Yanesen would be formed. They were joined by Yamasaki Noriko, who had come to Tokyo for work after high school and had moved to the neighborhood for its association with classic novelists, including Mori Ōgai and Natsume Sōseki. None of the three women was a member of any existing local organization. The three themselves wrote the majority of each issue. Mori Mayumi, the most prolific writer of the group, had witnessed the student movements on Tokyo campuses while in high school. She had thus seen the failure of left-wing radicalism and the disintegration of the mass public at an early age, and like many intellectuals who had powerful memories of the period, she held on to the ideals of organized action but directed them elsewhere.[8]

Beginning with the second issue, published in summer 1985, early issues of *Yanesen* opened with a statement from the editors that read, in part:

> Our town [*watakushitachi no machi*] still retains natural features rare in Tokyo—trees, birds, breezes—buildings that withstood the destruction of both the war and the earthquake, historic sites, and intangible ways of life, craftsmanship, and human feeling [*ninjō*]. We are publishing *Yanaka, Nezu, Sendagi* to survey and record these things, introduce them, and preserve a good environment to pass down to future generations. We are doing this not out of antiquarian interest [*kaiko shumi*], but in the hope that we may help the area in some way to develop as a place that is fresh and livable, while still retaining the good things of the past.[9]

The editors thus started as observers and recorders, in search of features to give the place a historical identity and foster a sense of community. In chronicling local history, they had forebears in the area, hinted at in this statement by the reference to antiquarianism. Yanaka had an organization called Group for an Edo Town (Edo No Aru Machi Kai), founded by the owner of Isetatsu, a successful local paper shop that was one of the few tourist destinations in the district. There had also been a short-run coterie magazine called *Aizomegawa* (Indigo dye river), named after the stream that once ran through the Nezu valley, printed by local literary men and distributed to their friends. Many residents of the area's narrow streets shared the kind of neighborly intimacy that sociologists and planners associated with strong local community. But these two things had not previously been conjoined: historical interest in the area was unconnected to neighborly community in the present, and communally inclined neighbors did not summon history to ground their neighborliness. The Yanesen community was latent rather than formally recognized; historical accident had created the conditions that made the area distinctive; and activists, starting with the three editors of the magazine, went about unearthing the objects, places, and stories from which evidence of community could be read and communal feeling fostered.

This conjunction of local history and community made Yanesen an exemplar of the new *machizukuri* ("town-making") movements emerging in the 1980s, which focused on the invention of local identity rather than the pursuit of common political goals. People from diverse walks of life found it easy to gather around local history and preservation. Core members of Yanesen's loose network of activists included the abbot of Kan'eiji, students from local universities, a sushi chef and former union activist, a veterinarian, the wife of a policeman, and the son of the head clerk at one of the neighborhood's oldest sake shops. Longtime residents and newcomers, regardless of age or background, found they could participate.

The fact that the editors were female also facilitated the building of common ground among residents. Local history writing had traditionally been the preserve of older men, several of whom took a paternalistic interest in the Yanesen enterprise and adopted the role of mentor to Mori and her collaborators. At the same time, as mothers of small children, the women had frequent occasion to meet neighbors and could speak with authority on everyday life (*seikatsu*) issues such as childcare and care for the elderly, schools, garbage, street safety, and parks, which tended to be viewed as belonging to the woman's sphere. They were thus positioned to play the role of what sociologist Robin LeBlanc has called "bicycle citizens": women whose politics is defined by the household and the neighborhood, given universal social legitimacy by their status as "housewives" (*shufu*).[10] The way they lived and worked itself presented a community model. By the end of the magazine's first decade of publication, the three editors had had ten children among them. The children were parented by the whole magazine staff and helped out with delivering the magazine and other tasks once they were old enough. *Yanesen*'s office occupied a small house rented from a loyal reader. In the daytime, it was a hive of activity, with neighbors coming and going, bringing stories and artifacts, and infants bedded down amid piles of printed paper and photographs.

Despite the community ideals expressed in the magazine's manifesto, Mori would later write that she and the others started *Yanesen* simply because they were seeking something to do. Like many women of their generation, the three found themselves in their late twenties with higher education but with little income of their own or chance of full-time careers, members of what Mori calls "a proletariat chained to the home and the neighborhood." Mr. Noike, the proprietor of a local sushi shop and a former national railway unionist, told Mori and her collaborators that the neighborhood needed a magazine. With the help of Noike and others already established in local society, they began to parlay their bicycle citizenship into a central role in the reinvention of the district.[11]

There was nothing inherently remarkable about a social movement led by women. Women had participated in large numbers in protest and opposition movements throughout the postwar period in Japan; women founded or were involved in founding several of the grassroots political organizations formed after 1960 Anpo; and the women's liberation movement itself spawned numerous groups pursuing diverse aspects of the feminist cause. Yet from members of the National League of House-wives' Associations (Shufuren) in the early 1960s, who carried rice scoops and wore aprons as they marched against hydrogen bomb test-ing, to housewife-led residents' groups in the 1970s, who fought devel-opers in court over sunlight rights (because sunlight meant dry laundry and healthy homes for children), women in Japan enjoyed the greatest public recognition and legitimacy as citizens in their role as *seikatsusha:* consumers, housewives, and mothers. The editors of *Yanesen* did not transgress these gender norms but expanded the field of *seikatsu* as a political issue beyond maintenance of their families and the domestic sphere. By involving themselves in the neighborhood through writing history—as investigators, interviewers, and chroniclers—they made local community an object of aesthetic and intellectual interest as much as an extension of the reproductive functions of the home.

SHITAMACHI—DOWNTOWN COMMUNITY

Behind the invented place "Yanesen" and entwined with its invention and reception loomed the older geographic invention of Shitamachi—a place that, over time, had encompassed the commoners' districts below the castle in Edo, the shopkeeping and working-class districts of modern Tokyo, and an ever-expanding industrial periphery mostly to the east of center city. It stood in contrast to Yamanote, the higher ground occupied first by samurai estates and in the modern period by housing for the new middle classes. Like Yanesen, Shitamachi was an informal designation, without administrative existence or firmly established boundaries. The conventional definition of Shitamachi in the Edo period—as represented, for example, in the official compilation *Gofunai bikō* (1818–1830)— referred only to the districts of Nihonbashi, Kyōbashi, and Kanda, which formed the heart of the commercial city. Asakusa and Shitaya, to the north, were also included as part of Shitamachi in a place-name dictionary published in 1894. In the twentieth century, as former farming villages to the east of the Sumida River urbanized with the influx of migrants, the boundaries of what was commonly referred to as Shitamachi stretched steadily to encompass new neighborhoods of the industrial working class. Thus, by the end of the century, Shitamachi was shorthand for almost all the city's working-class and shopkeeping districts.[12]

From early in its history, Shitamachi was more than a geographical designation. Late seventeenth-century fiction already distinguished Yamanote and Shitamachi people by their manners, the former being elite and the latter plebeian.[13] These stereotypes were further elaborated with each new addition to the social geography in the modern era. As Theodore Bestor put it in an essay on Shitamachi's late twentieth-century reinvention, "Ideas about Shitamachi as a *place* have been conflated with ideas about Shitamachi as a *way of life*."[14] That way of life, Bestor points out, was perceived by this time as threatened with extinction by forces of modernization disrupting and dismantling local gemeinschaft. Shitamachi, in other words, became in the late twentieth century a geographically fluid designation for neighborhoods in Tokyo bound together by traditional forms of social organization. To talk of Shitamachi in the late twentieth century was thus to talk of community.

On the official level, the Shitamachi revival involved efforts by ward governments in Taitō, Sumida, and elsewhere to promote places and events in their neighborhoods with the label "Shitamachi" and a vocabulary of common Shitamachi images, as well as the more serious business of archiving local history in the form of publications and museums. It also took nonofficial forms. The monthly *Shitamachi Times* (Shitamachi taimusu) was founded in 1973. The major daily newspapers later sponsored public forums and ran columns on Shitamachi.[15] Concurrently, Shitamachi was picked up by private enterprise and its image was used to market shops, restaurants, souvenirs, and other commodities.

Although it nurtured local memory, the Shitamachi revival contributed at the same time to a process of local forgetting that was under way in the 1980s. In the industrial era, Tokyo's map had been marked by sharp class divisions. From the late nineteenth century until the 1970s, Shitamachi was associated with the industrial proletariat, and with gangsters and prostitutes, as much as with the traditional craft producers and small businesses that comprised the active core of the revival. As the city's industrial labor force became increasingly marginalized or replaced by workers overseas, and the semilegal underworld itself dispersed (in effect, by gentrifying), Shitamachi's grittier past was put aside. The softer, sepia-lensed image that entered in its place idealized a waning world of frank and open-hearted working people, intimate and easygoing neighborly relations, and everyday life within an exclusively local ambit in communities sustained by common necessities, such as the shared use of a well, and local rituals, such as shrine festivals.

This fading from memory of Shitamachi's industrial-era class characteristics permitted the reclassification of Yanesen as a typical Shitamachi neighborhood. The districts that made up Yanesen had not always been considered part of Shitamachi. An opinion survey published in 1979 asking what districts Tokyo residents thought of as Shitamachi yielded Asakusa first, followed by a list of a dozen other places, but did not include Yanaka, Nezu, or Sendagi.[16] After the founding of *Yanesen* magazine, mass-market journalism (chiefly television and newspapers) and tourist media came to present the area as typical of Shitamachi, although *Yanesen*'s editors did not make such claims themselves. When the popular "Blue Guide" series published its first Shitamachi volume in 1987, it featured Yanaka and Nezu prominently.[17] Within the area, whether or not to embrace the popular designation remained a matter of dispute. The owner of Isetatsu objected to the association with the working-class city implied by calling Yanaka a part of Shitamachi. The name of his study group, "Group for an Edo Town," emphasized that the neighborhood's specialness lay in what it retained of the pre-Meiji past rather than in stereotypical traits of downtown community in the recent past. Regardless of whether they chose "Edo" or "Shitamachi," whether they preferred high cultural traditions or low, however, writers and activists located historical continuity with the past as a foundation for community in the present.[18]

NEIGHBORHOOD, COMMUNITY, KOMYUNITI

Troubled by what they perceived as the breakdown of community in Japan's burgeoning cities and suburban new towns, Japanese policy makers, sociologists, and urban designers in the 1960s began to study what kind of conditions made good neighbors. The idea of community acquired a new meaning at this time. Formerly, the Japanese local community had been seen as natural, ancient, and encompassing—or, within Marxist social science, as a feudal remnant. In the new urban discourse, it was reimagined as a civic solidarity in which people chose to participate, one that was now under threat and needed nurturing.[19] It also acquired a new name: *komyuniti,* a transliteration from English.

The existing collectivity in twentieth-century Japanese cities that could be labeled and studied as a "community organization" was the *chōkai* or *chōnaikai* (neighborhood association), one of which could be found in every district (*chō*) in Tokyo. Although founded originally in the early twentieth century without direction from the government—and in this sense, spontaneous and organic—*chōnaikai* had three fundamental characteristics that made them anathema to the new progressive community advocates and scholars: membership in them was obligatory, with all households in the *chō* expected to pay dues; leadership was patriarchal, with only male household heads representing their households; and the groups often followed the lead of municipal and state government. During the war, the Home Ministry had used *chōnaikai* as tools of mobilization and mutual surveillance.[20]

Japanese cities had thus long had strong community organizations, but little effort had been expended on the problem of *making* good community, because community had never been understood as elective. It was in the context of an unprecedented shift of population in the 1960s, together with the construction of large housing estates (the public housing blocks known colloquially as *danchi*) and bedroom suburbs—both settings where large numbers of families were starting life anew and choosing their place of residence without knowing their neighbors—that "community" emerged as an issue. The postwar state's engagement with new conceptions of community independent of the tradition of *chōnaikai* self-government began in 1969 with a report by the national Economic Planning Agency's Commission on Citizens'

Everyday Life (Kokumin Seikatsu Shingikai) issued under the title *Community: Human Regeneration in Places of Everyday Life* (Komyuniti: Seikatsu no ba ni okeru ningen no kaifuku). The commission treated *komyuniti* more as a goal than as an existing condition, defining it as "a body of people that is both open (*kaihōteki*) and [characterized by] trust among members, situated in the site of everyday life, whose agents are individuals and families aware of their autonomy and responsibility as citizens, possessing common locality and all forms of common objectives."[21] This report was followed in 1971 by a "model community" campaign, in which funds for construction of new community centers and other facilities were distributed to eighty-three selected municipalities or submunicipalities over three years, as well as the publication of a series of "community readers," which compiled writing by sociologists on the subject, in 1973, 1975, and 1977. Introducing the first volume, Miyazawa Hiroshi, an official in the Ministry of Home Affairs (Jichishō), asserted the need for community in a language that echoed popular works of American urban sociology of the time: the present, he wrote, was an era of "rupture, alienation, and isolation."[22]

The new notion of elective community implied by *komyuniti* was closely tied to *machizukuri*, another neologism that bridged local identities and national bureaucracy. The term was first used in the 1950s and 1960s by members of citizens' movements demanding infrastructural improvements or protesting against environmental damage in the areas where they lived. Like "community," it was a term whose vagueness was an asset. Starting in the 1970s, *machizukuri* came to serve as a catch-all term for residents' movements both opposing and collaborating with government. The city of Kobe passed the country's first *machizukuri* ordinance (*machizukuri jōrei*) in 1981, which was followed rapidly by analogous ordinances in Tokyo's Suginami Ward and other local governmental bodies.[23] These ordinances gave birth to voluntary councils through which citizens could participate in district planning decisions. Through the ordinance and councils, the term *machizukuri*, like *komyuniti*, was absorbed into the language and practice of government. The agent of *machizukuri* is ambiguous: both redevelopment plans handed down by planning departments and citizen antidevelopment movements claim the term. It is also ambiguous with regard to the existing townscape.[24] Some of the early, grassroots *machizukuri* movements sought demolition and reconstruction of old housing, but after the 1980s, preservation of buildings and local culture, both from the top down and from the bottom up, became common parts of *machizukuri*.

In the era of local image-making campaigns associated with "cultural administration" (*bunka gyōsei*), grassroots efforts to foster neighborhood identity were always co-optable to municipal and corporate boosterism. Many localities in Tokyo and elsewhere had their own "town magazines" (*taunshi*). Overwhelmingly, these tended to be promotional publications funded by government offices or chambers of commerce. While remaining an independent enterprise relying solely on sales and subscriptions, *Yanesen* magazine often published articles that made the area more appealing to visitors, like other *taunshi*. Yet the editors saw themselves as grassroots activists and refused to cooperate with initiatives that didn't come from among their neighbors.[25] Navigating this zone between citizen advocacy and the marketing of neighborhood appeal, *Yanesen*'s editors pursued a politics of locality, but one that denied conventional divisions of community insiders and outsiders.

SPATIALIZED COMMUNITY

Much as it did in the United States and elsewhere, architecture played a critical role in the late twentieth-century reimagining of urban community in Japan. Even at the height of the *danchi* lifestyle's popularity in the 1960s, intellectuals expressed anxiety about the alienating effects of life in large, socially homogeneous apartment blocks. Hani Susumu's 1963 film *She and He* (Kanojo to kare), for example, depicted a frightened and lonely housewife in a *danchi* who lets a vagrant into the apartment in order to break her isolation. The film juxtaposed vertiginous shots of the tall white slab blocks with a bird's-eye view of the warren of wooden shacks in a slum nearby. At night, the housewife bangs on the concrete bedroom wall, wondering whether anyone is there to hear her on the other side. Increasingly in the late 1960s and early 1970s, fiction, journalism, and social science came to portray the *danchi* as icons of an alienated, community-less existence in which, proverbially, one didn't know the person next door.[26]

The design of these popular yet vilified housing estates was not the product of a faceless bureaucratic machine, however, but of research by academy architects in a specialized field built around the study of how people use buildings and public space. Architectural planning studies (*kenchiku keikakugaku*) formed a discipline within architecture departments discrete from architecture, planning, and urban design, focused on public facilities. It treated schools, hospitals, and libraries, as well as housing estates, but the heart of the field was housing. Its roots lay in housing studies conducted by Kyoto University architect Nishiyama Uzō during the war. The field took formal shape in the late 1940s and 1950s at Tokyo University in the laboratory of Yoshitake Yasumi. Under the direction of Yoshitake, Suzuki Shigebumi and others designed the 1951 housing unit prototype known as the 51C, which became the icon of postwar public housing. Yoshitake and Suzuki continued afterward to have broad influence on public housing design.[27]

In the mid-1970s, Suzuki and his students began conducting surveys in both new neighborhoods and old ones to determine what spatial elements encouraged close neighborly relations (*kinrin kankei*).[28] With this shift in research focus, Suzuki turned from the new towns to the downtown, discovering in Shitamachi neighborhoods the antidote to suburban alienation. The housing glut and construction slowdown of 1973 marked a turning point for Suzuki. No longer pressed to generate designs for more units, Suzuki and his colleagues began to focus on integrating their studies of individual unit plans with their site studies. From this time on, Suzuki became critical of his own and his colleagues' former work, finding that architects had created homogeneous and overly insular (*heisateki*) housing by failing to adequately consider the desirable relationship between the individual dwelling and common space.[29] The problem, Suzuki believed, had been further exacerbated in the private housing market with standardization of the unit design formulae developed for *danchi* (the so-called *nDK* and *nLDK*, referring to a combined dining-kitchen space plus *n* additional rooms, and combined living-dining-kitchen space plus *n* additional rooms, respectively) in multi-unit housing and the proliferation of "mini-developments" (*mini kaihatsu*) of single-family houses on tiny lots. In short, both public and private sectors, Suzuki now believed, had standardized and optimized the private home as a commodity, and had destroyed community in the process.[30]

In surveys conducted in 1974 in the working-class district of Tsukishima and the following year in Yanaka, Suzuki's dwelling-planning researchers studied the physical setting of the prewar alleys and the tenement row houses called *nagaya* in relation to a range of behaviors, including how frequently residents went outdoors, how many neighbors they knew well, where and with whom they stopped to talk, where they sat to cool off on summer evenings, where they placed potted plants and who cared for them, whether they felt comfortable leaving the front door unlocked, the frequency with which they left the door

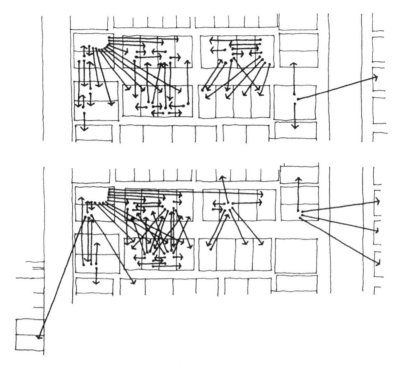

FIGURE 5. Diagrams of an alley in Tsukishima representing responses of residents to two survey questions about their relations with neighbors, 1974. Suzuki Shigebumi et al., *Ie to machi* (Tokyo: Kajima shuppankai, 1984).

open in summer, what they did when someone unfamiliar was seen standing in front of the house, and their degree of discomfort about being seen in their houses by someone outside.

Figure 5 plots the answers of residents in one Shitamachi alley to two questions: "Who would you ask to look after your house if you were going out, and vice versa?" (top) and "At which houses would you drop in for tea?" (bottom). Although Suzuki himself did not seek to translate his findings into preservation activism, these fine graphic expressions of intimacy among neighbors yielded material for a preservationist position. The survey results suggested that neighborliness correlated with traditional features such as alleys of under three meters width and lattice sliding-door entries facing directly on the alley. Suzuki's survey methods provided what subsequently became a standard set of measures for gauging community solidarity, used by others defending old neighborhoods in Japanese cities, as well as by those studying new ones.

These surveys sought new social and spatial terms to redefine community for an era in which local quality of life would take precedence over national development. Yet since neighborly solidarity had long been valorized by both local and state authorities, as well as by intellectuals and mass media, respondents knew what was sought from them and were likely to feel a duty to support the values of their interlocutors. Community studies started with the assumption that strong local ties were a prima facie good, with the result that questionnaires implicitly called upon residents to demonstrate their communitarian authenticity. The material conditions of surviving neighborhoods of early twentieth-century row houses were thus conjoined with reports of everyday habits in the present to solidify a new image of neighborhood built around physical vestiges of the local past and the relationships they fostered, separate from questions of class or family ties, and separate from the state and local institutions that had shaped previous understandings of community.

TOWNSCAPE AND COMMUNITY PRESERVATION

The first local efforts at townscape preservation in Japan similarly blended tangible issues of architecture with the intangible issues of community. Efforts to conserve houses and streetscapes in historic places followed a trajectory distinct from that of community studies while sharing a concern for building or maintaining local solidarity. But in Japan as elsewhere, when architectural preservation targeted private houses, it collided with private property rights. Maintenance or fabrication of a traditional streetscape often stood in tension with the sort of neighborly relations that depended on good fences. Where streetscape preservation movements did emerge, a crucial impetus tended to come from people outside the targeted districts, whose removal from local property relations permitted them to see buildings in strictly aesthetic terms, or to treat the entire streetscape as a new form of common property whose preservation would strengthen local community.

Japanese cities had had designated "scenic areas" (*fūchi chiku*) since this category was introduced in the 1919 City Planning Act. The designation targeted the natural settings of national sites—particularly sites of imperial significance, beginning with the newly planted woods surrounding Meiji Shrine in Tokyo. During the rapid urban development of the 1960s, the same concern for preserving scenic vistas reemerged in citizens' movements in Kyoto, Kanazawa, and other cities that had escaped firebombing and were known for their history. The Historic

City Preservation Act (Koto Hozonhō) was passed in 1966. Like the earlier designation of scenic areas, this law dealt only indirectly with protection of streetscapes, however, focusing first on vistas of important monuments.

It was in provincial places facing depopulation and economic decline, not in well-known historic cities threatened by development, that activists began the first local movements to create systems of restrictions and incentives for the preservation of residential streetscapes. The motive was to attract tourists. Tsumago, a former post town on the old Kiso Road in Nagano prefecture, became the vanguard case.[31] A preservation society, the Tsumago o Ai Suru Kai (Friends of Tsumago Society), was established there in 1968 under the guidance of Tokyo University architecture historian Ōta Hirotarō. In 1973, the town enacted a municipal preservation ordinance.[32] This was the country's first townscape preservation campaign, and its economic impact was enormous. After television features in 1969 and 1970, visitors came in droves. The number of tourist-oriented businesses in Tsumago leapt from three in 1967 to ninety-five in 1975, and the number of visitors per annum rose in the same years from 17,140 to 653,000.[33]

Despite this deluge, the resident population of Tsumago changed little. Most lots in the town had been held by the same families since the nineteenth century. Preserving houses and converting them to inns and shops aimed to limit individual property rights for the common good while allowing residents to stay in place. The Friends of Tsumago group explicitly worked to prevent the incursion of outside capital in the process. Private property was thus honored in the Tsumago movement as ancestral property, and the community invoked was one that had persisted over generations. In 1971, the town issued a "residents' charter" (*jūmin kenshō*), in which signatories vowed not to sell, lease, or demolish (*uranai, kasanai, kowasanai*) their houses.[34] Other provincial towns that organized their own preservation movements in pursuit of tourist revenues took a similar path (although other town covenants tended to be looser than Tsumago's). The National League for Townscape Preservation, or Zenkoku Machinami Hozon Renmei, was founded in 1974.[35]

The initial impetus for preservation in Tsumago and elsewhere had been local, and the National League for Townscape Preservation stressed the autonomy of the local groups, but in its conception, townscape preservation as a whole depended on an external gaze and was shaped by the mediation of forces outside the preserved towns.[36] Movement leaders in each town understood that a certain set of visual cues of historicity would appeal to visitors from urban Japan and beyond, and that the consistency of these signs was more important than the buildings' antiquity or their local significance. Much of what was preserved in Tsumago, for example, dated to the early twentieth century, well within memory for older residents, yet it belonged to a traditional mode of wood construction that marked it apart from contemporary urban building. Furthermore, academics and journalists from Tokyo played key roles in developing preservation programs and in promoting the towns. In addition to architecture historians like Ōta, *Asahi shinbun* writer Ishikawa Tadaomi reported frequently on the townscape preservation movement in the late 1960s and early 1970s, then himself became coordinator of the national league upon its founding.[37] Finally, national and international institutions provided the framework for pursuing local townscape preservation. The Ministry of Education's Cultural Affairs Agency announced in 1972 that it was beginning preparatory surveys to amend the Law for the Protection of Cultural Properties to recognize a new category of "groups of traditional buildings" (*dentōteki kenzōbutsugun,* abbreviated *denken*) by 1975.[38] The Cultural Affairs Agency's announcement followed the grassroots movements in Tsumago and elsewhere, but the enactment of the country's first municipal preservation ordinance in Tsumago, together with the formation of the national league of local groups and of the more urban Association of Towns with Historic Vistas (Rekishiteki Keikan Toshi Renraku Kyōgikai), during the three-year interval between the government's promise and the actual enactment in 1975, suggests the key role national law played in establishing local townscape preservation structures.

National laws emanating from Tokyo were further framed by preservation programs overseas. Revision of Japan's cultural properties law coincided with the United Nations' "Year of Cultural Heritage."[39] By the time that the Cultural Affairs Agency announced plans to revise the national preservation law, the *Asahi* had reported that the government wanted to institute a law like that which had been enacted for historic districts in France in 1962 under Minister of Culture André Malraux: Japan would have its own "Malraux Law," and the historic town of Imai in Nara prefecture would be remodeled in the manner of the Marais district in Paris, the newspaper reported.[40]

No part of Tokyo was among the districts involved in the townscape preservation movement of the 1960s and 1970s. Starting in the mid-1960s, however, there was talk of preserving Shitamachi history. Novelist Shirai Kyōji led a campaign to build a Shitamachi museum in time for the centennial of the Meiji Restoration in 1968. Speaking to an interviewer from the *Asahi* in 1967, he expressed anxiety that the old city was being lost. Like the bureaucrats of the Cultural Affairs Agency, Shirai took Paris as a point of reference. He began the campaign, he explained, after reading a letter in the newspaper from a French poet relating that France had developed plans to preserve Paris's "Shitamachi," and it was a pity to see Tokyo's Shitamachi destroyed. Unlike townscape preservationists, however, Shirai did not speak of local communities, streets, and houses. His concern lay instead with preserving the traditional arts and crafts of the old downtown and the "spirit of the ordinary people" (*shomin no konjō*). The museum, Shirai hoped, would stand alongside the historic cities of Kyoto and Nara as a place where foreign visitors could learn the history and feelings of the people (*minzoku no kokoro*) of Japan. Shirai's Shitamachi preservation vision was thus commemorative, fundamentally spiritual rather than material in focus, and for national rather than local ends.

Nostalgia for the backstreets of old Shitamachi was already common in literature, theater, and storytelling. Such nostalgia posed more of an impediment than an impetus to townscape preservation in Tokyo during the 1960s, however. In an era of national economic development, advocating preservation of streetscapes in the national capital could suggest an antiprogressive romantic decadence. Shirai avoided reference to nostalgic literature.[41] Rather than local community or the intimate spaces of the everyday, the museum Shirai envisioned would commemorate Shitamachi's contributions to national culture.

In the late 1970s and 1980s, as alleys of wooden row houses became increasingly rare in Tokyo, the aesthetic interest of the setting came to take a larger role in perceptions of Shitamachi. No longer identified only with an abstract "spirit" or with the specialized products of particular shops or districts, Shitamachi's character was now embodied in spatial and material traits like the ones analyzed by Suzuki Shigebumi and his colleagues in architecture and planning studies. The values and vocabulary of Japanese townscape preservation, forged in provincial towns like Tsumago in part to appeal to Tokyoites, thus found new soil in which to root within Tokyo, too.

RESIDENT TOURISM AND ACTIVISM

Unlike Shirai's Shitamachi, Yanesen began with a place on the map. For the editors themselves and for the place they had named, however, locality was still a question of definition in relation to other places. Mori discovered the Tokyo downtown through the suburban new town, much as urban designer Suzuki Shigebumi had done before her. In a writing job she held with a housing company before founding *Yanesen,* Mori had written a report titled "The Five Senses and the Town." As she would later recall, the research for this report made her realize how many things that appealed to her senses could be found in the Yanaka neighborhood where she was living but were absent in the new town about which she was writing the report: "wooden telephone poles, old wooden cisterns, traditional *kawara*-tiled roofs, enamel signs, the old style of trash boxes, hedges, and potted trees." With her infant daughter, her sister, and other new mothers with their children, she began exploring the backstreets of the area.[42]

Mori described these walks as a journey of discovery through the eyes of children:

> Toddlers let their curiosity take them into every alleyway they see. Follow them and you find alleys and old apartment buildings and row houses at the end of cul-de-sacs that you had never noticed in all the decades you'd lived nearby. Sometimes we'd be given plum wine or pickles by an old woman there. The town had inner recesses. People lived there. One couldn't know it just looking at the surface. . . . Things that one doesn't notice standing at the height of an adult appeared as if through a magnifying glass when I looked at them with my daughter at the age of one or two. . . . Even the trails [*kemonomichi*] that a cat takes through the alleys came dimly into view.[43]

This discovery led Mori to research her first book, *Yanaka Sketchbook* (Yanaka suketchibukku), and thereafter to found the magazine. As Mori's narrative of discovery makes clear, even though she was native to the area, it was the exoticism of what she found there that initiated her writing and activism, not its familiarity. This eye for the exotic, or pursuit and consumption of difference, is what sociologist John Urry has termed the "tourist gaze."[44] Critical anthropological and sociological studies of tourism since the 1980s have usually assumed that the tourist's perspective is predicated on distance, alienation, and the foreignness of its object. No absolute measure of physical or social distance determines the experience of exoticism, however. Although Mori had lived her life within a few minutes' walk of the streets she was now writing about, she and her coeditors brought to the Yanesen neighborhood all that was required for a tourist gaze: a level of cosmopolitan knowledge—which anyone in Tokyo by this time could readily acquire through television and other mass media as well as higher education—

and the consciousness of personal alternatives (that one might live in the suburbs rather than downtown, for example). This awareness enabled a "resident tourism" that gave exotic appeal to old houses and old people's styles of life, like the lives of the artisans and shopkeepers of Yanesen.

When Mori began interviewing her neighbors about local history, she knew none of them. Mori and her collaborators were young residents of modern apartment buildings, and they lacked family ties to local shops or positions in the neighborhood associations. From the perspective of most of their interviewees, they were community outsiders. Yet they spent their days in the neighborhood and already knew its geography. Because of this in-between position, their writing in *Yanesen* magazine oscillated between the voice of the tourist and that of the neighborhood activist and advocate. This also reflected the divided nature of their readership, which encompassed long-time residents and new ones, day visitors, and distant subscribers, particularly former residents. Nothing, however, put these different relationships to the neighborhood inherently in conflict with one another.

Actual conflict of interest arose only with the arrival of big capital, in the form of real estate developers. By 1987, the speculative rush on Tokyo real estate was in full swing, and its effects were conspicuous along Shinobazu-dōri, the main artery through the Yanesen area. Since 1985, mob-connected land sharks called *jiageya* had been going house to house pressuring owners to sell their lots, then reselling them in larger parcels to real estate companies. In a special issue on the real estate rush published in the summer of 1987, *Yanesen* moved beyond community news and history to take on the role of community defender. Among testimonials of harassment by *jiageya* and statements both for and against development (most quoted anonymously), the magazine featured a long interview with Hattori Hirohisa, the resident-owner of a tobacco and sundries shop on Shinobazu-dōri who refused to sell his land to a company that had bought the rest of the houses on his block and demolished most of them for high-rise construction. Hattori had received threats, had garbage thrown into his shop, and seen a neighboring house bulldozed so that a party wall formerly shared with that neighbor was left exposed and had to be covered with tarpaulins. When the new landowners blocked the back alley that had been used communally by Hattori's family and several other households, he sued for recovery of the right to passage (*tsūkō chiekiken*). Not all of Hattori's neighbors were supportive. Rumors spread that he was just holding out for a higher offer, and people asked why he had to make such trouble when the rest of the block had already been sold. In the magazine, he gave several reasons: this was his hometown; his family had owned this land for three generations; until the recent wave of speculation and demolitions, they had always been close with their neighbors, having suffered through the war together; he was too young to retire and wanted to continue his business; and he wouldn't sell to ill-mannered outsiders he'd never met before.[45]

The magazine had earlier run a feature on the threatened removal of the "Boddhisattva of Peace" (Heiwa Jizō), a small Buddhist memorial built on the same block in memory of residents who had been killed there by an American bomb in March 1945. The issue included interviews recalling the circumstances of the bombing in detail and listed the names of the dead. Before the special issue on the land crisis, Mori had tried contacting mass media outlets about the threat to the memorial but had been rebuffed. By offering reporters the present-day human drama of an individual citizen battling predatory speculators, Hattori's story brought the wanted attention. Following publication of the interview in *Yanesen*, NHK and TBS television and the *Mainichi* newspaper all did stories on the shopkeeper's battle. Subsequently he won his suit, passage through the back alley was preserved, and the shop and the memorial survived while the rest of the block was rebuilt.[46] Hattori reported to *Yanesen*'s editors that, thanks to the media attention, formerly suspicious neighbors now came to him for advice on dealing with land sharks.[47] The magazine did follow-up issues on land speculation and high-rise construction, and the editors started a column on preservation and redevelopment issues called "Neighborhood Ombudsman."

Three aspects of the Hattori incident reveal how ideas of community and preservation functioned in *Yanesen*. First, no existing collectivity or organization rallied people to the cause. Hattori happened to have previously collaborated with neighbors in forming a group to respond to redevelopment plans put forth by the ward planning office. That group's aim, however, had not been preservation but gaining a say in the redevelopment process. It failed because of disagreements among residents.[48] Second, the object of preservation in the Hattori case was neither a historic building nor a memorial of widely recognized significance. It was Hattori's right to keep his land rather than the shop building itself that was championed. The peace memorial was not a significant rallying point, since it was unknown by all but its immediate neighbors before the magazine printed the news that it was threatened. Finally, the campaign was refracted through and magnified by external mass media before returning to have an impact within the neighborhood. Television and newspaper reporters learned of Hattori from *Yanesen,* and area residents learned of the incident from television and newspapers as well as from the magazine. A photograph taken for the magazine was eventually used to aid Hattori's case in court. The plight of an individual shopkeeper thus became metonymic of the neighborhood's battle against developers. Community was defined in the process, fashioned from local stories mediated through mass media.

Yanesen was quickly becoming a widely recognized voice in grassroots *machizukuri* activism. The magazine was awarded the NTT (Nihon Telegraph and Telephone Corporation) National Town Magazine Prize in 1985 and again in 1988. In 1986, the Toyota Foundation funded a "neighborly environment study" (*shitashimareru kankyō chōsa*) of the Yanesen area by the editors of *Yanesen* in collaboration with architecture students from the nearby Tokyo University of Fine Arts. Compared to traditional architectural planning specialists, the group took a less scientific approach to the community study—including, for example, a tally of what they termed "communal cats," fed by more than one household, and coming up with nicknames for the various unnamed alleys in the neighborhood on the basis of distinctive features and stories told by residents. In place of the standard academic report, the group published a miscellany called *Yanesen Alley Encyclopedia* (Yanesen roji jiten), which was based on site and house plans and interviews in twenty alleys. Alleys that fulfilled several or all of the following criteria were chosen:

1. Cul-de-sac or street that few people use as a thoroughfare.
2. Street less than four meters wide.
3. Houses on both sides face directly on the street.
4. Alley itself on private property.
5. Residents think of alley as their common space.
6. Residents care for potted plants and cleaning of street space.
7. Change of level or some other marker indicates alley entrance.
8. An outsider would hesitate to enter or might be watched suspiciously by residents.[49]

This list of attributes, determined by the survey group, stressed markers of intimacy, insularity, and collective use and maintenance. Within

FIGURE 6a. Neighborhood child and alley in the *Yanesen Alley Encyclopedia*. Edo no aru machi Ueno Yanesen kenkyūkai, *Yanesen roji jiten* (Tokyo: Sumai no toshokan shuppankyoku, 1987). © Yanesen Kobo.

these spaces, the group catalogued features of traditional construction and signs of long-term habitation, including working wells, wooden clapboards, stepping stones and wooden gutter boards, sliding-door entries (which were both traditional and easier to leave open than swing doors), potted plants, and household items such as washing placed out in the alley, showing the "overflowing" (*afuredashi*) of domestic life outdoors (see figure 6).

FIGURE 6b. *Nagaya* row houses in an alley nicknamed "Dr. Hassai's Alley," after the NHK television morning series for which it was used as filming location. Edo no aru machi Ueno Yanesen kenkyūkai, *Yanesen roji jiten* (Tokyo: Sumai no toshokan shuppankyoku, 1987). © Yanesen Kobo.

Much of the list could also be read as a catalogue of fire code violations, beginning with the critical fact of the narrow street width itself. The national building code required setbacks to guarantee a street of over four meters wide and a uniform building-to-ground ratio of 60 percent. The desire to avoid losing land from already small lots militated against rebuilding, since the law applied whenever owners rebuilt. Under these Ministry of Construction standards, it was impossible to rebuild and maintain the scale of common street space in old urban districts. Wooden houses facing narrow streets thus tended to survive together until a landlord or developer demolished the whole row.[50]

Preservation campaigns, led by the magazine editors and by groups involved in the *Alley Encyclopedia* collaboration, developed concurrently with the survey work. Yet the effort to preserve architecture in Tokyo on aesthetic grounds—especially in the instance of Yanesen's alleys—posed a dilemma on several levels. To begin with, it confronted dominant attitudes about property rights. Calling for the preservation of a building meant telling others what to do with their property— something not unlike the offense cited when *Yanesen*'s editors had defended Mr. Hattori's right to resist selling his. The problem was exacerbated by the fact that, in Tokyo at the time, a low-rise building on a downtown lot had negative value as real estate. A landowner or speculator who could combine three or four of the small house lots in a Yanesen alley could build a three-story apartment block that would yield more rent than the existing houses, which therefore represented little more than a demolition and removal cost. If a portion of the assembled lot fronted onto a wider thoroughfare, zoning laws permitted the owner to build to ten stories.

Furthermore, the issue was not simply someone else's property, but someone else's lifestyle and standard of living. As Dean MacCannell has observed, the tourist visiting exotic places seeks authenticity.[51] This is no less true of the ethnographer or the resident tourist. The occupant whose potted plants and laundry and neighborly habits are made a research subject, the old woman at the back of the alley who offers the curious visitor refreshments, becomes as much a part of the scene as the houses. The longer she has lived there, the more authentic: her habits of life can appear as natural as the marks of time on the houses and the alley. The appeal lies in her antithesis to the deracinated position of the tourist, writer, or researcher, who comes to the alley by choice, as a consumer, and admires it precisely for its difference from other lifestyle choices that present themselves to modern consumers. Any form of institutionally organized preservation threatens to thwart the exoticist desire for authentic difference. The exotic everyday object is only precious as long as it is ordinary for someone else. That someone else, however, may not wish to live in the past or be made part of the scenery.

As intractable as these problems were, they were nevertheless common ones in preservation, only made more extreme by the hyperinflated land values and disparities between old and new building materials and technologies in late twentieth-century Tokyo. The negative real estate value of Yanesen's old houses was counterbalanced by their value in terms of what legal scholar Carol Rose has called "un-real estate" or "illusory property": a right claimed by virtue of the fact that the site can be seen.[52] The financial balance still tipped heavily toward pure land value, but the social balance, in which multiple proprietary claims could be made on bases other than possession of a land deed, was more even. Alley occupants learned from the survey and the magazine that their houses and alleys were valued for their visual interest by a growing number of their neighbors as well as by visitors from elsewhere. This engendered local pride and a sense of being an important part of the "Yanesen community." At least two alleys in the area had also served as the locations for period dramas on television, contributing further to residents' sense of their historical importance.[53] Local pride, in turn, affirmed the existence of the community that preservationists sought in the alleys, creating a natural symbiosis with the appreciation of resident tourists and outsiders.

Mori and the editors of *Yanesen* struggled in print with the contradictions inherent in local preservation, refusing a fixed position either as champions of old buildings in themselves or as defenders of sovereign property rights.[54] The magazine campaigned publicly for preservation only in instances of publicly owned property or buildings that required public support to preserve. For private houses, they printed what they termed "love calls": short features with façade photos and architectural descriptions that let owners know that their buildings had fans.[55] Their preservation and other campaigns were further shaped by the magazine's policy of criticizing government, politicians, and large businesses unhesitatingly but never writing critically of people they considered members of the community.[56] This itself was a community-building policy.

COMMUNITY IN PRINT

In twenty-five years of activism led by *Yanesen* magazine, no part of Yanaka, Nezu, or Sendagi received a historic district designation, and only a handful of historic buildings received either funding or official protection. In the case of one or two large buildings, high-rise construction plans were altered, and a small number of old houses were preserved by their owners. For the most part, though, real estate speculators continued to acquire land and front-street owners continued to rebuild to maximum height limits unimpeded by the preservationist ethos that had developed through the efforts of *Yanesen* and related local groups.[57] In some respects, the community activism catalyzed by *Yanesen* functioned like the political movements built around "minicommunications magazines" (*minikomishi*) in the 1960s and the residents' movements (*jūmin undō*) of the 1970s, but unlike these earlier activists, Yanesen neighborhood activists generally sought and anticipated no official response, and the many years of their activism yielded no decisive change in public policy. Instead, *Yanesen* magazine gradually built a space of encounter in print, involving the editors and authors, the artists who provided illustrations, the interviewees, readers both inside the neighborhood and outside, and letter writers.

If this community in print lacked a single unifying goal, it was not without a focus. Locality—both in the sense of a bounded place on the map and in the sense of localness as a framework for action—defined what *Yanesen* magazine did and what it brought about. Print redefined the neighborhood, beginning with the editors' choice of boundaries and the magazine's name. The editors had originally considered other adjacent districts, but having once provided the name, the Yanaka-Nezu-Sendagi trio remained at the core of the community identity that developed around the magazine and came to determine tourist itineraries.[58] Sendagi was included in part because two of the editors were living there at the time they founded the magazine. Since Nezu and Sendagi were part of Bunkyō Ward and Yanaka was in Taitō Ward, there had been no administrative connections tying the three pieces of Yanesen together. The ward governments showed no interest in Yanesen as a district until *Yanesen* magazine had made the name commonplace. With the success of the magazine, Bunkyō and Taitō Ward governments collaborated for the first time on a Yanesen-area "Shitamachi festival," and Taitō Ward published a "Yanesen map" in imitation of maps published by the magazine.[59]

The magazine also invented or resurrected and popularized colloquial street names, like "Snake Street" (Hebimichi) for the winding road through the low land of Nezu that followed the path of the old Aizome River. The name was introduced in a special feature on the river, appeared on maps in the magazine from the third issue, and became popular afterward.[60] The map that appeared in each issue (subsequently printed and sold separately) also contributed to the definition of the district. Over the first decade and a half of publication, the map accumulated increasingly dense notation of shops, historic sites, and streets that had appeared in the magazine's pages, thus graphically representing the inscription of locality (see figure 7). Partly influenced by *Yanesen*, ward governments in the 1980s and 1990s posted more historical markers on the neighborhood's streets. In contrast to the magazine's participatory approach, these more conventional commemorative markers defined local history by a canon of important sites and events.

A strategy of maintaining and enhancing localness permeated the production and distribution of the magazine itself. In addition to interviewing local residents and soliciting essays from local writers, *Yanesen* used illustrations by local artists and was printed by a printer in the neighborhood. With the exception of a few large bookstores downtown, copies were sold only at shops to which the editors could deliver

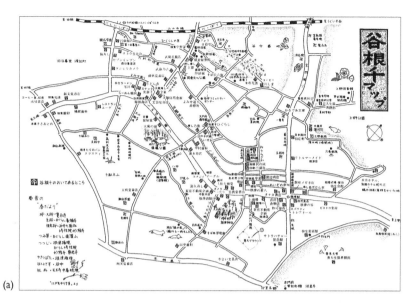

(a)

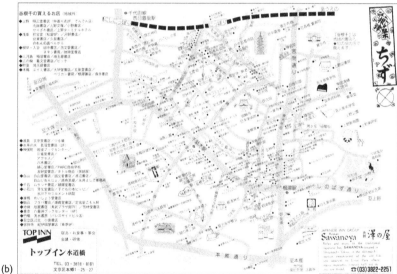

(b)

FIGURE 7. Localness represented in density of information: maps of the Yanesen district from (a, *above*) 1985 and (b, *below*) 1995. *Chiiki zasshi: Yanaka, Nezu, Sendagi* (Neighborhood magazine: Yanaka, Nezu, Sendagi) 3 and 45. © Yanesen Kōbō.

them by bicycle. Shops that advertised in *Yanesen* sold copies of the magazine instead of paying for ad space. By 2005, three hundred shops participated.[61] Most of them did not deal in other printed matter; some targeted tourists with handicrafts or antiques, but others were shops with an obviously local clientele, such as butchers, liquor shops, and a large number of restaurants. Marketing in this manner personalized the exchange. Although relationships between local merchants and a *taunshi* (town magazine) were common in Japan, most *taunshi* were explicitly promotional, their pages given over predominantly to glossy advertisements, and shops distributed them for free. *Yanesen*'s editors, by contrast, had to persuade merchants to sell their magazine, since the magazine depended on sales and subscriptions. It was printed on matte paper without color. Advertisements occupied a small part of the page and were generally handwritten.[62] To keep costs down, the editors (who laid out the magazine themselves) packed the maximum possible text on each page. In each phase of production and distribution, *Yanesen*'s editors thus chose to invest personal labor beyond what would have been necessary to simply print and sell magazines, and to accept the transaction costs for the goal of heightening the local element in the magazine's character and its distribution network.

A typical issue of the magazine often quoted several dozen interviews. The magazine's heavy reliance on interviews created a distinctive vernacular historiography, with stylistic elements of oral history and journalism combined in a text without a unified story line or narrative closure. A feature on a subject about which many residents had stories to tell would often be made up primarily of direct quotations, the language of speech rendered with colloquialisms intact, and each interviewee's words set as a single paragraph followed by a name (appended with the suffix *–san*, implying polite familiarity) and an identifier of some kind, such as the *chō* where the interviewee lived and a shop name if the person managed a business. Several pages would be taken up by quotations, printed in direct sequence without the intervening words of the editors, which were often set in different typefaces or in separate columns when they appeared. With so many interviews quoted in each issue, after a few years of publication, hundreds of local readers would find their own words in print, many for the first time.

Readers were brought further into *Yanesen*'s vernacular historiography through the letters and supplements published in the magazine. Mori, who came to write columns in the *Asahi* and *Mainichi* national newspapers (publications with readerships orders of magnitude larger than that of *Yanesen*) following the success of her writing about the neighborhood, remarked in 2009 that she always received more reader response to pieces in the magazine than she did to pieces she published elsewhere. Readers would write detailed letters, adding stories of their own experience to the accounts of others in the magazine, or would call the office with corrections and more stories. Unlike the case of a large publication like a newspaper, readers contacting *Yanesen* knew they would get a response from the editors.[63] Every issue included corrections, some penned into the printers' block copies (*hanshita*) by hand at the last minute. Letters sometimes became articles or the basis of new features. Features that brought responses with new stories resulted in follow-ups or supplements (*hoi*) and occasionally supplements to supplements (*hoi no hoi*).[64] Reader feedback thus not only contributed to what the magazine printed but sometimes took over and redirected it.

The editors' desire to hear particularly from residents with long memories of the area tended to situate a particular era—focused on the first half of the twentieth century, and pivoting particularly around the crisis of World War II—at the core of the neighborhood history *Yanesen* told. War memory anchored narratives of the past and brought neighbors together around common experiences. One of the topics that received the most extended treatment over the twenty-five years of the magazine's publication, for example, was the evacuation of children in anticipation of the bombing of Tokyo. School classes had been evacuated together. *Yanesen*'s editors traced records and stories through Tokyo school alumni groups and through investigation at the rural schools where the children had been sent. This was an important and understudied chapter in the lives of millions of Japanese. A larger number of special issues on history, however, were devoted to events and places in the area that had only footnote significance in the standard history of Tokyo or Japan as a whole: accounts of the dyers' businesses that once lined the Aizome River, the history of all the pawn shops or bathhouses in the area, the origins of the chrysanthemum dolls that were once a popular festival feature in Yanaka, or the colorful life of local banker and landlord Watanabe Jieimon.

Since the magazine asked old people to recount their memories and the editors' policy was not to criticize or interrogate, certain tropes cultivated by mass media and repeated in daily conversation—about the "good old days" before the war, the simpler lifestyle before high economic growth in the 1960s, or Shitamachi's traditional community spirit—sometimes colored the stories residents told in *Yanesen*. Childhood memories were, by their nature, often nostalgic.[65] To the critical historian, the whole enterprise might appear essentially to be about nostalgia, and doubtless it was consumed by some readers as such.[66] However, the intensity of the feedback process between editors, local readers, and members of a growing Yanesen "diaspora" distinguished *Yanesen* markedly from the library of nostalgic writing by Shitamachi strollers and chroniclers in the tradition of Nagai Kafū. *Yanesen*'s multivocal historiography asserted a collective claim that the district belonged to its residents.[67] By also presenting a history that reached beyond present residents' experience and incorporating the letters of subscribers outside the neighborhood (and overseas), *Yanesen* constructed a community that was simultaneously geographical and virtual, founded on the *idea* of the locality called "Yanesen" but not bounded by its actuality. Elective solidarity around an invented place fit an era in which all urban experience was mediated and organic community existed more as a utopian image than a functioning reality.

MEDIA, THE PAST, AND TOKYO TOWN MAKING

In the 1980s and 1990s, movements elsewhere in Tokyo mobilized pieces of the past and the environment of alleys and wooden *nagaya* tenements to assert local identity in similar ways. Other *machizukuri* plans began with the issue of fire prevention but grew to involve preservation of the marks and vestiges of local history. Kyōjima, for example, a working-class district to the east of the Sumida River that had some of the highest densities of wooden housing in the city, shifted from municipal plans for wholesale redevelopment in the 1970s to a locally based *machizukuri* plan in the 1980s. The new plan allowed for narrower streets and proposed "community housing" (*komyuniti jūtaku*) that would be smaller in scale and retain the mix of commercial and residential use characteristic of the area. In the 1990s, it then went through further revision to make the community housing match the scale of existing *nagaya* and to incorporate tiny "pocket parks" and squares (*hiroba*). Architecture and planning students from Chiba and Waseda Universities came in the 1990s to work with residents on new ideas for retaining the traditional character of the neighborhood. They published the *Kyōjima rojikomi mappu*, a map and walking guide showing all the area's alleys (some of which, as private passageways, did not appear on official maps), surviving *nagaya*, and historical points of interest.[68] In nearby Higashi Mukōjima, which had been designated a "model district" for *machizukuri* plans in 1985, a local group collaborating with the ward government began a project in 1988 to place rainwater cisterns in small backstreet common spaces (again referred to as *hiroba*). The cisterns were designed to be reminiscent of cisterns that had once been maintained in every alley as a precaution against fire, making them symbols of both local tradition and fire safety awareness. They were dubbed with the neologism "alley shrines" (*rojison*). This term was also used in the name of a local newsletter published by the ward government and printed in the style of an Edo broadsheet.

Beginning in the late 1990s, the district became the venue for international symposia on town planning and for an art festival in which artists worked in and around surviving *nagaya* tenements. Some artists set up permanent ateliers in them.[69] The arrival of artists renting or buying local property suggests the early stage of the bohemian-led gentrification pattern seen in cities in Europe and the United States since the 1960s.[70] In Higashi Mukōjima, however, the artists came following an official cleaning up of the area's image, beginning with the place name itself. Formerly known as Tamanoi or Terashima-chō, it had been the home of an illegal prostitution district from World War I until the 1950s. Terashima-chō was renamed Higashi Mukōjima as part of the citywide revision of postal addresses in 1970. Tamanoi Station became Higashi Mukōjima Station in 1987. This erasure of the old prostitution district from the map accorded with the broader "de-classification" of Shitamachi memory. Promoting links to the Edo past helped culture bureaucrats in the ward government bypass a socially undesirable modern history. The artists also came through the efforts of local government, and their focus on the physical environment of the alleys and row houses helped recast the area as a typical Shitamachi neighborhood rather than a place of clandestine activities.

Yanesen, too, saw an influx of artists in the 1990s. This was less of a break with the past than in Mukōjima, since the Yanesen neighborhood's proximity to the University of Fine Arts had long made it a popular place of residence for art students and professors. What was new for Yanesen was that art now became part of the public face of the district. This cultural development did not lead to the rise in property values and displacement of lower-income residents that have characterized full-blown gentrification in U.S. cities and elsewhere. The old low-rise wooden housing stock that gave the neighborhood historical value to outsiders and made it distinctive continued to hold little real estate value. As a result, beginning in the late 1990s, Yanesen experienced something better described as "boutiquification" than "gentrification."

Population composition altered little overall, but small shops and galleries appeared, often in formerly noncommercial spaces, designed to attract visitors. *Yanesen* magazine and its ripple effect in mass media brought weekend strollers from elsewhere in Tokyo, sometimes in numbers large enough to create pedestrian traffic problems. In the early 1990s, at the height of the magazine's popularity, the editors had campaigned successfully to keep out tour buses. Nothing could prevent tourists coming on their own, however.

Several developments in national policy contributed to a change of climate around preservation and community activism in the Yanesen area and other urban neighborhoods after the burst of the bubble in 1990. In 1996, the Cultural Affairs Agency again amended the cultural properties law, this time to create a registration system akin to the U.S. National Register of Historical Places, making it possible to recognize historically significant buildings without a binding obligation being placed on either the owners or the state for their preservation. This permitted looser standards of historical significance and allowed citizens' groups to campaign for registration of buildings without worrying that designation would require sale of a majority stake in the property to the government for conversion into a museum, which had been the most common result for individual buildings given national "cultural property" designations under the old system. The so-called NPO Law of 1998 allowed small volunteer organizations to incorporate as nonprofits, and under a subsequent amendment, it permitted them tax breaks. This led in 2003 to the incorporation of the Taitō Rekishi Toshi Kenkyūkai (Taitō Historical City Research Group), a Yanesen-based nonprofit preservation group organized chiefly by University of Fine Arts architecture faculty and students who had worked on surveys and *machizukuri* proposals both with *Yanesen* magazine editors and independently since the 1980s. One strategy this organization used to engage neighbors in its activities was to sponsor walks and seminars they called "Searching for Good Places" (Ii toko sagashi). Participants were asked to identify spots they liked in the streets of the area and bring the group there to point out their appeal. This townscape appreciation game cultivated the resident tourist gaze.[71]

Yanesen was a local history project unique to its district and participants yet at the same time a summation of many of the trends that brought ideas of community, locality, and history together in Tokyo. Urban community as a positive value and a choice, based on shared space and freed from the gendered and semicompulsory institutions of the *chōnaikai,* had emerged as a response to new social and political conditions in the city of the 1970s. The focus on townscape, which emerged in the late 1960s and 1970s as part of the new era of domestic tourism, informed the perspectives of Yanesen activists and provided models for their activism. Both of these 1970s concepts—community (*komyuniti*) and townscape (*machinami*)—contained an ideal of the city as the common property of local residents. Shitamachi served as the fluidly bounded site and dominant figure of these ideals in Tokyo. Because of the energy of *Yanesen*'s editors and the local preservation activists around them, these elements came together in their most artic-ulate form around the newly invented Yanesen district, although Yanaka, Nezu, and Sendagi had not stood out previously as a distinc-tive district, much less a Shitamachi icon. Local history grounded the imagined community of Yanesen. Its success was measured less in pres-ervation of buildings—in contrast to the controversial Tsumago, Yane-sen property remained unsequestered from the real estate market—than in the creation of a virtual community in print. True to the way in which local community had itself become a media product, through the recording and distribution in print of local residents' memories, the media space of *Yanesen* engendered the physical space of "Yanesen" and its many social possibilities.

CHAPTER 3

Deviant Properties

Street Observation Studies

This city can be known only by an activity of an ethnographic kind: you must orient yourself in it not by book, by
address, but by walking, by sight, by habit, by experience;
here every discovery is intense and fragile, it can be repeated
or recovered only by memory of the trace it has left in you.

—Roland Barthes, *Empire of Signs* (1970), translated by
Richard Howard

MAKING, FINDING, INTERPRETING

Another trajectory away from the politics of the public square and into
the everyday city lay through personal appropriations of vestiges of the
past found in the streets. Despite the inherent fragmentation of the
masses that such a move implied, people could be mobilized into active
publics around the personal and the intimate as well as the communal,
and rallied to the cause of overlooked, unvalued, and seemingly insignificant things, precisely because they survived, yet to be claimed and
given meaning. This chapter examines the popularization of this
approach to the city in 1980s Tokyo through a movement called street
observation studies (*rojō kansatsugaku*), whose objects of study, as a
participant informed the press, included "manhole covers, hydrants,
animal forms in building ornament, useless staircases, *karugamo* ducks,
street botanical gardens [potted plants], paper signs, and all the unconscious expressions of the city."[1] The objects of street observation studies were defined generically as "inexplicable protuberances and con-
cavities connected to buildings and streets in the city, which, while
purposeless, have been beautifully preserved."[2]

If one detached the logic of the vernacular urbanism of Itō Teiji and others from a conventional agenda for architecture or planning, idiosyncratic objects like these could be placed on the same conceptual plane and treated as deserving the same attention as waterways, open lots, alleys, market spaces, and the long idealized public square. This is what street observation did. Members of the Street Observation Studies Society (Rojō Kansatsu Gakkai), formed in 1986, rejected the theoretical approaches of architects and planners because they saw them as co-opted into a society of managed consumption that could be challenged only through a radical rethinking of how the city was made and how the individual encountered it. The "consumption empire" was the enemy, as architecture historian Fujimori Terunobu wrote in his introduction to the *Primer on Street Observation Studies* (Rojō kansatsugaku nyūmon). It was "strategizing to commodify the entire town," and it had already succeeded in consuming urban theory itself.[3]

Despite the apparent lack of public significance to the group's objects of interest, the Street Observation Studies Society launched itself into the public eye with prepossessing ceremony. On June 10, 1986, fourteen members gathered in morning coats on the steps of the University Club (Gakushi Kaikan), the downtown Tokyo alumni club of the national universities. There, they unfurled a banner bearing the society's name and made a statement to the press announcing its inauguration. Members of the group had notified the major newspapers and television networks, and since they counted several well-known public intellectuals in their number, reporters and cameras were present to record and broadcast the event. As artist and founding member Akasegawa Genpei later noted, it looked like the formation of a new cabinet.[4]

The scientific-sounding name of the group was as tongue-in-cheek as the academic pomp of the inaugural meeting. The same parodic style marked the street observationists' "studies," which involved photographing and documenting oddities in the streets and grouping them into cleverly named categories. The group included three cartoonists, a popular science fiction writer, a literature scholar, and a dentist who had built a prodigious collection of fragments from demolished buildings, along with Akasegawa, who had been a leading figure in the artistic avant-garde of the 1960s and had subsequently had a successful career as a novelist, and Fujimori. Still, despite their eclecticism and humorous self-presentation, the street observationists were earnest enough about their investigations to publish their results, prefaced by manifestos announcing their intent to rediscover and reclaim the city. The challenge raised by the Street Observation Studies Society—a challenge its members put to themselves, and, by extension, a challenge their writing and photographs put to their public—was to find what could still be discovered in the streets of Tokyo that had not already been claimed by the state or capital. This challenge pointed directly back to founding theoretical issues of property. In Hegel's terms, property originates in the capacity of individuals to extend their will over external things by making and manipulating them. What part of the city did individual citizens still make for themselves? Over what fragment or vestige in the streets of Tokyo in 1986 could they still hope to extend their wills, when it all seemed to have been claimed and repackaged for them already?[5] By setting out to find and interpret the traces of others' interventions in the planned regularity of the contemporary city, the street observationists allied themselves with an imagined army of anonymous citizens claiming space by altering the streetscape.

To a degree that members of the group themselves had not anticipated, their activities proved popular. The response revealed that they had given a name and a rationale to a sensibility about the city that was already widely shared. Searching for undiscovered places and curious surprises in the streets of Tokyo had a new meaning in the 1980s. Since the opening of the fashionable, youth-oriented department stores and boutique complexes at Shibuya and other west Tokyo rail hubs in the 1970s (particularly by the Seibu-Parco group), youth consumption had transformed the face of the city. The generation that had come to Tokyo from the countryside for higher education and jobs in the 1960s and early 1970s, and had taken its causes to the streets in Shinjuku and elsewhere, was being replaced by a new generation of youth. The majority of this younger generation had been raised in the Tokyo suburbs, with money to spend and more interest in window-shopping and people watching than in political organizing.[6] The weekly event guides *PIA* and *City Road* began publication in 1971, shortly after the suppression of student movements and the reestablishment of police authority on campuses. With copious information on theater, film, and event venues major and minor, and with detailed neighborhood maps, these guides presented Tokyo as a vast assemblage of places to be explored.[7] *PIA Map*, a periodical volume of "play spot" maps, began publication in 1982, reflecting the expansion of consumption opportunities and the demand for related geographical data.[8] "Town walking" (*machi aruki*)—meaning in particular exploring in search of sources of entertainment, places to eat, and things to buy—was one of the buzz-words of this new information economy.

In 1983, Disneyland, the apotheosis and global icon of managed leisure consumption, opened in the suburbs of Tokyo, drawing huge crowds. West Tokyo's new commercial complexes offered an experience comparable to Disneyland in many respects: a completely enveloping, safe, clean environment tailored in every respect to young people's tastes.[9] Yet as managed consumption spaces flourished, so did the interest in escape from them. Reviewing the *Primer in Street Observation Studies* in the young men's magazine *Popeye,* writer Yamazaki Kōichi captured this paradox for trend-conscious youth:

> In Shibuya and Harajuku on the weekend, with everyone walking on the same streets and going around the same stores, it's such a pedestrian traffic jam that plenty of times you've got to wait through two lights to cross the street. And you're cursing "How come it's so damn crowded? Bumpkins go home!"—but leaving aside the fact that you're there too. . . . Well, sure, that's what they call "the carnivalesque nature of the street space in high consumption society," or something like that, and it's an important part of what makes cities fun, but if you think about it, it's totally obvious that a place where capital and functions and information are concentrated like Tokyo is going to be "fun." It's just that taking it just as it is and treating *that* as fun is not fun.

Yamazaki endorsed street observation as a "more advanced *machi aruki*" that would "reveal the secrets of the city." His review was titled "The Back Alleys Are More Fun than the Tidy Main Street."[10] As the crowds flocking to places recommended in the weekly guides and magazines grew, the search for the next new thing extended into slumming in unfashionable neighborhoods and consuming obviously unchic products. The restaurant and shopping guide *Hanako* had a hit with a series of books called *B-Grade Gourmet,* which promoted the hunt for the most authentic sources of proletarian meals like ramen noodles and rice omelets (*omuraisu*). Seibu-Parco's trend-watching magazine *Across* (Akurosu) reported in 1984 that the tastes of the present "prodigal age" were resolutely "B-grade," and it linked this to demand for no-brand and nostalgia goods, the "ethnic boom," and even a fascination with Communist countries as the antithesis to Japan's consumerism.[11] The currents of fashion in urban leisure thus generated desire for spaces and activities outside the dominant fashion, and—as the writer in *Popeye* recognized—the market continuously circled back to reincorporate the unfashionable within fashion. This insatiability of consumer capitalism presented a dilemma for the street observation studies group, whose members sought to resist it by identifying and claiming only objects that appeared uncommodifiable. Yet by documenting and popularizing them, they made commodities of them.

PROPERTY AND APPROPRIATION

Members of the group referred generically to the uncommodified objects that they photographed and documented as *bukken,* a word for "property" appropriated from the argot of real estate. A *bukken* is an item, a material instance of property, rather than property in the abstract. The group's use of the term masked political intent, since this eccentric word choice highlighted the materiality of the city they investigated while questioning how value came to be invested in material things and places.[12] There were actually layers of appropriation involved, since the objects of street observation themselves claimed space, and the observationists claimed those objects by naming and interpreting them, through language that was itself appropriated from elsewhere. Henri LeFebvre describes appropriation as an act of opposition against the static formulation of ownership implied by the term *property.* "Appropriation," he writes, "implies time (or times), rhythm (or rhythms), symbols, and a practice."[13] An act of appropriation questions the stability of property, whereas property itself is the product, or the instantiation, of claims made through appropriative acts and the recognition of those acts in law. LeFebvre correlates appropriation with use and property with exchange. Yet this is an artificial correspondence: the intent either to use or to exchange can motivate the static claim of property as established fact just as much as either can motivate the appropriative gesture that precedes or challenges that claim. Appropriation—the gesture of claiming something as property—simply draws attention to property's madeness, its artifactual nature. The appellation *bukken* was thus ironic both because of its reference to real estate, which holds a special place as spatial commodity and foundational form of property, and because of its reification: the materialist term *bukken* made value seem to inhere in the "thing" captured by street observation when, in fact, the object had no inherent value, having been made by some unidentified person or by natural accident, then only incidentally found, photographed, and interpreted by the observationist. This sequence of actions—more exchanges or *transactions* than signs of use value—bound observationists intimately to anonymous past appropriators and embedded itself in their identification of the objects they photographed as "properties."

Since Marcel Duchamp exhibited a urinal under the title "Fountain" in 1917, numerous artists have explored the idea of using unmodified everyday objects ("readymades," to use Duchamp's term) to challenge the institutional boundaries of art. The street observationists' "properties" lent themselves readily to interpretation in this conceptual tradition, particularly because Akasegawa was known as an artist. But the observationists eschewed the usual marks of artistic authorship. Street observation did not entail physically removing the object or altering the streetscape. Akasegawa wrote that the observationists maintained a strict "moral rule" to remain in the role of passersby, not even touching the "properties" in question.[14] They displayed and published their photographs with text but without signs of authorship, such as unique titles for individual images or identification of the photographer. Flyers advertising their first exhibition announced that they had taken more than ten thousand pictures and listed the districts they had covered, implying that this was not a display of carefully framed artworks but part of an ongoing documentation of the city as a whole. By simply recording, classifying, and describing their discoveries, the observationists left the city itself as the primary frame, suggesting the potential existence of innumerable similar instances in the same classification scheme, as an archeologist interprets fragments for what they suggest of the whole to which they once belonged, not for the intrinsic interest or beauty of the fragment itself.[15]

Authorship was further diluted by the fact that the street observationists worked as a group. In his "hyperart" project, a precursor of street observation studies, begun in the 1970s and serialized in the magazine *Photo Age* (Shashin jidai) in the early 1980s, Akasegawa had solicited photographs and descriptions of odd finds in the streets from his students and readers, using a standardized data form similar to something that might be used to record information about artifacts in an archeological or geological survey. The Street Observation Studies Society did not solicit contributions, but it continued to treat the activity as participatory. Street observation properties were collected in planned expeditions in which the group focused on a city or district for a few days, scouring the streets with their cameras and notebooks individually by day, then gathering at night to compare and interpret their findings. The "society" had no official membership list. People interested in joining were encouraged to start their own groups. As the title

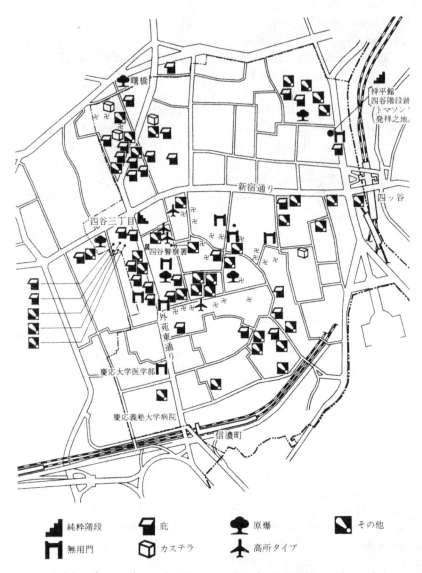

FIGURE 8. Map of street observation "properties" in the Yotsuya area. The symbols indicate (reading vertically from the top left): (1) pure staircase; (2) purposeless gate; (3) pent-roof type; (4) pound-cake type; (5) A-bomb type; (6) airborne type; (7) other. *Rojō kansatsugaku nyūmon* (Tokyo: Chikuma shobō, 1986).

of the group's first publication, *Primer in Street Observation Studies,* implied, street observation was presented as an activity to be taken up by anyone who wished to learn its methods (see figure 8).

Most of the members belonged to the student movement generation, and even if the master narratives of that era of political activism were dead, the impulse to translate ideas into group action—replete with published manifestos—remained. Individually, the choices and interpretations made by each observationist were clearly a kind of artistic work, but collectively they constituted a critical statement on urban property, along with the capitalist economy and national policies that manipulated it. Their collective presentation as an opus and as the basis of a method signaled a utopian attempt to recover or reconceive the city as a commons from which residents could appropriate as they pleased. Street observation thus carried forward some of the political ideals of the public square as commons into an era in which mass consumption had replaced the mass rally as the city's grandest spectacle and defining experience.

EMPIRICISM AS ETHOS

Real estate speculation and the policies that encouraged it viewed urban space dematerialized, in the abstract terms of economic calculation. The bubble economy of the late 1980s thus provided a fertile milieu for street observation's eccentric activities to develop into something like a movement, since those activities, by fixing on concrete material details of no economic significance, posed a precise antithesis to the real estate speculator's vision. Individually, however, members of the group had been exploring a microlevel empirical approach to the Tokyo streetscape since the early 1970s.

A central figure in the artistic avant-garde of the 1960s, Akasegawa had become a cause célèbre in 1966 when he was prosecuted for counterfeiting because he had distributed a reproduction of the face of a thousand-yen note as an announcement for an art event. During the four-year trial that followed, which resulted in his conviction without penalty, Akasegawa found himself caught between the courts and the art world. The experience left him estranged from the artistic avant-garde, which, like the state, had its own sanctioning institutions and ideology.[16] Starting in 1970, he began leading students, friends, and fans into the streets of Tokyo to photograph objects that he termed "hyperart" (*chōgeijutsu*): signs, street furniture, and elements of structures or road construction that looked like

they could be contemporary art.[17] To express their beautiful purposelessness, he subsequently named these objects *tomason,* after an American
baseball player (known in the Japanese press only by the transliteration of
his last name, Thomasson) who had been brought to Japan amid much
fanfare and had spent a season on the bench before returning to the United
States.[18] *Tomason* hunting was a communal activity in which the personal
expression of the artist was decentered, offering Akasegawa a mode of
aesthetic intervention in the city free of the onus of playing the individual
genius and martyr to Art.

Both in their evocation of the irrational and in their reliance on the
camera, hyperart and street observation bore echoes of surrealism. Akasegawa noted the resemblance, as well as a difference: while surrealism
had pursued the unconscious in the human body, street observation
sought the unconscious of the city.[19] *Tomason* photographs were reproduced in black and white, characterized by a documentary flatness, with
little shadow or movement.[20] Each "property" was typically represented
with two or three photographs, showing the setting and the anomalous
detail that delivered the "punch line." Descriptions often anthropomor-
phized the object or imputed will and intention to it. The plainness of the
visual presentation invited viewers to recall objects from their own surroundings and imagine them in the same light, redirecting their attention
to things on the periphery of consciousness. It was a practice of "awakening the eyeballs," Fujimori observed. Akasegawa later recalled feeling
so overwhelmed and excited after the group's first expedition that he
couldn't sleep, and the group's publisher, who was also a participant,
recalled returning to the office exhausted because everything he saw on
the habitual route to work had suddenly become new and fascinating,
demanding attention.[21]

Like Akasegawa, Fujimori had begun walking and documenting in
Tokyo in the early 1970s, when he set out with a colleague to identify
every surviving example of Western-style architecture in the city built
prior to World War II. He coined the term "signboard architecture"
(*kanban kenchiku*) for the most common vernacular type they found,
the two- and three-story shop houses that dominated commercial streets
in the old downtown. Built between the world wars, signboard architecture was constructed in wood by native carpenters but fronted with
ornamental façades in brick, tile, and copper that made the buildings
superficially Western. Since signboard architecture lacked the pedigree
of either a trained architect's design or a native tradition considered
pure, it had no place in the national patrimony of buildings then regarded

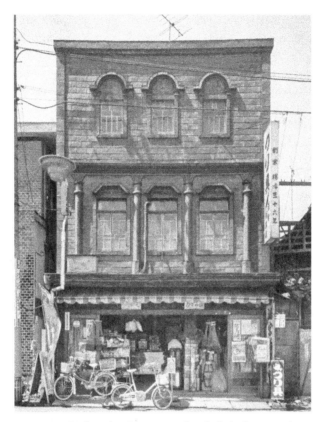

FIGURE 9. Signboard architecture: a shop built in the 1920s in the Kanda district. Photograph by Masuda Akihisa. Fujimori Terunobu and Masuda Akihisa, *Kanban kenchiku* (Tokyo: Sanseidō, 1988). © Masuda Akihisa.

as historically significant. Senior scholars criticized Fujimori, questioning whether these uncanonized modern buildings were worthy of scholarly study.[22] Fujimori held his ground on the basis of empirical method: these buildings were there to be documented, he asserted, yet academics had constructed a Whiggish history of architecture based on texts rather than on what stood right around them.[23] Fujimori stayed in the academy, but he resolved to reject the hierarchy of expertise and specialization of the human sciences. He also began writing popular essays about his Tokyo explorations, conducted together with a group he referred to as the Architecture Detective Unit (Kenchiku Tanteidan) (see figure 9).[24]

In many parts of the world after the late 1950s, avant-garde movements in art, architecture, and urban writing sought critical positions outside consumer society yet grappled with the paradox of its inescapability. Taking their art beyond the walls of art institutions, artists hoped to challenge the complacency of everyday life in mass society. Although the street observationists' ideas emerged primarily from a Japanese intellectual context, they shared both social concerns and modes of engagement with avant-gardists elsewhere. In performance pieces in the 1960s, Akasegawa had attempted an art that raided and critiqued the everyday. Like Guy Debord and members of the Situationist International, Akasegawa and Fujimori believed that new techniques of walking and documenting the city were necessary to challenge the "colonization of the everyday" by bureaucratic rationalism.[25] The fragments they collected spoke of a vanishing past, which was another thing they shared with Debord, who began his explorations in "psychogeography" out of a sense of the loss caused by the demolition of working-class neighborhoods like the Les Halles market area in Paris.[26]

Yet the intellectual context, cityscape, and consumer culture of 1980s Tokyo presented a different set of issues from the Paris of the 1950s and 1960s. Despite aesthetic common ground, street observation took a markedly different stance from its precursors in France. In the situationist *dérive* the walker did the deviating, whereas the street observationist treated the object as deviant and took the position of discoverer.[27] The difference did not necessarily dictate different practices, since both groups set out to wander without destination, and the identification of the deviance as an event and the deviant object as a discovery equally depended on the walker making it so. Still, it reflected a basic contrast in the position of the protagonist, as even the two movements' names suggested: the situationists saw themselves as radical agents engaged in reinventing urban space; the observationists saw themselves as bringing to light an urbanism already latent. Compared to Paris, where the layers of the past were everywhere recognized—if not all equally valued—in Tokyo the fact that the city contained layers of the past at all appeared to be a new discovery making the streets pregnant with possibility.

The street observationists differed most strikingly from Debord in their complete rejection of abstract theorization. From Akasegawa and Fujimori's vantage point in 1986, the ideas of French urban theorists were themselves imported commodities, conspicuously consumed in Japanese intellectual circles and beyond. Jean Baudrillard's apocalyptic interpretation of contemporary mass culture, clearly indebted to Debord's *Society of the Spectacle,* was read in a positive as well as a negative light in Japan.[28] Effectively turning Baudrillard on his head, literary critic Yamazaki Masakazu's widely discussed theory of "soft individualism" claimed that the shift to postindustrial society had liberated Japan from its feudal past, making Japanese consumers free subjects who defined themselves through their choices and made capitalism their servant. Marilyn Ivy has noted the symbiosis between Japanese mass culture critics and marketers in their readings of the new consumer's hedonism.[29] The influences went both ways: while some sociologists wrote about Japan's new consumerism in ways that accorded well with the interests of marketing and contributed to Seibu-Parco's mythic status as cultural catalyst, Seibu chairman Tsutsumi Seiji, a former student radical, wrote theoretical critiques of consumer society, quoting Baudrillard and Bataille.[30]

The further commodification of theory itself was exemplified by the popularity of the intellectual wunderkind Asada Akira, whose 1983 study *Kōzō to chikara* (Structure and power) sold over one hundred thousand copies, prompting the popular press to speak of the "Asada phenomenon."[31] Most of the book was a digest of French works in semiology. Readers reportedly read only the introduction, which invited them to treat the acquisition of knowledge as play.[32] Addressing a sold-out crowd at a department store in Ginza, Asada described contemporary society as a "Klein bottle"—an enveloping and cyclical space with neither inside nor outside—and advocated escape (*tōsō*) as the only means of establishing one's humanity, since human beings were innately distinguished from other creatures by their tendency toward "deviance" (*zure*).[33]

With the collapse of Marxist universal history, with racialist theories of Japanese culture in the ascendancy among conservatives, and with imported theories themselves seeming mere fashions to be consumed and discarded, the street observationists judged empiricism alone as the progressive intellectual's legitimate strategy of escape. As science fiction novelist and society member Aramata Hiroshi put it, there was "something terrifying" in the actual discovery of a real thing, something that was absent in semiotics and other theory. "The strength of fieldwork," Fujimori added, lay in this power of discovery, "that before the person who has seen something the person who hasn't can only be silent and listen."[34] Street observation's antitheoretical stance, which was itself a theoretical stance, reflected a disillusionment with theorizing more than an active opposition to Marxism or any other specific political theory (see figure 10).

Rather than citing European theoretical and architectural writing, Fujimori and Akasegawa proclaimed themselves the heirs of the Tokyo-based

MAZU
TOKYO
O
ARUITE
MIRU

FIGURE 10. Colophon to *Natural History in the Tokyo Streets* (Tōkyō rojō hakubutsu-shi) (Tokyo: Kajima shuppankai, 1987). The caption reads "First Walk Tokyo and See." Engraving by Harui Yutaka. © Paper Studio.

urban investigators Kon Wajirō and Yoshida Kenkichi, whose studies of public behavior and streetscapes during the 1920s went under the name "modernology" (*kōgengaku*). Modernology offered a precedent for the street observationists' witty visual and verbal style as well as for their minute empiricism. Working in the streets of a Tokyo rapidly rebuilding after the earthquake of 1923, Kon and Yoshida had attempted to attune themselves to every new detail of street life that could be recorded, sketched, or enumerated. Modernology treated the social world as an entropic, fluid form on which no overarching schema could be imposed—one could only trace trajectories through it and collect fragments from it.[35] Yet, whereas the modernologists had attempted to capture the fleeting present, their 1980s descendants looked back.

Street observation's empirical approach, which treated the contemporary city as a site for exploration and fieldwork, attracted a mass audience in 1980s Tokyo for two seemingly contradictory reasons. On the one hand, their empiricism had a populist appeal that put it in a long tradition of postwar democratic thought and practice. The circle movement of the 1950s had gathered small groups of ordinary citizens to create a people's literature.[36] Amateur historians had played the central role in the regional history movement of the 1960s, assembling documents and chronicling the non-elite histories of their prefectures, towns, and villages.[37] Grassroots movements in natural sciences such as geology had advocated an antitechnocratic "democratization" of science that placed the authority of the field researcher—who did the walking, digging, collecting, and observing—above that of the university-based scholar. Antipollution citizen groups had applied this kind of mass democratic science to monitor pollution levels in the 1960s and 1970s.[38] In parodic form, street observation offered a comparable democratic science that promised to wrest control of the city from technocrats. On the other hand, the fashion for appropriation as a response to consumer society in the 1980s placed street observation comfortably alongside the postmodern theorists, part of a new mode of intellectual hedonism that took the contemporary city as its playground. Responding to mass consumer society by appropriating and resituating its products or vestiges was a major part of the international art scene of the 1980s, a strategy rife with political ambiguity. In the domestic context, the politics of appropriation were no less ambiguous. Conservative Yamazaki Masakazu's proconsumerist theory of "soft individualism," after all, also championed appropriation.

DEVIANT PROPERTIES

Viewing the contemporary city as under siege by the "consumption empire" and state-driven urban development, the street observationists sought out deviations (*zure*) from the hegemonic logic of these adversaries. Anything that could be read as anticonsumerist, antirational, or antiplanning qualified potentially as a deviation. Fujimori defined the deviation in aesthetic terms, as an object at odds with its expected place or scale, something that possessed an "expressive excess."[39] The deviation was not only aesthetic, however, since it often also involved an element of trespass. Some instances revealed people trespassing in actual legal terms, claiming public property for unintended private purposes— truck gardens, for example, that were found being furtively maintained on the grounds of the National Diet or the banks of the Imperial Palace moat. Other trespasses were more casual or incidental, as in the category the street observationists called "animal trails" (*kemonomichi*), referring to the signs of foot traffic where people had taken shortcuts across grass or gravel-covered public areas.[40]

For Fujimori, the street observationist map also revealed a recognizable yet uncharted iconography of overlooked objects, properties "amortized and forgotten" yet still scattered through the city. In the 1987 book *Natural History in the Tokyo Streets* (Tōkyō rojō hakubutsushi), he and Aramata Hiroshi documented statues of forgotten historical figures, mounds built as miniature versions of Mount Fuji, public baths, abandoned subway stations, and what Fujimori called "fossil shops" or "miserable shops"—places of business that appeared hardly to be in business—which he described as sites that "throw at the passerby the existential question 'what is trade?'" and "expose the essence of the commodity."[41]

Akasegawa focused more on the accidental and uncanny. But Akasegawa's *tomason*-hunting component of street observation took its cues from the same vernacular city that Fujimori documented. *Tomason* tended to appear in places where the street was treated as a commons more than a thoroughfare. The dictum "purposeless, [yet] beautifully preserved," which Akasegawa used to describe his selection principle, gave a special place to surviving features of the streetscape that planned development would ordinarily eradicate. The anomalies he uncovered extended Fujimori's palimpsest of vernacular building regimes and overlooked monuments by revealing everywhere a more evanescent palimpsest of minute acts of construction and preservation. Hand-drawn or hand-painted signs posted on telephone poles, markings on the street itself, stones, pieces of concrete and other objects placed in public space to mark private use, along with unusual repairs and modifications to gates, fences, walls, and steps, provided hints to the observant passerby of the hand of some anonymous bricoleur (see figure 11).

In contrast to the usual forms of documenting architectural heritage, the street observationists never investigated the circumstances that lay behind the sites they photographed, and they never sought their physical preservation. What they preserved instead was the object's enchantment as an inexplicable presence. Its aura lay in the confluence of happenstance and human effort—effort that was sometimes futile, yet beautiful in its pathos. Conventional historical research and preservation would have entailed demonstrating that these objects were important examples of a style, relics of some significant event, or useful contributions to the present townscape. Research, in the minds of the street observationists, lay on a trajectory to exploitation for other purposes, destroying the capacity of the found object to speak directly.

A distinct historical conception of the "originary landscape" nevertheless lay implicit in the group's reclassifying of these things and places

FIGURE 11. Hyperart *tomason* no. 1: the "pure staircase of Yotsuya." Note repair to hand railing on right. Akasegawa Genpei, *Chōgeijutsu tomason* (Tokyo: Chikuma shobō, 1987).

as new urban landmarks. For Fujimori, the source of the street observationist's urbanism lay in a time when Tokyoites had been able to build what they needed without relying on municipal authorities. After the earthquake of 1923, people had constructed their own temporary shelters, and merchants had created improvised shops, hanging out banners announcing their trades. Kon had started his modernology work by sketching these handmade shelters, noting the ingenuity with which people had accommodated themselves using available materials. These skills of self-sufficiency, Fujimori believed, had been all but lost by the 1980s.[42] The traces of subtle appropriations and transgressions of public space thus spoke of an imagined past when individuals established their rights to the city through the labor of shaping the environment themselves.

Such a story of origins could find its philosophical foundation in John Locke's liberal individualist theory of the origin of property at the moment that man first mixed his labor with nature, improving it and thereby making it his own. The city, Aramata noted, was a "second nature" awaiting its own naturalists.[43] The anonymous makers of Tokyo's properties, the observationists found, had mixed their labor with the second nature of the street, and without the sanction of the state or the intervention of capital, had made it their own. Writing in the early 1980s, Fredric Jameson called culture in postmodern society a "second nature," since the capitalist economy, after it had completely cultivated and exploited the resources of the natural world, turned toward the products of culture.[44] In contrast to Jameson's bleak story of ineluctable exploitation, the observationists conjured for second nature a redemptive story of return to the beginnings of property, as if the decline of the industrial era had offered humanity a second chance, with a new nature to be appropriated.[45]

Signs were abundant at the time of the Street Observation Studies Society's inauguration that the vernacular city was being dismantled and replaced by one over which individuals would have less control. Still, Tokyo remained a complex and irregular city in visual and formal terms, lacking an overarching street plan and shot through with oddities and accidental juxtapositions. Seeing these irregularities rather than the encroaching corporate homogeneity was a matter of figure and ground. High-rise construction in steel and concrete made low-rise wood buildings stand out as figure against the ground of a faceless modernism, and the incursion of corporate and commercial capital made formerly overlooked quirky local shops seem worthy of note. At the same time, the international context of postmodernism in art and architecture made the historical trace desirable and quotable. Photographers and journalists had recorded the survival of a one-story shack nestled into a residual triangular lot on the flank of the 109 Building in Shibuya, which was one of the most conspicuous icons of the high-tech city of consumption. The shack housed a bar whose owners had set up shop in the black market after the war and refused to give up their land when the Tōkyū Corporation redeveloped the site in 1979.[46] Remnants of the black market district that rose up on the south side of Shinjuku Station in the immediate postwar period were documented by photographer Araki Nobuyoshi, among others.[47] Intellectuals haunted tiny bars in one- and two-story shacks in another district in Shinjuku, known as "Golden Avenue." Part of the appeal of these places lay in the fact that they survived in improbable settings—in the case of Golden Avenue and the alleys of the former black market, a stone's throw from Shinjuku Station and surrounded by office buildings.[48]

The street observationists' photographs thus partook of an emerging aesthetic of the fragment. Araki, the most famous and prolific of Tokyo photographers, had started walking and compiling his voluminous oeuvre in the late 1960s.[49] Much of his work during the 1970s and 1980s documented the layers of occupancy and use in Tokyo streetscapes and buildings. He rejected framing and sought a mode of unposed shot devoid of subjective content, directing the camera at what he called the "skin of the city" and permitting the streetscape to speak for itself. To the extent that there was an overall artistic consistency to Araki's photos, it was the very ordinariness that was an inevitable product of sheer volume and lack of stylization. The kind of scenes and objects toward which he turned his camera followed a certain pattern, however. Araki's streetscapes, critic Iizawa Kōtarō writes, were dominated by three things: "details," "stains," and "lumpiness" (*dekoboko*).[50] Although Araki published photographs throughout the 1960s and 1970s, his work became widely known only in the early 1980s, with the publication of the magazine *Photo Age,* the same magazine in which Akasegawa's "hyperart" project was initially serialized. Araki's documentary style and attention to irregularities had clear affinity with the aesthetic of street observation.

Just as the project of street observation took marginal objects and made them prominent, the street observationists were unabashed about the marginality of their own enterprise. Like the concept of deviance, marginality had no shortage of intellectual champions in the 1980s. Street observation made these intellectual sensibilities accessible by taking them out into the streets. The accumulated material traces of the past, particularly fragments that failed to conform to present urban patterns and functions, were the one thing irrefutably present in Tokyoites' immediate surroundings to assert difference amid homogenization. Street observation provided a framework, a language, and tools to take some of these fragments and make them meaningful, appreciating them for their stubborn resistance as well as their absurdity. Deviant properties reaffirmed that individuals made their environment, while street observation as a practice reaffirmed that the individual consumer could be more than a passive beneficiary (or victim) of capitalism.

STREET OBSERVATION AS MASS COMMODITY

The activities of the Street Observation Studies Society were widely reported and imitated. Since several members of the group were popular in the media already, the mere fact that they had banded together to form a "society" was newsworthy, and the objects they pointed out, by extension, acquired the aura of celebrity. But the mass media's version of street observation was apt to be less cunning and wrapped in paradox. Interpretations tended to tip either toward tragedy or toward comedy, since thoroughgoing irony was difficult to sustain. In tragic mode, street observation was read as drawing attention to parts of the old city threatened by modern urban development; in comic mode, street observation simply offered a new sort of pastime. In either case, one inescapable irony for the observationists themselves was that their success as crusaders against the commodification of the city streets derived commodity value from the purportedly valueless "properties" they had photographed. The *Street Observation Primer* sold well enough to go into multiple printings. The first exhibition of their discoveries, titled "Tokyo Fun Museum" (Tōkyō omoshiro hakubutsukan) was held at a gallery in the new Shitamachi location of a Seibu department store—the very embodiment of the "consumption empire" encroaching on a previously unconquered working-class neighborhood. Magazines, newspapers, and television contributed further to the commodification, reappropriating street observation and its objects in the process. When the location of a "property" was known, Akasegawa wrote in apparent frustration, reporters from the television stations and glossy weeklies would go looking for it, treating it as a riddle to be solved. Interviewing local residents to determine how a particular oddity had come about reduced the element of mystery that gave the practice itself the surrealist resonance Akasegawa valued. "Since street observation is completely useless," he wrote, "it only exposes the emptiness of the so-called 'correct answer.'"[51]

Journalists and reporters seeking to make sense of the street observationists' activities as a news story groped for the vocabulary with which to derive a general message. For most, it was about what the title of the group's first exhibition announced: the "fun" of the city. Some read this fun itself as serious business. Reviewing the *Street Observation Primer,* writer Egawa Kōichi found that it taught him "what it meant to live free in the city."[52] In contrast, the *Asahi shinbun* article covering the group's inaugural event treated it as salvage archeology and possibly an antidevelopment crusade. The article was headlined "A Sense of Crisis at the Disappearing Townscape: United Front Formed with Founding of Street Observation Studies Society." It noted that Tokyo was in the midst of a process of urban redevelopment not seen since the earthquake of 1923 and quoted Fujimori speaking of "standing on a precipice." In this late twentieth-century reincarnation of Kon Wajirō's modernology, the *Asahi* writer proposed, "one glimpses a suspicion of the type of city-building that uproots all the weight of history, the breath of nature and the smells of everyday life."[53] This interpretation prompted other journalists to view street observation as nostalgic—a view that rankled the observationists, yet was hard to dispel entirely, in light of the patina and hand-craftedness of many of the objects they chose.[54] Street observation's objects were not always antiquated, but they showed the passage of time: human labor reworking the fossilizing forms of second nature—as in bricked-in doors and staircases to nowhere—and first nature working its effects slowly on human products—like the roots of a tree that have enveloped an iron fence, reclaiming spaces that humans in their hubris had attempted to claim to themselves. And since the observationists often noted that the practice involved coming at the landscape with the fresh eyes of a child, it was natural enough to see these adults playing at being children as nostalgists seeking to reconstruct the "originary landscape" of their youths.

Popular magazines treated street observation as an open-participation game. "Calling All Street Observationists!" announced the headline in *Hot Dog Press* shortly after the group's launch. To underscore street observation's cultural legitimacy, the magazine pointed out that the group's "properties" had already appeared in venues such as the art journal *Geijutsu shinchō* and the media review *Kōkoku hihyō*. Readers of *Hot Dog Press* were invited to submit their own discoveries to the editors, to be sent on to the group. "If you are the possessor of an 'observer's eye' that causes you to stop whenever you glimpse a carpenter or house painter at work or road construction going on," the advertisement said, "then you can appreciate that every 'street' conceals the possible presence of a 'problematic property.'"[55] A review of the *Primer in Street Observation Studies* in the comic magazine *Manga akushon* similarly emphasized street observation's availability to all, noting that its great virtue was that it was a game that cost no money.[56] This was the populist version of the group's anticonsumerism.

The popular press had in fact provided a venue for similar urban ephemera collecting prior to the 1986 founding of the Street Observation Studies Society. Part of the group's success derived from its easy fit within this genre of participatory observation in print. A feature in the monthly magazine *Takarajima* called "Voice of Wonderland" (abbreviated "VOW"), for example, had been printing reader's letters and photographs since 1973. In the 1980s, VOW turned to printing oddities that readers had discovered, eventually publishing them separately in a book series subtitled "Strange Things in Town" (Machi no henna mono). In the afterword to one of these volumes, writer Enokido Ichirō noted the precedent of Kon Wajirō and observed that the world was flooded with meanings that our eyes normally fail to see. Writer Naka-jima Ramo proposed in the same volume that VOW was creating a time capsule of the sorts of trivial and quotidian things that people in the future would really want to know about the present era.[57] The only stylistic difference between the way the editors of VOW collected oddi-ties and the street observationist approach was that VOW's punch lines were simpler—the object in question tended to be treated as someone's laughable mistake, to be labeled *baka* (stupid) or *hen* (weird). VOW's readers pursued, in a less cagey and sophisticated form, the same types of anomalies and deviations that street observationists did.

Street observation's pursuit of the useless could thus be made use-ful in various ways by others. The movement was featured in news-paper and magazine copy about the crisis of uncontrolled real estate development and the destruction of the old city, as well as in the occasional quirky local-interest television feature. In a few places, government, too, saw value in the group's activities. Members were brought in to conduct training seminars in municipal and prefectural government offices, and ultimately in the national Ministry of Trans-port. The western Tokyo suburb of Suginami Ward commissioned Hayashi Jōji, a member of the group who had exhaustively docu-mented the designs of manhole covers, to design new manhole covers for a walking route through the ward. street observation thus also became a potential tool in urban design and in what is sometimes called "place branding."[58]

Inert and for the most part unremarkable without their labels, street observation's objects were essentially conjured into existence by the observationists themselves. The very peculiarity of the observationists' claims on their behalf as anonymous appropriations from the managed environment of the city thus made the observationists' own reappropria-tion conspicuous, implicitly inviting further appropriation. Since the actual history of the original appropriations of street space whose results they documented was left a mystery, the group's publications drew atten-tion to the entertaining and simple practice of claiming things by naming and documenting them, with camera and notebook, so that others—adopting the street observationists' idiom as the street observationists themselves had adopted the techniques and sensibilities of nineteenth-century naturalists, Kon Wajirō's modernology, and surrealism—could construct their own city of personally selected fragments and deviations.

The bricoleurs who made the city that street observation uncovered took their pieces from the second nature created by industrial society. By connecting these sites to one another, street observation composed a third nature: a city made of the fragments of industrial society reconstituted and reinterpreted to suit the needs and desires of postindustrial society. And just as the street observationists could appropriate the objects of earlier citizens' appropriations of second nature, others could appropriate the objects of the street observationists' third nature.[59] Indeed, there was no reason not to imagine a fourth or fifth nature. The further orders of appropriation came not simply in the form of popular imitations of their practice, but in television, film, and museum displays that drew upon the iconography that street observation had helped establish. Just as the streetscape itself was made up of layer upon layer of small acts of building, altering, and marking space, street observation had revealed that in postindustrial Tokyo, property rested on no ontological order of individuals' making, but existed virtually, in a spiraling sequence of appropriations upon appropriations.

Amid these unending appropriations, was there in fact redemption in finding the "properties" left by the city's bricoleurs? Did the discovery provide tools for reclaiming urban space from the forces of global capital and state developmentalism? The street observationists never pursued these questions programmatically. Yet appropriation in itself, as a mode of reinvention through consumption, was not what they celebrated—rather, it was the creative handiwork of anonymous Tokyoites and the strange wonder of the natural and artificial environment they inhabited. In the end, the street observationists must be called optimists, for without a belief in the possibility of redemption in individuals' reshaping the city to their own ends, they would not have taken to the streets to investigate.

CHAPTER 4

Museums, Heritage, and Everyday Life

Starting in the 1980s, museums in Tokyo began to collect everyday objects and reconstruct everyday scenes of the past. This was a new kind of public investment. It also established a new public commemorative language for Tokyo, built around the everyday and the ordinary. This new public history drew from a longer intellectual tradition of the study of everyday life, which, after 1970, converged with a developing exhibit design industry that made scenes of everyday life one of its specialties. The confluence found fullest expression in the planning and design of the Edo-Tokyo Museum, completed in 1993 (see figure 12). With lavish funding from a municipal government flush with property tax revenues, scholars, designers, and bureaucrats in cultural administration collaborated to create the first comprehensive museum of the city. The Edo-Tokyo Museum was designed to serve as a new monument for the city at the apex of its four-hundred-year history and as an architectural icon of Governor Suzuki Shun'ichi's "World City Tokyo."[1] It thus presented an official summation of how the city's past was to be remembered, symbolically ending the period of experiments in using Tokyo's past to claim the city as the property of its citizens. The monumental and the everyday, two poles of meaning configuring urban space since the 1960s, came together here, but the terms were reversed, as a privatized everyday was given monumental form.

Monumental expression of the city's history did not, however, close it off to further appropriation. In continual flux before the Edo-Tokyo

FIGURE 12. The Edo-Tokyo Museum. Photograph by the author.

Museum's completion, history and nostalgic memory continued to evolve afterward as well. This chapter traces the intellectual currents and institutions that produced exhibits of everyday life in Japanese cities, particularly in Tokyo, from 1970 through the years that the Edo-Tokyo Museum was planned and built, and into the first decade of the twenty-first century.

Although everyday life has been represented in museums in many countries since the nineteenth century, the way it was represented and contextualized, and the meanings derived from it, changed significantly in the latter half of the twentieth century. The first great sea change, noted by many museologists, reflected the populist turn in preservation by shifting from an antiquarian focus on the document and the artifact to an emphasis on reconstructed settings. Writers on museums have referred to this change variously as a shift "from object to experience," or "from knowledge to narrative," but both connote the same overall trend.[2] The reconstructed interior, house, or streetscape had its roots in ethnographic displays at nineteenth-century expositions—some involving living human beings—and in folk-house museum parks like Sweden's Skansen (built in 1873), but in public history museums it became common only in the latter half of the twentieth century.[3]

In Japan and around the world, this trend coincided with development of the notion of "cultural heritage" (*bunka isan*) as a way of describing things recognized as constituting a valuable shared past for some community of people in the present (including, potentially, the global community of all humanity). International diffusion of the concept of cultural heritage following the 1972 UNESCO Convention Concerning the Protection of the World Cultural and Natural Heritage encouraged a more holistic understanding of the usable past. "Heritage" also signified a new view of national and international publics as the heirs to historical artifacts and places—recipients of a history passed down to them in things—rather than as passive audiences to be instructed by monuments, historic sites, and museum exhibits.

Exhibits of everyday life in Japan prior to the 1970s were primarily folkloric or ethnographic in nature. Museum contents were presented as belonging to a culture exotic to the curator and viewer, and distant in geographical and class-cultural terms if not in time. In the 1920s, Shibusawa Keizō, grandson of the Meiji industrialist Shibusawa Eiichi and future minister of finance (from 1945 to 1946), built the country's first modern museum collection of native everyday artifacts, which he called the Attic Museum. Shibusawa had begun by collecting traditional handmade toys (*kyōdo gangu*). He formed a collectors' society, which in its early days had the character of a hobbyists' club more than that of a scientific organization. Ultimately judging toy collecting by itself to be a dead end, Shibusawa moved on to systematic collection of rural folk implements generally. Shibusawa and his colleagues took a taxonomic approach to ordering and displaying the collection, following the approach established in natural historical and ethnographic exhibits at the British Museum and elsewhere.[4] Since the Attic Museum housed objects from around the Japanese archipelago, it represented a national heritage, but it also highlighted the unevenness of national space. Wealthy, urban, and cosmopolitan, Shibusawa enjoyed a life far removed from the rural places where he did his collecting. The social and cultural gap between rural and urban Japan was pronounced in the interwar years, and this gap was felt keenly by Shibusawa, as it was by folklorists like Yanagita Kunio. Shibusawa collected out of fear that artifacts and folk practices of the Japanese countryside would soon be lost to modernization.

Toys readily evoke nostalgia for childhood. They are also for many people the first private possessions in life, the first external property we acquire as our own and manipulate as we please. Thus, Shibusawa's movement from toy collecting to ethnography can be seen as recapitulating a process in human development from what psychoanalysts call "transitional objects" to fully autonomous property ownership.[5] The transition in the Attic Museum collection may also be taken as a microcosm of a social development from private antiquarianism to public preservation. With the addition of folk tools, Shibusawa's collection became "cultural heritage" to be maintained and passed down to future generations.

One further dimension to the Attic Museum collection reflected twentieth-century social concerns, along with Shibusawa's own involvement in industry. In the newly named *mingu* (implements of the people), Shibusawa sought objects of use value, and saw them as embodying an everyday life founded in productive labor. The collection documented and commemorated a nation of productive agricultural households and villages. This focus led him to avoid artifacts available for sale and to collect only directly from the makers and users of the implements themselves, so that the implements' authenticity as folk tools would be untainted by the market.[6]

In ethnographic displays like Shibusawa's, the absent owner was himself or herself an object of inquiry and preservationist interest, with the consequence that artifacts like tools and clothing had special valence for the intimate connection they bore to the owner's body. In contrast, the heritage approach that emerged in the 1970s shifted attention from the productive labor of the peasant maker and user of farm tools to past lifestyles generally. Accompanying this was a new focus on consumption and domesticity, embodied in houses and household items. The reconstructed house created the impression of a whole and knowable past, suggesting a milieu the museum visitor might inhabit. Household objects placed in situ in reconstructed interiors added to that impression. In situ display also helped sever the relationship between the artifact and its original owner, making the museum's contents available to anyone.

Models of domestic interiors in Japanese museums were first introduced as part of a global move toward making museum displays more entertaining and approachable. The 1970 World Exposition in Osaka brought this trend to Japan. In 1937, Shibusawa had donated the Attic Museum collection to the Japan Ethnological Society, proposing construction of a national museum.[7] His plan lay dormant for a quarter century, but it was revived in the 1960s and carried forward in the exposition. This ultimately resulted in the National Museum of Ethnology, which opened on the former exposition grounds in 1977. Umesao Tadao, who led a study mission to look at methods of display in historical and ethnographic museums around the world in preparation for the exposition, noted with enthusiasm the trend away from what he called "dead museums." He also observed that the time was ripe for an ethnology museum at home because of the growth of interest in museums on the part of the Japanese public, which he attributed to the spread of postsecondary education and an increase in leisure time for cultural activities.[8] As museums became a part of mass society, they lost their privileged status as preserves of high culture and became one of many available forms of edifying leisure, competing with theme parks and television.

The supplanting of cases of authentic artifacts by reconstructed scenes and mock-ups might appear at first to thwart the museum's role as a site of heritage, but in fact the opposite was the case. "Heritage" in its new usage referred as much to the linking of past and present effected through artifacts as it did to the actual artifacts transmitted. The capacious ideal of "heritage" as historical identity came to overlay the earlier focus on objects of monumental value ("cultural properties," in the postwar Japanese terminology) or of ethnographic significance, just as museums shifted from being repositories of rare artifacts to being sites for the staging of popular educational experiences. Rather than enshrining the relics of an illustrious past or of exotic people and places, populist public history sought to compose a past that contemporary audiences could feel belonged to them. Where artifacts alone could not convey this, full-size reconstructed settings promised to offer an experience of connectedness to the past derived from lifelike settings. Artifacts and reconstructions were combined to impart a sense of the past's immediate presence.[9]

This ultimately set the stage for a second shift in Japanese history museums that followed in the 1990s, in which everyday life exhibits moved from teaching a communal past to providing material for personal reminiscence. Each moment in this evolution of exhibits of everyday life possessed an iconic object or display style, reflecting the preoccupations of museum professionals and their advisers as well as contemporaneous trends in popular culture. In the 1970s, exhibit designers sought to present a timeless core of everyday life that resisted the effects of Western modernity. Their key device was a model farmhouse. At Tokyo museums in the 1980s, memories of poverty and local community were evoked in reconstructed wooden tenements (*nagaya*). This trend was followed in the 1990s and 2000s by representations of everyday life in a domestic interior centered on a dining table (*chabudai*), which served to embody family togetherness. Museum presentations of domestic life after the 1990s also increasingly featured displays of mass-market commodities from the recent past, together with displays that referred to television programs and movies, designed to awaken personal nostalgia.

Throughout this evolution in exhibit style after 1970, however, museums persistently located the heart of past everyday life in the domestic sphere, usually as a site of consumption and reproduction rather than production. The home was where historians of everyday life and exhibit designers sought to give expression to community in intimate and familiar form. Privileging the home as the site of everyday life elided other sites of community and spaces of commonality, and made possible the reinscription in objects of ideological bonds between the individual and the state.

THE CULTURE OF EVERYDAY LIFE AS IDEAL AND MISSION

In Shibusawa's original plans for a national museum of ethnology, the collection was to combine the garments, tools, toys, and ritual implements already in the Attic Museum with an outdoor museum of folk houses modeled on Stockholm's Skansen.[10] To be completed in time for the twenty-six hundredth anniversary of imperial rule in 1940, the museum would also have included Ainu and Korean folk houses, reflecting the expanded purview of Japanese ethnology under the empire. Kon Wajirō, who had visited Skansen in 1935 with a guidebook given him by Shibusawa, did design sketches.[11] Japan's first international exposition was also planned for 1940, but it was ultimately canceled due to the deepening austerities of total war.[12] Eventually, the project was set aside, to be revived by others decades later. The Attic collection lay in storage until the national museum finally opened in Osaka in 1977.

By the 1970s, the vision of the museum had altered, affected by the postwar intellectual climate and by the ideals of the 1970 exposition. Instead of representing the folk culture of Japan and some of its colonial territories, the new museum sought to represent folk culture from the entire world. Sculptor Okamoto Tarō, appointed to serve as chief producer of the Theme Pavilion for the exposition's central "Festival Plaza," authored the plan to install ethnographic exhibits of the peoples of the world there. A survey team was dispatched to collect artifacts, and a separate team of subproducers, including Metabolist spokesman

Kawazoe Noboru and several other figures in the Metabolist group, was chosen to work on particular exhibits.[13]

Planning for the national museum went on concurrently with exposition planning, which began in 1964. With realization of the exhibit of cultures of the world in 1970, the groundwork was complete for a permanent museum, which would be built on the site after the exposition ended. Museum director Umesao Tadao hired Kawazoe to oversee the design of Japan-related exhibits. In moving from exposition planning to museum exhibit planning, Kawazoe left behind his role as spokesman for the Metabolism movement and its future-oriented architectural utopianism and turned his energy toward the representation of past and present everyday life.

Since the 1960s, Japanese intellectuals in various positions had come to feel keenly the need for a living quotidian culture that could have political meaning, and, in the museum context, for a mode of display that would allow visitors to experience that living culture directly. This encouraged museums to focus on the commonplace and the familiar rather than on the vanishing and exotic. The new museums aimed to give visitors a sense of the actuality of the life represented, as opposed to the antiquarian authenticity of the artifact. Kawazoe's exhibits at the Museum of Ethnology, designed under the direction of Umesao, reflected this political idealization of the everyday. Two seemingly minor curatorial moves here established an approach that placed intrinsic value in the commonplace: first, house models incorporated the surrounding lots and trappings of occupancy; and second, models reconstructed the state of the sites on which they were based as they were found at the time of the survey rather than reconstructing their past. Curators thus treated the detritus of an ordinary household as no less worthy of being in a museum than a historic folk house, and presented history itself as existing in unbroken continuity with the present. The Japan exhibit centered on four empirically precise $1/10$-scale models of farmhouses, chosen because they were typical of the major regional types in the archipelago. For the fieldwork, Kawazoe mobilized students of the folklore scholar Miyamoto Tsuneichi—who enjoyed cult status among youth in the 1960s—and young architects who had done design surveys in the countryside during the student movement days in order to escape the turmoil on Tokyo campuses. Rural Japan at the time was experiencing an unprecedented tourist boom, inspired in no small part by the success of Miyamoto Tsuneichi himself in encouraging young urbanites to reconnect with their national roots by visiting farm villages.[14] Riding the wave of the new rural tourism, one farmhouse the students surveyed for Kawazoe had recently become an inn, and it was shown at the museum as such. A bicycle parked outside another was replicated in miniature.[15]

The turn toward populist themes and the common use of reconstructed settings in U.S. museums in the 1960s and 1970s has been related to the triumph of "bottom-up" social history in universities and to a new educational mandate given by government agencies and school boards to make history accessible to a wider audience. Similar influences were at work in Japan as well, but behind this contemporary international context, valorization of the everyday at Japanese museums had deep native philosophical roots. Between the time of the exposition and the opening of the museum, Kawazoe had founded an academic society for the study of everyday life (*seikatsugaku*), built around the legacy of Kon Wajirō, who had been his mentor at Waseda University. Kon had proposed such a field in an essay published in 1951. Since the 1920s, Kon had built the foundations of this field through his graphic microstudies of everyday patterns of behavior in public and private settings. The minute empiricism of Kawazoe's everyday life studies and of the reconstructions in museums after 1970 derived from this tradition of scholarship as well as from the work of folklorists and collectors like Shibusawa.[16]

Kawazoe also regarded *seikatsugaku* as a political tool. Like scholars of the new "people's history" (*minshūshi*), and, in a different sense, like Henri LeFebvre in France, Kawazoe believed that the last possible site of resistance to bureaucratic modernization lay in the everyday. Quoting Marx's observation that the abstraction of labor under capitalism had made it possible for the first time to understand labor in past historical eras, Kawazoe proposed that the contemporary stage of Japan's development had brought about for the first time the abstraction of everyday life itself, giving the history of everyday life both a new significance and a new interpretability. In this moment of crisis, when traditions were being destroyed, a discipline of everyday life study was needed to give direction to national life, he maintained. Kawazoe believed that the abstraction of everyday life called for a concrete response that was both scholarly and political, much as Marx's political economy had responded concretely to the abstraction of labor under capitalism. The empirical work of representing *seikatsu* in museums flowed from this commitment.[17]

Kawazoe emphasized that the social and technological transformations of the 1950s and 1960s had made it impossible to return to an agrarian society. His object of concern was a thoroughly urbanized everyday. Thus, he focused not on the makers of hand tools and their craft but on consumers in a complex society, whom he called *seikatsusha*, employing the term that had gained currency in municipal bureaucracy and consumer advocacy.[18] Everyday life in *seikatsugaku* included the consumption of mass-manufactured commodities. Yet Kawazoe held the conviction that at the foundations of the contemporary Japanese lifeworld lay cultural continuities still untouched by either market fashions or state rationalization. *Seikatsugaku,* Kawazoe explained in the Everyday Life Studies Association's first bulletin, was a peculiarly Japanese concept intended to provide a "filter" for coping with the relentless pursuit of efficiency, or "Western rationalism." Everyday life was the site where cultural "stock" accumulated—not merely ephemeral things "like last year's refrigerator," which gets thrown out next year.[19]

These ideas themselves were not new. The concept of a "culture of everyday life" or "living culture" (*seikatsu bunka*) had emerged in the late 1930s. Intended as the antithesis to a modern urban lifestyle that embraced every new image or commodity to come from overseas, *seikatsu bunka* provided a touchstone for discourse on both aesthetics and social transformation in the increasingly fascist climate of the era.[20] For philosopher Miki Kiyoshi, writing in 1940, culture and everyday life in Asia had always been unified, and westernization threatened to destroy this unity. Japan needed revitalization, he maintained, through a resurgence of culture "from below," where tradition was a dynamic force, part of a culture of production, rather than merely an object of veneration.[21] Updated for postwar mass society, Kawazoe's manifestos for *seikatsugaku,* penned in the early 1970s, displayed the same anticonsumerism combined with rejection of nostalgia, the same belief that true culture resided in the most ordinary things—not in elite art or imported philosophies—and the same unquestioned native essentialism.

Although the museum's elevation of everyday life possessed this long intellectual pedigree, the confluence of individuals and institutions in 1970 around the exposition exhibit and the ethnology museum was new. Expo '70's Theme Pavilion was the birthplace of a collaboration between bureaucrats, academics, and culture industry figures that would form a lasting institutional structure for Japanese museums. To design the exhibits, Kawazoe worked with film set designers, including Ono Hitoshi, who had left the Tōei film company to join the Theme Pavilion team, and who subsequently established Total Media Planning, the country's first and largest museum design firm.[22] Kawazoe became Total Media's senior adviser soon after Expo '70. Film industry participants in turn brought in prop suppliers like Takatsu Decorative Arts, which created a museum supply division in 1971 in response to demand from Total Media.[23] Through Kawazoe, designers from the Metabolist group and intellectuals involved in exposition planning were engaged as an informal consulting board for the newly established design company, using it at the same time as their think tank.[24]

Total Media was formally commissioned to design and fabricate exhibits for the Museum of Ethnology in 1972. During the period between the exposition and the construction of the museum, Kawazoe lectured the company's young designers and managers on everyday life culture. Total Media president Ono Hitoshi distilled Kawazoe's message into a company mission to engage in "forming everyday life culture" (*seikatsu bunka no keisei*) and a corporate philosophy of "making culture an enterprise" (*bunka no jigyōka*).[25] In the hands of Total Media's chief executive, then, the study and active creation of "everyday life," which ran together in Kawazoe's rhetoric, were recast as sources of commercial value.

Expo '70 also brought together key figures in the postwar planning and policy establishments, who formed relationships that would live on in large public projects. Suzuki Shun'ichi, Expo '70's secretary general (*jimu sōchō riji*), was already a veteran of state pageant management, having planned the unrealized first international exposition in 1940 and managed the 1964 Olympics. Tange Kenzō was put in charge of the master plan. Suzuki would become governor of Tokyo in 1979, then hire Tange to design the new Tokyo City Hall in 1988. Suzuki first announced his plan to build an Edo-Tokyo historical museum as part of his "My Town Tokyo" campaign at a tenth-anniversary gathering of planners and designers who had been involved in the 1970 exposition. Soon after the announcement, Total Media president Ono Hitoshi visited the newly created "Offices of Everyday Life Culture" (at that time called the Seikatsu Bunkabu) in Tokyo City Hall to begin negotiating a role for the company in this project. Once this objective had been achieved, Ono restructured Total Media to direct all resources toward the Edo-Tokyo Museum. One major cultural project thus linked seamlessly to the next, with many of the same individuals leading the way.[26]

Planning of the Edo-Tokyo Museum spanned the decade of the 1980s. Between the completion of the Museum of Ethnology and the completion of the Edo-Tokyo Museum, Total Media built a large portfolio of history museum projects, beginning with the Shitamachi Museum, opened in 1980, fourteen years after the idea had first been proposed by novelist Shirai Kyōji. The Shitamachi Museum, the first urban history museum in Tokyo to feature a life-size architectural reconstruction, was unusual among Total Media's projects for its level of local involvement. Much of the collection was built from donations solicited by Taitō Ward, and individual donors' names were included in display labels. To build the reconstructions, Total Media worked with local carpenters who volunteered their services.[27] This museum and the Fukagawa Edo Museum (completed in 1986), which was built by another Shitamachi ward government following Taitō Ward's success, served as the company's trial runs for the Edo-Tokyo Museum.

As the exhibit design industry and the budgets for local museums grew, subsequent projects came to rely more on purchased artifacts and building expertise brought in by Total Media and other design firms. Beginning in the 1970s, prefectural and municipal governments around the country incorporated museum plans in centenary commemorations.[28] Many of these came to fruition in the 1980s. In these projects, Total Media developed formulae for representing everyday life history that would subsequently be applied at the Edo-Tokyo Museum. Much of the material substance of everyday life, particularly recent urban everyday life, was not sharply determined by local factors. Total Media and its rivals thus built a national industry for representing locality using variations on a few common themes.[29]

Takahashi Hiroshi, Total Media's senior designer for the Edo-Tokyo Museum and participant in a number of other regional museum projects, has noted the connection between national planning, local history, and commemoration in the proliferation of everyday-life exhibits. Large public works projects driven by the third and fourth Comprehensive National Development Plans (Zensō, 1977 and 1986) broke ground in many untouched sites, sparking a wave of last-minute salvage archeology. In Tokyo, the first major excavation of the Tokugawa-period capital was done in 1975. The results of the excavation were published in 1985 in a report titled, simply, "Edo."[30] Reconstruction by private developers of large parts of the old downtown replaced basementless wood structures with buildings of reinforced concrete, requiring excavation of sites where the earth had not been turned before. The city's wood construction and long history of fires meant that little remained of old structures, but archeologists found a wealth of metal and ceramic artifacts, from hand mirrors to sake bottles.[31] The artifacts unearthed most frequently, Takahashi points out, were the odds and ends of commoners' lives rather than relics of the elite past. Since these could not be ordered into a strict historical chronology, museums developed thematic exhibits.[32]

Although interest was sparked in part by rapid redevelopment and the trove of minor and comparatively recent artifacts it yielded, most of the new local museums of everyday life built in Tokyo, as elsewhere during the 1970s and 1980s, in fact started not with a collection needing preservation but with a commemorative agenda for which artifacts were then assembled and dioramas fabricated. Their purpose was to create narratives of identity through a common heritage. The Shitamachi Museum, among Total Media projects the museum most intimately tied to a sponsoring community of nearby residents, began (like Shibusawa Keizō's Attic Museum) by collecting toys and other personal memorabilia, then expanded to include all artifacts of daily life. Things that Tokyo residents had previously thought too recent and insignificant to merit research or preservation came in the process to be viewed as significant history. This extended to people's trash: the Shitamachi and Edo-Tokyo Museums both collected items such as old washboards and rice cookers that Tokyoites were putting out on the street for the sanitation department.[33]

COMPOSING THE EDO-TOKYO EVERYDAY

Tokyo's new identity as a site of "everyday life culture" broke significantly with the way the national capital had been officially represented, narrated, and invested in before the 1980s. Academics and amateur historians, rather than culture bureaucrats and curators, were the first to shape a historical image of everyday Tokyo. The germ of the Edo-Tokyo Museum's historiography lay in "Edo studies" or "Edo-ology" (Edogaku), a field that gained academic legitimacy in the 1970s, but built on a tradition of folklore and antiquarianism that had flourished earlier outside the university setting. This tradition posed Edo culture as an alternative to the alienation of modernity, a path not taken.[34] Edo scholars championed the denizens of the old capital—the so-called Edokko, or "children of Edo"—who had seen their city transformed by newcomers (led by the revolutionary leaders from the distant provinces of Satsuma and Chōshū) after the Meiji Restoration. Historian Nishiyama Matsunosuke, who founded the Research Group on Edo Townspeople (Edo Chōnin Kenkyūkai) in 1966, brought Edo studies to the academic context. He trained a generation of Edo scholars, several of whose members would form the core group of historical consultants at the Edo-Tokyo Museum. Their work combined empirical social history with a mission to rehabilitate the culture of the pre-Meiji city.[35]

Like Kawazoe, scholars of Edo studies idealized local traditions and the everyday past while distancing themselves from overtly nostalgic language. Writing in 1991, Ogi Shinzō, director of the foundation that managed the Edo-Tokyo Museum and the central figure in its realization, explained their reappraisal of Edo:

> Since Meiji, Japanese have denigrated the Edo period and poured their energy relentlessly into leaving behind feudal tradition. From the time that the high economic growth of the postwar era came to an end, people gradually began to look back and reflect on the life of Edo people and the peaceful world they enjoyed. Certainly, we should be proud of the people of Meiji, who pushed forward Japan's modernization at a record pace, yet it is difficult to suppress resentment at the fact that they absolutely refused to acknowledge the cultural heritage of the Edo period.[36]

Ogi's Edo-Tokyo studies followed from his mentor Nishiyama's Edo studies, seeking to comprehend the culture of the city as a whole and to show its legacy for modern Japan. In contrast to nostalgists who sought a private refuge in the city's past, Ogi wanted Edo's legacy publicly recognized. Yet he found the elements of this heritage in the same places that nostalgists cultivated: alleys, tenements, and downtown working-class communities. These places constituted the city of what Ogi and other Edo-ologists called the *shomin,* or common folk. Ogi's major historical study, *Tōkei shomin seikatsushi kenkyū* (Studies in the everyday life history of Tōkei's common folk), reflected this determination to establish a heritage for modern Tokyo by demonstrating the continuities in everyday life among common residents of the city across the political divide of the Meiji Restoration.[37] Seeking to express the same message, the museum set political history aside, putting the restoration itself and the city's role as national capital in the background. No model was included of the Imperial Palace, for example, and its occupants went practically unmentioned. The everyday life of ordinary people, in Ogi's perspective, was unconnected to emperors.

Exhibits at the Edo-Tokyo Museum presented the history of the city from 1590, when the first Tokugawa shogun made it his castle town, until roughly 1960, the beginning of the era of high economic growth. Since the modern capital was founded in 1868, the city of the old regime had survived until recently enough to be recorded in photographs. Some visitors in the 1990s would have had grandparents born in the Tokugawa period. Yet after more than a century of rapid modernization Edo had become a world almost as far away and exotic in the minds of Tokyo-ites as the "Orient" was to nineteenth-century Westerners. Only a small minority of Tokyo residents by this time could claim the status of Edokko, descendants of Edo residents. Although Ogi and other scholars of Edo-Tokyo studies sought to awaken appreciation of the city's distinctive local heritage, for most Japanese, regardless of whether they came from Tokyo or elsewhere, Edo was part of a distant and generalized national past.

Since the museum had no existing collection, planners sought to attract visitors with reconstructed streetscapes and interiors and exquisitely crafted architectural models, including miniatures of famous sites in Edo and a portion of the shogunal palace. Life-size reconstructions of *nagaya* tenements enjoyed prominent positions in both the pre-1868 area, called the "Edo zone," and the modern "Tokyo zone," a sign of the centrality of the domestic sphere in the museum's image of everyday life. The *nagaya* was the only type of structure to appear twice in the museum, and the Edo-zone *nagaya* was the only reconstructed interior with life-size mannequins. Whereas in Kawazoe's Japan exhibit at the Museum of Ethnology common heritage had been embodied in a farmhouse, in the Edo-Tokyo Museum—as in the Shitamachi Museum—heritage resided in a backstreet tenement.

Reflecting the Shitamachi Museum's emphasis on childhood memory, the first unit in the Shitamachi Museum *nagaya* had been a penny candy shop, but at the Edo-Tokyo Museum, the emphasis was instead on family domesticity. Over the postwar years, the small urban home had become the iconic site of everyday life, which was understood increasingly as synonymous with private life. As Japanese became more prosperous and left the volatile era of urban migration and mass politics behind, everyday life had also become more spatially segregated. The bureaucratic state stood on one side as the sole public authority, while the nuclear family household stood on the other as the site of reproduction, a women's sphere more than the household had ever been before. The heritage of everyday life that most modern Japanese visitors could readily connect to their own present lives thus lay in reconstructed small urban dwellings.

Like the English word *tenement,* the Japanese *nagaya* had long connoted lower-class housing, sometimes with the suggestion of slums. But as the structures themselves rapidly disappeared in the 1970s and 1980s, the stigma of poverty receded. The picturesque version of *nagaya* life that now came to dominate drew upon fiction such as Edo *rakugo* comic monologues, which had been further popularized in period dramas on television and in the general commodification of Shitamachi by newspapers, magazines, and local government. Although most Japanese had never lived in one, the *nagaya* as a site of nostalgia was available to everyone as an icon of a simpler urban life.

The apartments in the Edo *nagaya* exhibit were placed back to back under one gabled roof. Of the two households portrayed, one belonged to a single craftsman and the other to a family. The craftsman mannequin sat alone on the floor, planing a wooden box. On the other side of the wall was a small nuclear family in which the mother was shown having just given birth. She lay in one corner, her upper body propped against a folded futon. A midwife washed the infant. The father and a male child knelt nearby, their bodies bent solicitously toward the mother and infant. Seeking to give drama to the prosaic history of private life, exhibit designers had chosen the most dramatic moment of family reproduction. Although home birth was rare in Japan after the 1950s, the intimacy in this scene echoed normative images of nuclear families projected by mass media and government. Media in the 1970s proclaimed the emergence of the "new family" (*nyū famiri*), a small nuclear household centered on a couple who had married for love rather than family duty. At the same time, anxieties about the "collapse of the family" were rising, linked to the advent of private rooms for teenage children and subsequently to modern apartment blocks made up of one-room units (*wan-rūmu manshon*).[38] Museum exhibits did not directly address these issues, but exhibit choices reflected contemporary ideas about family, rendering material the concerns of the era.

Lifelike scenes in historical exhibits inevitably invite questions of typicality. Were these people representative of Edo *nagaya* occupants? Were nuclear-family households usual? Were fathers in Edo often in attendance when their wives gave birth? Although little quantitative data describing Edo backstreet families survives, fragments might be assembled from the historical record to support the authenticity of this particular scene.[39] The historical plausibility of an endless number of other scenes of everyday life might also be established. Determining where a museum object begins and ends is, as museum scholar Barbara Kirshenblatt-Gimblett has put it, "an essentially surgical issue."[40] Every preserved artifact is a fragment of something larger. In the same way, the reconstructed period interior populated with human figures makes a temporal cut through the undifferentiated continuum of the past. The variables are multiplied: which people to represent, in which moment in their lives, or in the course of a day; which momentary gesture to represent and leave standing in for the rest?

The choices made in the museum's *nagaya* exhibit contrasted markedly with the way that Edo life was represented by artists in the Edo period. Family portraiture as a genre was alien to Edo artists. Without the tradition of representing particular patrons in family groups, the notion of representing a typical family would have had little meaning. Visual sources for life in Edo are plentiful, but they are weighted toward the life of the prostitution and entertainment districts. A woodblock print reproduced in the museum catalogue, for example, showed a birth scene that appears to be a source for the one shown in the *nagaya* reconstruction. Here, however, all the figures are gaily dressed and coiffured women. This is not to say that this print should be taken as any more typical or authentic a representation of birth or everyday life in Edo than the museum's diorama. It suggests instead that what registered to the eye of the nineteenth-century artist as worthy of depiction differed from what registered as significant to the eyes of late twentieth-century exhibit planners (see figure 13).

Late twentieth-century representations of the ordinary and the everyday also diverged from the museum's monumental agenda. The tension between the museum's twin goals of commemorating the history of ordinary people's Tokyo and serving as a monument for "World City Tokyo" is evident in the reaction of architect Kikutake Kiyonori to the exhibits installed in his building after completion. "One has no sense of the global dynamism of cultural formation," he told Umesao Tadao in a dialogue published shortly after the museum opened. The *nagaya* exhibit, Kikutake complained, left visitors with the impression that Japanese housing conditions were poor, when in fact, until the sixteenth or seventeenth century, they were better than

FIGURE 13a. A birth scene in the Edo-zone tenement, as depicted in the children's guide to the Edo-Tokyo Museum (*Yasashiku tanoshii Edo Tōkyō hakubutsukan annai*). Courtesy Tokyo Metropolitan Edo-Tokyo Museum.

in Italy, where six people slept in one bed. In Kikutake's eyes, cultural comparison was needed to bring Japan due recognition for its contributions to world civilization, and to make the Japanese themselves more aware of the greatness of their own past.[41] *Nostalgie de la boue* for the simpler life represented by the *nagaya* had no place in the museum he envisioned.[42]

Yet the antiheroic mode of history that Kikutake rejected bound the longer tradition of everyday life studies to the aims of Total Media and other exhibit design firms. Scholars made everyday things into a heritage worthy of museum display while exhibit designers used the everyday to make visitors feel at home in museums. Brought from the comparatively distant Edo period into the recent Shōwa period, which was still fresh in audience minds, this arrangement would engender a more intimate form of spectacle, one tied to each visitor's memories and imaginings of childhood.

FIGURE 13b. A birth scene depicted in a nineteenth-century woodblock print reproduced in the museum catalogue (Utagawa Kuninao, "Hinoe uma doshi no setsu," ca. 1847). Courtesy Tokyo Metropolitan Edo-Tokyo Museum.

THE DOMESTIC INTERIOR AND THE INTIMATE NATION

Reconstructions of modern interiors from ordinary houses, first seen in the Shitamachi Museum and repeated at the Edo-Tokyo Museum, would become a standard formula in history museums, exhibits, and theme parks in Tokyo and other Japanese cities beginning in the early 1990s. The exhibit design firms had made life-size reconstructions their big-ticket items: museum administrators wanted them because they were accessible and appealing to visitors, and museum visitors came to expect them. Most of these new reconstructions portrayed houses of the twentieth century, some less than a generation old. Representations of small domestic interiors, especially rooms where families shared meals (the *cha-noma* and the *dainingu-kitchin*), resonated with nearly a century of popular idealizations of the home and reformist rhetoric about the importance of family intimacy, making these reconstructions seem like natural embodiments of everyday life. At the same time, Shitamachi neighborhoods became sites of nostalgia in the mass media of the 1980s. These two developments combined to popularize domestic scenes of a less affluent urban Japan. Nostalgia was deepened and given a national cast in the 1990s by the sense of lost innocence as Japan's global economic power diminished and brought down individual hopes in the "lost decade."[43] A new material vocabulary of nostalgia was established in the process.

The death of the Shōwa emperor (Hirohito) in 1988 inaugurated a national trend of nostalgic representations of the Shōwa era.[44] Although Hirohito's reign had spanned six decades, retrospective media images of Shōwa-era everyday life concentrated increasingly on the late 1950s and early 1960s, or Shōwa thirties, a choice of period that skirted memory of World War II and the Allied occupation. This decade was also a convenient historical destination for purposes of marketing: it preceded the trade wars, the oil shocks, and the full recognition of the environmental crisis caused by rapid industrialization, all of which marked the end of Japan's postwar rush toward prosperity. The Shōwa thirties closed with the Tokyo Olympics in 1964, which were simultaneously a national triumph and a local cataclysm, since urban redevelopment in preparation for the event transformed old neighborhoods throughout the city. The decade prior to the Olympics and the city's rebuilding was historically reinscribed as a time of innocence and optimism, when citizens were bound by a sense of national purpose and faith in progress, but life was still rooted in traditional communities. As Laura Neitzel has noted, "Looking back from the 1990s, people felt nostalgia for the feeling of 'looking forward.' "[45] As early as 1992, Kawamoto Saburō, one of the most prolific of Edo-Tokyo historical essayists, dubbed the era the "Tokyo Belle Epoque."[46]

Shōwa nostalgia presented a new challenge to the museum exhibit design and supply industry by creating demand for recent mass-produced artifacts—many of which, unlike the typical folk tool, had been made to be used and thrown away.[47] Japan during the 1960s and 1970s had produced vast quantities of mass-manufactured ephemera, few items of which had acquired antique-market value. Since they were not intended to be handed down, the objects museums now sought to display also lacked the marks of heirloom care, making it difficult to resituate them in a heritage system. For audiences that had grown up as urban consumers surrounded by these things, however, the stimulus to memory could be just as powerful regardless of their low value to traditional modes of preservation.

One iconic object that straddled Shōwa mass-market nostalgia and the folk historical mode of previous museum-based heritage was the *chabudai,* a low wooden folding table designed for taking meals seated on the floor that had been common in urban homes from the 1920s through the 1950s. The simple, handcrafted character of the *chabudai* made it readily universalizable as a folk object, although a mass-produced one. *Chabudai* were also plentiful in the antique market, since they were made of durable materials and had been manufactured by both large factories and small shops until the 1960s, when most households replaced them with taller kitchen tables and chairs. *Chabudai* came to play a central role in museum displays of everyday life in the 1990s. They were heavily invested with nostalgic meaning by popular media.[48]

In local museums, Shōwa everyday life exhibits centered on what curator Aoki Toshiya has called the new "three sacred regalia" (*sanshu no jingi*) of museum display: the *chanoma* (family eating room), the *chabudai* table, and the television set.[49] These exhibits highlighted the homogeneity of national consumption habits in the 1950s and 1960s, binding the nation into an implicit community. A common memory of the postwar era from the consumer's perspective made it possible to speak of television "coming" (*terebi ga kita*) and refrigerators "coming" (*reizōko ga kita*) in the Shōwa thirties, as if these technologies had fallen from the sky into people's homes.[50] Remembering the Shōwa thirties through a litany of commodities—first acquired by a handful of households, then gradually by more, and eventually by almost 100 percent of households—reinforced the sensation created by mass media that each family's life history was a microcosm of the history of the nation.

Everyday memories of the home and household goods also underwrote selective national memory in a way that made them political instruments. The National Shōwa Memorial Museum (Shōwakan), a state-funded museum built in response to years of lobbying from Nippon Izokukai, the national organization of bereaved families of World War II soldiers, and opened in 1998 in central Tokyo, used the home to recast the history of imperialism and war. Dedicated, according to museum publications, to "conveying to future generations the everyday sufferings of the nation during and after the war," the Shōwa Memorial Museum devoted its four floors of photographs, films, and reconstructions to sacrifice on the home front and the struggle up from poverty after 1945. Despite the museum's wartime theme, displays contained no weapons or evidence of death. The war's victors were not depicted and went almost entirely unmentioned. Instead, the

FIGURE 14. Home-front domesticity under glass: the heavily guarded but humble display of national life during World War II as represented in a meal at a *chabudai* folding table in the Shōwa Memorial Museum. Photograph by the author.

museum highlighted the spare domestic interiors and the appliances whose acquisition punctuated popular narratives of Japan's hard-won postwar prosperity. Life on the home front during the war was represented by a reconstructed typical meal scene, with the low *chabudai* that had become a fixture of Shōwa nostalgia in other museums and popular media. Since the dining arrangements of most Japanese homes changed little between the 1930s and the 1950s, the exhibit could not be faulted for historical inaccuracy in empirical terms. Yet in the context of a national museum funded by the Ministry of Welfare to commemorate World War II, everyday scenes and goods served to hide the era's politics, painting the war itself in soft sepia tones (see figure 14).[51]

Comparison to the everyday life exhibits at urban museums in places with different political histories makes it evident that these museums, which constructed a national heritage of family meals and home appliances, were doing their nation work in a way specific to the late twentieth-century Japanese context. The Hong Kong Museum of History, for example, which opened in 2001, used similar techniques and style of presentation, emphasizing everydayness with reconstructed shops and streetscapes, yet showed few domestic scenes. It was divided into ethno-graphic and historical sections—the ethnographic section containing farm implements and examples of traditional costume, while the historical section included what the museum guide described as "models of different modes of transport, industrial and commercial products," along with life-size dioramas of shops, restaurants, and movie theaters.[52] In short, the sites of ethnography at the Hong Kong Museum lay outside the twentieth-century cosmopolitan environment, while modern everyday life was located not in domestic interiors but in commerce and the street. Meanwhile, a large section of the exhibit space was devoted to the island's prehistory, constructing an indigenous identity for the islands that tied them culturally to southern China. The museum thus helped Hong Kongers imagine their nationhood in association with China after years of colonial ambiguity. The one reconstructed domestic interior in the modern section was a room from the Shek Kip Mei resettlement estate, built in 1953 to house slum dwellers after their district was destroyed by fire. Home in Hong Kong was portrayed as a place of sojourn, and collective memory of the everyday located more in public and commercial spaces. In contrast, in Japanese everyday life museums of the 1990s and after, the nuclear family home stepped in to function as the national community writ small.

THE NOSTALGIA DILEMMA AND THE DEMISE OF PUBLIC HISTORY

Some museum professionals viewed the nostalgic effect produced by everyday life exhibits beginning in the 1990s as a dilemma. Kaneko Atsushi, curator of the Parthenon Tama History Museum, a public museum in the largest of Tokyo's planned suburban new towns, chose not to include any reconstructed domestic interiors because he believed that life-size displays of the "three regalia," regardless of the context, created an apolitical history that deflected attention away from real historical questions.[53] As Kaneko observed in an essay on war exhibits, since visitors understand the history museum as "authorizing" an official history, the meanings of everyday scenes and objects displayed there are universalized and made normative—usually as part of a story of the nation that implicitly suppresses difference and dissent—so that even the intent "not to exhibit things that have the potential to contain historical judgment" (as promised by the Ministry of Welfare in planning documents for the Shōwa Memorial Museum) produces "the message of containing no message."[54] The history of a postwar suburb, although less hotly contested than the Second World War, has the same potential for politicization, and therefore also for the politics of depoliticization. To thwart this depoliticizing effect, Kaneko displayed video footage of a thatched farmhouse being bulldozed to make way for new town construction in 1972 instead of reconstructing scenes of domestic life in the apartments that replaced it.

Given a similar postwar suburban history to exhibit in Matsudo, a satellite city to the northeast of Tokyo, curator Aoki Toshiya reconstructed as precisely as possible a section of one of the public housing blocks (*danchi*) that had made Matsudo a bedroom community, complete with the furnished interior of one apartment. In the interest of authenticity, Aoki had wanted to exhibit the possessions of one Matsudo household, but he was unable to acquire a complete set of furnishings from a single source (in part because the apartments had little storage space where residents might have kept old things), so the décor was a composite of what seemed typical and in period for the time of the building's construction. Artifacts were chosen on the basis of surviving surveys of several households. When the exhibit opened in 1993, Aoki found to his dismay that the public and press described it simply as "nostalgic" (*natsukashii*). In 2000, he responded with a more sharply honed empiricism, mounting an exhibit based on photographs from a single household in which the father had carefully documented home life through the 1960s and 1970s. Unhappy with the thought that visitors were making the museum what he called a "stage for pursuing personal memories" (*omoide sagashi no butai*), Aoki thus sought to convey a precise, properly historical message about changing everyday life by narrowing the exhibit focus to the history of one family. Writing in 2003, he acknowledged, however, that he had no indication that this had produced any different effect on audiences.[55]

Even in such an exhibit, the problem Kaneko observes—that public history museums are expected to provide an "authorized," and therefore generalizable, history—remains. Since history exhibits are thus a kind of apparatus of typicality, and museums in Japan have tended to conspire with other media to enhance the image of a nationally homogeneous everyday life, this problem often takes the form of doubts cast by museum visitors who find that the everyday life presented does not match their personal memories. "That's not how it was" or "We didn't have that" are common responses.[56]

Audiences came to depictions of the recent past in films and other media, as well as in museums, with the same expectations, seeking a personally verifiable authenticity regardless of the context. The most successful evocation of Shōwa nostalgia in visual media was the 2005 film *Always: Evening Sun over Third Street* (Always: Sanchōme no yūhi). This film presented an imaginary Tokyo street in the year 1958, when Tokyo Tower was under construction. The filmmakers themselves acknowledged that the film's success derived from its ability to conjure the images and feelings of urban life in the Shōwa thirties. The star of the movie, in essence, was the set.[57] *Always* director Yamazaki Takashi noted a response issue like the one that troubled museum curators: audience members and critics claimed either that real living standards at the time were lower than depicted in the film or that they were higher.[58] Although the film was fictional, the filmmakers had invested as much in accurate reconstruction as any museum—using many of the same devices and props—and viewers demanded that the typical past they believed it to authorize conform to their own, often disparate, pasts.

The audience's response of "That's not how it was" presents a more fundamental dilemma for museum curators than it does for film directors. As Aoki Toshiya's frank self-criticism shows, the curator staging recent everyday history performs a balancing act between the desire to appeal to visitors by creating opportunities to associate the exhibit with their own experience and the museum's didactic mission, which fails if visitors focus exclusively on personal experience. The risk that everyday history will verge into private memory is always latent in the notion of a heritage of everyday life. If what the museum presents is the common property of a local or national community of citizens, it is not surprising that some of those citizens will want to test the vague promises of common heritage concretely—to claim their portion of the inheritance, metaphorically speaking—by seeking only the objects with which they have a direct personal association.

One of the first Shōwa-themed museum exhibits built in the 1990s was the most iconoclastic in this regard. In 1993, the Shikatsu-chō History and Folklore Museum, a local museum in a Nagoya suburb, began an approach to collection and display that embraced, rather than struggling to overcome, visitors' privatization of the exhibit message. Curator Ichihashi Yoshinori, an archeologist by training, decided to make the preservation of commonplace artifacts from the recently ended Shōwa era the museum's mission. He launched the new collecting policy with an exhibit titled "The Orange Crate in Your Attic is a Treasure Chest" (Yaneura no mikan bako wa takara bako), which showed samples of the range of things the museum was seeking to collect and appealed to visitors to bring artifacts to donate.[59] The museum covered the whole Shōwa era (1926–1988), but Ichihashi chose to focus particularly on the Shōwa thirties and forties (1955–1975), when electrification and new appliances were transforming the home most visibly. In 1997, the museum adopted the unofficial name Shōwa nichijō hakubutsukan, the Shōwa Everyday Museum.[60]

In contrast to the many museums built after the 1970s primarily to teach or to celebrate local history and secondarily to serve as repositories of artifacts, the Shōwa Everyday Museum was driven by Ichihashi's determination to preserve as much as possible of the material remains of a passing era. He soon faced the problem of surfeit rather than scarcity. Locally, museum staff went to collect things wherever houses or shops were being demolished. The museum paid shipping for donations from farther away. By 2008, museum storage held thirty thousand items from roughly ten thousand donors, with more arriving daily. Ichihashi reported that the warehouse was filled to capacity and that the museum had stopped accepting some bulky objects, such as sewing machines.[61]

To persuade local officials of the value of building a Shōwa collection, and to overcome concern that he was making the municipal museum into a junk shop, Ichihashi invited scholars for a series of lectures introducing the work of Kon Wajirō and other scholars in everyday life studies. Little further persuasion was needed, however, once the museum began receiving media attention. Local and national television crews came dozens of times each year for the first few years after the Shōwa exhibit opened in 1993. Requests came from other museums for advice and loans of objects. Film companies requested permission to borrow objects or to use the museum as a set. Antique dealers also began coming to see what was now being recognized as having museum value.[62]

Ichihashi explicitly chose personal nostalgia as the organizing principle of the museum visitor's experience.[63] The museum had two reconstructed interiors: one a domestic scene with the "three regalia," the other a part of a farmhouse. It also contained a life-size streetscape. A large part of the exhibit space was given over, however, to open cabinets filled to overflowing with objects grouped generically. Ichihashi chose to provide a minimum of wall text and to make what text was provided of the most general nature. A cabinet filled with electric and hand fans, empty soda bottles, wind chimes, and dolls in summer kimonos, for example, was labeled simply "Summer in Japan." The

FIGURE 15. Wall cases of cosmetics, radios, souvenirs, cameras, and miscellaneous
Shōwa memorabilia at the Shōwa Everyday Museum. Photograph by the author.

more explanation the museum provided, Ichihashi believed, the more it,
"reduce[d] the element that appeals to the emotions." For the same
reason, the museum omitted labels identifying donors, to avert attention from the fact that the artifacts had belonged to anyone in particular.[64] Visitors were thus encouraged to experience the museum with as
little mediation as possible between themselves and the objects—to lay
personal claim to them in every form short of outright ownership (see
figure 15).[65]

In 2001, the Shōwa Everyday Museum began organizing gatherings
of senior citizens to look at and handle museum objects as part of a
mental health exercise known as "reminiscence therapy" (kaisō ryōhō),
which used recollection of the past to strengthen the patient's faculties
and general sense of well-being. Reminiscence therapy had been
explored already for roughly two decades by psychologists in England,
who used storytelling to exercise patients' memories.[66] With the rapid
aging of Japanese society and major changes in health care policy filling
the news, interest in reminiscence therapy was growing in Japan.
Ichihashi's innovation was to bring it into the museum and focus on the

mediation of memory through material objects. This drew media interest and attracted imitators once again. The museum received funding from the Ministry of Welfare in 2002 to construct a reminiscence therapy center in a building next door. Events at the center included training seminars for both museum curators and mental health professionals. The museum also began renting out "reminiscence kits"—which contained household items such as washboards, hot-water bottles, hand scales, abacuses, and toys—to nursing homes and community centers, together with instructional videos for using them in reminiscence therapy.[67]

Similar installations and activities subsequently appeared at other museums. In 2004, the Edo-Tokyo Museum added a "hands-on experience corner" (*taiken kōnaa*), consisting of a three-room house built on the permanent exhibit floor and furnished with a *chabudai* and a few other items common in middle-class houses of the first half of the twentieth century. The rooms and objects were all newly fabricated for this exhibit and bore no individual wall text. Unlike in the rest of the museum, however, here visitors were allowed to step into the tatami-floored interior and touch the exhibit. Although the exhibit had been built for reminiscence therapy, curators soon found that many younger Japanese enjoyed it as an exotic experience, since they had never lived in houses with tatami mats.[68]

These new installations made up a small part of the total exhibit area at the Edo-Tokyo Museum, but they represented the second major shift in the museum display of everyday life, of which the Shōwa Everyday Museum was the vanguard. Put in extreme terms, this was the abandonment of the museum's didactic mission altogether, and, with it, of public history itself. Since the local museum boom of the 1970s, historians and curators had endeavored to compose a common heritage through artifacts and carefully reconstructed settings. Some measure of fiction was unavoidable in reconstructions, but museums preferred experts' research and empirical precision as guarantees of a faithful representation of the collective past. No one in these institutions had questioned the founding assumption that the advising historians and museum curators who selected what to display and how to display and identify it were, and should be, the proper sources of historiographic authority. Departing from this traditional understanding of the relationship between museum and audience, the Shōwa Everyday Museum proposed instead a model that ceded authority to the visitor's memory, giving it precedence over the historians' narrative constructions.

At the Edo-Tokyo Museum's suburban annex, the Edo-Tokyo Open Air Architectural Museum in the Tokyo suburb of Musashi Koganei, curators took their own steps away from didactic display and toward popular memory. Opened in 1993 together with the Edo-Tokyo Museum, this outdoor museum assembled twenty-four freestanding buildings from the early twentieth century, saved from demolition and transported from sites around the city. Director Miyazaki Hayao's 2001 animated film *Sen to Chihiro no kamikakushi* (English title: *Spirited Away*), changed the open-air museum's audience. Animators from Miyazaki's Studio Ghibli had used elements of a reconstructed bathhouse and a shop at the museum as models for drawings in the film. As news of this got out, Miyazaki fans began coming to see the buildings themselves. Many came on tours that combined the museum with a visit to Miyazaki's own Ghibli Museum, built by the production company in the same year and located by coincidence in the same part of the city. The Edo-Tokyo Open Air Architectural Museum responded to the attention by mounting a special exhibit on the making of the film.[69] In a similar vein, when the museum reconstructed an open lot in 2003 and 2004 with scattered pieces of concrete pipe (a vital piece of the postwar "originary landscape," or *genfūkei*, of Tokyo nostalgia), visitors responded that it reminded them of the popular comic *Doraemon*. The following year, the museum created an exhibit called "*Doraemon* and Open Lots" (*Doraemon* to harappa), with models of the comic protagonist's house, as well as exhibits and activities connected both to the comic and to childhood in the era that it depicted. Since even in the time that it was serialized, *Doraemon* itself had tended to show the landscape of urban childhood through a nostalgic lens, this exhibit offered cues to private memory of an already backward-looking mass media product—nostalgia for nostalgia.[70]

The fact that private reminiscence in these instances operated through clearly mass-mediated memories does not make these extensions of the museum's purview fundamentally distinct from reminiscence therapy done for senior citizens using washboards and abacuses. Memory in any generation is constituted by more than just bodily experience. For the generation that grew up in a world dominated by movies, television, and mass-manufactured commodities, particular characters, programs, and brands were as likely as anything else to serve as the proverbial madeleine. In either case, the visitor was given the pleasure not only of seeing (or, in some cases, touching, entering, or climbing on) an artifact and remembering the past, but of personalizing and laying claim to something that now inhabited the public realm of the museum, which sanctified it as heritage. The didactic contract between the museum as historical authority and museumgoers as citizens encountering and learning from their collective heritage was replaced here by an arrangement in which the museum made available historical material for museumgoers to take and interpret in relation to personal experience. In a way it had not before, the museum thus made good on the promise of heritage as a bequest.

WHOSE PROPERTY IS THIS HERITAGE?

The Edo-Tokyo Museum was the high point of Tokyo history museums in its physical scale and grandeur, as well as in the scale of the urban community it represented. Yet the dioramas and reconstructed houses that dominated the permanent exhibit space portrayed the national capital primarily as a site of everydayness, echoing the early 1980s slogan "My Town Tokyo" and the trend outside official circles to find useful pieces of the city's past in humble forms. Ogi Shinzō and the team of other historians involved sought to teach the history of Edo-Tokyo everyday life, transmitting the heritage of the *shomin* (commoners) of the past to a *shomin* population in the present.

Ogi's commoners' history was challenged by academic historians, mostly champions of a more left-leaning social history in which the people were called variously *jinmin* ("the people") and *minshū* ("the masses"). These historians criticized the museum narrative as too "bright" and the style of presentation as too calculated to entertain. Although these historians advocated a people's history, on the relationship of the museum to its audience, they were, if anything, more didactic in tone than Ogi and his colleagues. One statement of protest, issued by the Historical Science Council (Rekishi Kagaku Kyōgikai) in 1989, pronounced: "We oppose unscientific plans or exhibits designed for mere amusement, ungrounded in the results of historical research. If scenes severed from the structure of history are reconstructed as 'spectacles,' not only will historical consciousness not be correctly formed, it may even be distorted."[71] Although populist Edo-Tokyoologists saw their mission as didactic, they never spoke of "correctly" forming popular historical consciousness. Championing the ordinary, in their eyes, was sufficient to correct an Edo-Tokyo history that had been distorted by the modern state, which had devalued the continuities in everyday life and promoted a heroic narrative of modernization. In municipally sponsored discussions held in the Edo-Tokyo Museum's early planning stages, academic and nonacademic participants alike spoke of making the museum a means to preserve "ordinary people's architecture" (*shomin kenchiku*) and "the culture of daily life"—things "so ordinary that they go almost unrecognized as cultural heritage."[72]

Meanwhile, official rhetoric in the museum's planning phase—using the bureaucratic fiction of the *tomin*, or "people of the metropolitan region"—conjured a museum narrative created not merely for, but *by* the people. Although at the time this was little more than rhetoric, after the early 1990s, history museums in Japan began to grope in this direction, in a way that few historians of everyday life had imagined in previous decades. With this curatorial invitation to private reminiscence, the notion of a Tokyo citizenry or of a unified national public to be the designated heirs of the museum's heritage itself seems to have begun to disintegrate.

Yoshimi Shun'ya has written of the "disappearance of 'Japan' as a historical subject" in the context of economic and cultural globalization since the 1990s.[73] The concurrent sea change in museums agrees with Yoshimi's observation. Japanese museum visitors now looked at exhibit objects for their personal value as much as for their broader historical meaning. With the content of exhibits dictated by forces in mass media or produced by a kind of "crowdsourcing" collection strategy, the inculcation of narratives of community, either local or national, receded in importance. Yet rather than being erased by globalization, the national community as historical subject at these museums was more often simply assumed, as something requiring neither assertion nor refutation. Although the coherence of national community as a force in the present may have been dissolving, the prominence of "Shōwa" in the name and conception of the Shōwa Everyday Museum, first and boldest of the new history museums of the 1990s, belies any notion that the nation was being erased as a framework for reflection on the past. Just as the nation underwrote the *chabudai* in popular stagings of the recent past at the Shōwa Everyday Museum, the Shōwa Memorial Museum, and elsewhere, the nation was still there in the background of personalized, privatized museum experiences, able to flow in and fill the gaps between fragmentary memories, engendering spectral but unified histories.

Can museums ever completely abdicate their authorizing position, even if curators were to consider such a development desirable? The issue originally at stake in collecting artifacts and reconstructing scenes from the past at history museums was the creation of an officially recognized heritage for the museum community, whether that community was a Nagoya suburb, Tokyo's Shitamachi, Tokyo as a whole, the Japanese nation, or (as at Expo '70) the community of "mankind." The Tokyo Metropolitan Government's large investment in a permanent exhibit at the Edo-Tokyo Museum reflected the fact that Governor Suzuki felt—and to a greater or lesser extent the culture bureaucrats and historians involved must also have felt—that the city had arrived at an appropriate point from which to look back in triumph. Because of the populist historical conviction that the true Tokyo community's history resided in everyday places and things, everyday history was the history celebrated.

The conjunction of the impulse to commemorate the communal past and a philosophy of history that elevates (and in some instances fetishizes or mythologizes) everyday life yielded a heritage in ordinary things: folk houses and tenements, dining tables, and more recently, particular brands of mass-produced goods and particular children's television shows. The museum arrests objects in the processes of circulation, appropriation, and decay or destruction, preserving and managing them for transmission from one generation to the next. Reconstructions blended with original artifacts serve their purpose in history museums like those built in Tokyo in the 1980s because these museums aim to transmit communal identity as much as to preserve artifacts. This contrasts with traditional ethnographic exhibits, which display authentic artifacts as indexical traces of the exotic people who made them, and with art museums, where the authentic object in itself is everything, preserved against both the ravages of time and the claims of other collectors.

Of course, actual transmission in museums is indefinitely deferred: visitors cannot go home with the things they find there, and, with the exception of experimental hands-on exhibits, they usually cannot handle them, either. As historians have noted, modern museums were conceived for a disciplined mass public, which was supposed to understand that the objects were displayed for general edification. The universality of the tradition of public heritage is part of what made the attempt to break with it by the Shōwa Everyday Museum and its imitators so radical. As history museums, their true radicalism lay less in the fact that they were experimenting with various kinds of hands-on activities, however, than in their abandonment of public edification as the foundation of a compact between museum and audience.

By reconstructing the everyday past and enshrining it in the name of cultural heritage, Japanese history exhibits in the 1970s and 1980s—

from Kawazoe's models for the National Museum of Ethnology to the permanent exhibits at the Edo-Tokyo Museum—sought in essence to embody ideals of national and local community in architecture and artifacts. The ideals they invested in museum exhibits implicitly substituted for the ideal of a broad urban citizenship that had been defeated with the collapse of the student movements and the evacuation of Shinjuku West Exit Plaza in 1969. They located in the home the continuity of everyday life and a common social space shielded from the forces of capitalism and the modernizing state. But museum audiences were as easily drawn to the validation of personal memory as they were to attempts to constitute collective memory. During the Shōwa boom, mass media, theme parks, and some museums played readily to this desire. With the privatization of audience expectations at the museum, the notion of heritage splintered, spinning fragments off in whatever direction audience memories wished to go. Museum curators were left to respond either by picking up popular trends and creating exhibits and events that reinforced them, or by remaining aloof and risking obscurity. In the effort to create a truly inclusive notion of heritage, populist history opened the way to a public history with no public at all. The saga of efforts since the 1970s to conjure new publics through the use of the past thus returned to its point of origin, confirming once again the loss of the public with which it had begun.

Conclusion

History and Memory in a City without Monuments

> I must not leave the truth unstated, that it is again no
> question of expediency or feeling whether we shall preserve
> the buildings of the past or not. *We have no right whatever
> to touch them.* They are not ours. They belong partly to
> those who built them, and partly to all the generations of
> mankind who are to follow us.
>
> —John Ruskin, *The Seven Lamps of Architecture* (1849)

John Ruskin states the ethos of historical preservation in the epigraph above in stark terms. Presented in this categorical fashion, the imperative to preserve would bring history to a stop, leaving us with an untenable accumulation of detritus. We would have to become nomads to escape it.[1] Of course, Ruskin was arguing primarily for preservation of particular kinds of buildings: the Gothic churches of northern Europe, the stone and stucco palazzi of Venice and Florence, or the ruins of imperial Rome—piles of stone and mortar that had stood for centuries or even millennia. By the end of the twentieth century, the range of objects of preservation had expanded vastly worldwide, and with the accelerating speed of technological change, the time necessary for something to be recognized as belonging to a distinct and valuable past had shrunk from the centuries that separated antiquity from nineteenth-century Europe to the decade it now took for a fashion to be recovered as "retro."[2] Tokyo in the late twentieth century occupied the opposite pole of the urban spectrum from Venice and Rome in terms of evidence of antiquity. The city's physical state at the end of the millennium not only challenged the usefulness of Ruskin's conservative dictum but invited yet more basic questions: When do things of the present become historical? And, after all, why preserve anything?

If, in participating in the global cultural turn toward the past, Tokyo was faced with a desire for memory but a lack of monuments that could constitute a heritage, then one might view the entire project of preservationism in Tokyo as based on a misrecognition, an attempt to transplant values from elsewhere into infertile soil. Perhaps, that is to say, the dominant trait of the landscape of Tokyo was not the fragile accumulation of fragments of the past but ephemerality itself, together with repeated destruction so complete that it left no ruins. If this were the case, then the sensibility that would be truer to the city's cultural and material character—one that might serve as the counterpart to the appreciation of ruins in a city of stone—might rather be the apocalyptic perspective of Godzilla, the science fiction epic *Akira,* and other examples of film, literature, and *manga* in the large body of fictional works that have dwelt almost lovingly on Tokyo's destruction and resurrection.[3] Yet to portray Tokyo as a city without the traces of memory would be to overlook the ways that the past in this city has constantly evolved as citizens gave new meanings to its tangible and intangible traces. Despite Tokyo's repeated destruction and rebuilding, Tokyoites, too, have searched for history among surviving places and material things.

When preservationists began to make public cause of the remains of Tokyo's past in the 1970s and 1980s, they did so for political reasons tied to the city's present rather than because of the intrinsic architectural importance or inviolability of the objects of preservation themselves. This was not peculiar to Tokyo, since preservation in modern capitalist cities is always a field of political contention. Tokyo's search for a usable past came in the context of moves to reclaim space and redefine participation in the imagined communities of urban and national citizenship. It derived from a set of attitudes about everyday life: everyday life as the location of deep social bonds sheltered from bureaucratic modernity; as a realm of discovery, where the familiar became exotic and the ordinary bled into the extraordinary; and ultimately, as a site of native authenticity. Yet as its most celebrated theorist, Henri LeFebvre, emphasized, the concept of everyday life is politically ambivalent, for it encompasses both the "organized passivity" of mass consumer society and the historical resources for emancipation from that passivity, located in a world before the dominance of consumerism and the bureaucratic state.[4]

The student radicals and antiwar protesters of the late 1960s stood on the cusp of a transition from idealization of the heroic and the monumental to idealization of the everyday. In the symbolic figure of the *hiroba* and in the actual site of the Shinjuku West Exit Plaza, a space of citizenship in the center of the city had been granted and then taken away, compelling citizens to locate new sites and invent other figures. The turn toward local history, marginal spaces, and recovered objects thus began when urban space could no longer be imagined within the progressive narrative of a heroic national subject.

In political terms, these vernacular preservationist activities were successful insurgencies—in the sense of movements at the margins—successful in mobilizing micropublics and giving them new ways to participate in the city. Yet they were also fragile. None offered a total politics of urban citizenship or a way to theorize it. This reticence compromised the idea of everyday life as a basis of critique. It lay everydayness open to appropriation for reactionary purposes. As Michael Taussig has noted, despite the obvious fact that each person's everyday is different, as a conceptual tool, "the everyday" easily serves "to erase difference in much the same way as do modern European-derived notions of the public and the masses."[5] In Tokyo, from the early 1970s forward, championing the everyday for its own sake supplanted championing the masses or the democratic national public. Since the 1990s, Japanese museums, film, and other mass media have popularized a vision of the everyday centered on nostalgic stereotypes of the nuclear-family home in the Shōwa era. This "Shōwa thirties boom" shows the way that the potentially homogenizing effect of everydayness as a foundation for politics permits it to be simultaneously privatized—narrowed to the domestic sphere and to private memory—and nationalized—used as the basis for coercing memory into the mold of supposedly common national experience. The layers of habitation and habit, handed-down knowledge, practice, and objects in everyday life provided the material for staking out new political turf and creating new solidarities apart from existing social and political hegemonies. Yet the project of recovering and preserving the everyday was always at risk of a fatal compromise that would allow ideologies of natural community to recolonize it.[6]

PRESERVING JAPAN'S CENTER POINT

Ideals of the historically layered vernacular city manifested themselves in more central sites as well as on the margins. The evolving perceptions, representations, and inscriptions of Nihonbashi, the bridge that traditionally marked the center of Tokyo, illustrate this. Physically dwarfed before it was recognized as a monument, preserved without ever having been threatened with demolition, Nihonbashi shows that preservation need not be about the material object itself and that the historical site is a mental space as well as a physical one. As much as any marginal or forgotten place, this central site also acquired meaning through vernacular reinterpretation. Here, too, the politics of the everyday were pitted against the politics of monumentality.

Nihonbashi crosses the Nihonbashi River (Nihonbashigawa), a canal opened when Tokugawa Ieyasu established the capital. In 1604, the bridge was designated the point of origin of the "five highways" (gokaidō) radiating from the city, the country's zero-mile marker. It was named Nihonbashi, meaning "Japan bridge," in 1659.[7] Built of wood, it was destroyed by fire eight times in the course of the Tokugawa period. The wooden structure was replaced with a stone one in 1872. This stone bridge in turn was replaced in 1911 by the present-day Nihonbashi, a double-arched stone bridge in Renaissance style with iron ornament designed by architect Tsumaki Yorinaka.

The roadway that passes over Tsumaki's bridge forms one of the two main shopping streets of the Ginza district. By the late twentieth century, it had been rendered inconspicuous by the growth of the modern city around it. It was traversed by a constant flow of motor traffic, it passed over a polluted waterway that served for no more than passage of the occasional garbage barge, and it stood in the shadow of the Metropolitan Expressway, surrounded by high-rise commercial buildings.

Architecture critic Hasegawa Takashi hypothesized in 1975 that Tsumaki had clandestinely expressed his alienation from modern civilization, embodied in paved roads and vehicle traffic, by designing the original bridge as an "ironic monument" intended to be appreciated from the water rather than from the road. Hasegawa read the bridge as encoding a message about the vanishing city of waterways. What Hasegawa imagined as the designer's gesture toward a deeper history gave the bridge an aura of mystery in an arid and rationalized modern everyday: "Skepticism or revulsion toward Meiji, and a corresponding longing for Edo," Hasegawa proposed, "turned the designer's point of view from the everydayness of Meiji civilization found at the road level to the cultural extraordinariness (hinichijōsei) of Edo that lay at the water level."[8] Like a street observationist identifying a "deviant property," Hasegawa fixed his gaze upon an ordinary sight until it yielded signs of the uncanny.

In chapter 1, I introduced Hasegawa as one of the canonical writers who retheorized the city in its post-1969 move away from the politics of the public square. The bridge and its surroundings underwent significant change during the 1960s and 1970s, providing another context for Hasegawa's urbanism. Construction began in late 1962 on an elevated section of the Metropolitan Expressway (Shuto Kōsoku Dōro) that ran above the Nihonbashi River on pylons set in the riverbed and passed directly over Nihonbashi.[9] The highway was completed in time for the 1964 Olympics. The Nihonbashi Preservation Society (Meikyō Nihonbashi Hozonkai), led by the chief executives of the Mitsukoshi department store and other old businesses in the vicinity, was established in 1968, at the time of the Meiji centennial. The 1911 bridge was not under threat, and the preservation society made no mention of its architecture in its founding statement. Instead, the statement spoke of recognizing the historical significance of the site as the center point of the city's commercial district since the Tokugawa period, and the importance of maintaining the bridge for future generations, despite its having been overshadowed by the highway. In 1971, the group began an annual tradition of mobilizing local youth and neighborhood association members to wash the bridge's road surface with buckets and brushes (see figure 16).[10] This group emerged not in protest against construction of the expressway, but several years afterward, when the expressway had already become an ordinary piece of the cityscape. Hasegawa himself acknowledged in 1975 that at the time the expressway was constructed he had thought little about its visual impact.[11] The preservation society chose as its public gambit, moreover, a symbolic act of reclamation based on local ties to the site rather than a challenge against urban development founded on aesthetic, environmental, or ethical claims. Just as Yanesen activists in the 1980s first sought to build a neighborhood identity from the material of local history, and only subsequently found themselves battling against demolition and redevelopment, Nihonbashi preservationists first engaged in claiming local meaning for the bridge rather than defending it from a physical threat.

In 1983, in an era of large-scale infrastructural development plans and increasing interest in water as an urban amenity, the preservation society called for removal of the portion of the expressway passing over the bridge. Their demand went unheeded until the beginning of the twenty-first century, however, when Nihonbashi became a key case in

FIGURE 16. The annual washing of Nihonbashi by members of
the Nihonbashi Preservation Society and local youth groups,
1983. Photograph courtesy Meikyō Nihonbashi hozonkai.

discussions in government and city planning circles about improving
the appearance of the capital. This official interest had an international
context: examples were cited of overhead highways being rerouted
underground in Boston, Seattle, and San Francisco. Seoul's Cheonggye-
cheon project, completed in 2005, which involved removal of an
overhead highway and creation of a waterfront pedestrian area in
its place, was perhaps most directly influential on Nihonbashi's case.
Seoul was seen as a closer rival than U.S. cities, and old notions of cultural hierarchy—although not stated explicitly—dictated that Japan's

capital should not be preceded by Korea's in an urban modernization project. In 2006, Prime Minister Koizumi Jun'ichirō threw his weight behind the idea, proclaiming the ambition to "bring the sky back to the Nihonbashi River," and assembling a group of powerful advisers to look into it. The group, led by Waseda University planning professor Itō Shigeru, called itself Group to Return the Sky to the Nihonbashi River (Nihonbashigawa ni Sora o Torimodosu Kai).

Since the years of the economic bubble, municipalities throughout Japan had been enacting local ordinances to protect historical and natural landscapes (*keikan jōrei*), creating guidelines and setting up consultation offices for new construction or modification of the existing landscape in designated districts. Tokyo enacted its own ordinance in 1997. By 2002, there were 298 such municipalities nationwide (slightly under 10 percent of all municipalities in Japan). Over half of all prefectures had created analogous laws.[12] The national Vistas Protection Law (Keikan Hō) was passed in 2004, following the Ministry of Land, Infrastructure, Transport and Tourism's "Creating a Beautiful Country" policy initiative (Utsukushii Kunizukuri Seisaku Taikō), which sought to establish a national basis for the disparate range of local policies on landscape and to incorporate them into the government's agenda to attract more international tourists. The Vistas Protection Law represented the first time that the national government had concerned itself with the vernacular landscape in general, contributing to a nationwide effort to harmonize signage, façades, and roofing materials, to remove utility poles and other visual obstructions, and to create what were called "symbol roads," overhauled to focus the eye on historic landmarks.[13] The Nihonbashi campaign was closely tied to these developments in national policy. Concurrent with passage of the law, the Group for Creating Beautiful Vistas was formed under the leadership of the same Itō Shigeru who would soon also be appointed to lead the Group to Return the Sky, with the aim of reviving the "unique beauty" of Japan that had been destroyed by postwar development and fostering an awareness of beautiful vistas as the common property of the nation. One of the group's first gestures was to publish on the Internet a list of one hundred bad vistas as object lessons in what needed improvement. The expressway passing over Nihonbashi topped the list.[14]

Reacting against this state-led management of aesthetics, architecture theorist Igarashi Tarō sparked controversy by questioning whether the 1911 bridge was a significant enough landmark to warrant the public expenditure necessary to remove the overhead expressway. He further speculated that in time the expressway itself might come to be seen as the greater landmark. Strictly in terms of monument value, this provocative assertion was not easily rebutted, since little was being said in the Return the Sky campaign to champion the architecture of the 1911 bridge, and regardless of how it was viewed aesthetically, the overhead expressway certainly represented a monumental achievement of construction for its time.[15] Proponents of removing it to expose the old bridge to the sky spoke of the site's potential to "signal to the world" the city's appeal, but as Igarashi noted, Tsumaki's bridge had little to distinguish it from any number of late Victorian bridges in Europe. Moreover, if the fact that it had appeared in several European and American films was any indicator, the expressway bore greater interest for Westerners than the bridge underneath it.[16]

Architect Ōta Hiroshi responded to Igarashi by broadening the issue beyond the merits of the particular case of Nihonbashi, arguing that aesthetics were really just a device for designers to focus on urban "activities" (akutibitii) and propose how people could better inhabit and use the site. Public space, he asserted, was a network of human interaction. This conception of space as defined by "activities" bore echoes of Itō Teiji's notion, articulated more than forty years earlier, of kaiwai as a distinctively Japanese form of "activity space." Ōta also defended the Vistas Protection Law, pointing out that unlike so many top-down government initiatives in Japan, the law had emerged from local streetscape protection ordinances and represented part of a global trend toward "citizen governance," founded in greater municipal and regional autonomy. "Introducing the concept of the 'citizen' in Japan may be no more than an experiment," Ōta wrote, again recalling hoary Japanese debates about public space and civil society, but it was the only alternative to either "bureaucratism or populism."[17]

Questioning the value of the bridge highlighted the fact that claims of historical significance were themselves historically situated.[18] What, ultimately, was historically significant in this site, and for whom? Proponents of removing the expressway had made an ambiguous case, turning sometimes to the Meiji-period bridge and sometimes to the longer history of the site in Edo, advocating its significance as a national landmark on the one hand and associating it with the local "everyday life culture" of the Shitamachi districts surrounding it on the other.[19] In a painting parodying the fashion for imagining the postmodern landscape of Tokyo steeped in memories of old Edo, artist Yamaguchi Akira depicted a Nihonbashi district in which the waterway, the Meiji-period bridge, and the expressway had become layers of the past, with a steep wooden bridge arcing above all of them like a fantastical future Edo reclaiming the center of the city. Historian and urban chronicler Kobayashi Shin'ya offered a similar parodic solution by proposing on his blog that if the government was seriously going to spend money on making a tourist landmark of the site, they should tear down the 1911 bridge and build a replica Edo-period wooden bridge in its place, and then—in the name of historical authenticity—forbid vehicle traffic. In response to an earnest reader's suggestion that residents' opinions should be surveyed first, Kobayashi concurred that resident participation was vital to urban design, but that in this instance the question was "Who are the residents?"[20] As had been the case in defining the museum community of the Edo-Tokyo Museum, locating collective memory in a feature of the cityscape raised the problem of who had claim to its heritage. Was this modest historical structure at the center point of the old city a matter of concern for its neighbors, for all residents of Tokyo, for all Japanese citizens, or, as some Return the Sky proponents would have it, was it a global cultural heritage site with the potential to raise Japan's position in the international competition for tourists?

The shopkeepers and local business executives who made up the Nihonbashi Preservation Society clearly viewed the bridge as their own local heritage first and foremost. In October 2011, the preservation society sponsored a festival celebrating the centennial of the 1911 bridge. The events included displays of samurai arms as well as hundred-year-old automobiles, a procession led by the oldest resident of the district (himself one hundred), and fleets of traditional wooden boats that had once carried fish and produce from the bay and the city's northern hinterland to the market that occupied the riverbank until 1923. The anniversary of the modern bridge thus provided an opportunity to display a miscellany of signs of age value asserting historical continuity between the old city and the present day, emphasizing Nihonbashi's place in the vernacular landscape rather than its significance as a monument.

Just as the debate over the highway and the bridge revealed that the real concern lay less with the preserved object itself than with different ways of imagining the usable past, the gestures of the preservation society to mark, make visible, and celebrate the site reached well beyond conventional architectural preservation. Although Nihonbashi was anything but marginal geographically, and its historical significance was not exclusively or even primarily local, the history of its historicization began with local residents and businesses seeking to claim it for themselves after its marginalization by modern infrastructure development. Its historicization gained further depth through Hasegawa's influential interpretation, which overlaid an explicitly antimodernist meaning on the bridge. The expressway that passed over Nihonbashi was unchallenged in the years of construction prior to the Olympics, when national interests took precedence over all else. Subsequently it came to symbolize the loss of locality, not only because it dwarfed the old bridge and left it in shadow, but because it cut through the district without benefiting local residents. The local response, when it arose, took a form that underscored everydayness through the act of cleaning, a consummately quotidian statement of proprietorship over a prized possession, like polishing the family silver. Finally, in an era of cultural competition and transfer of planning ideas among global cities, both the bridge and the highway—bearing with them the traces of these earlier readings and acts of appropriation—were lifted out of their local context and into the orbit of national cultural policy and debate.

AUTHENTICITY AND CO-OPTATION

The dominant line of critique in the recent history of heritage argues that in the burgeoning culture of preservation, reconstruction, recycling of historical styles, and museum construction since the 1970s, the past has been co-opted. Places and things of the past have long been put to the service of the nation, but the postindustrial era, or "postmodernity," is identified with a new commodification of the past in the context of global tourism and the saturation of urban space by leisure consumption.[21]

Everywhere that Tokyo's past was rediscovered in the 1970s and 1980s, sites and artifacts were recycled in the mass market as commodities. Old neighborhoods became tourist destinations; surviving anomalies in the cityscape popularized by street observation became the subjects of magazine and television features; museums provided the material for popular films and theme parks. Once recovered, nothing could be pinned down and sequestered from the market. This total commodification not only of historical objects but of historical and ethnographic discourses and practices became visible in Japan during the economic bubble, when both corporations and individual consumers found themselves with excess cash and sought ways to invest it, sparking speculation and free spending in everything from real estate to wine, and catalyzing unprecedented growth in product stylization, market differentiation, and new forms of leisure.[22]

Antimodern and anticonsumerist at first appearance, movements for neighborhood preservation and local history, exploration of the vernacular streetscape, and preservation of the history of everyday life seem readable as reactions against the cultural environment of the bubble. Viewed this way, the story of preservationism in these years becomes one of market co-optation: grassroots efforts using history to sustain or recover local identities respond to consumer capitalism, only to be swallowed into it and recycled as historical simulacra. An authentic past, once discovered, is replaced by a falsified one. The mass public in this portrayal is easily imagined as happy to be duped, unconcerned about the difference between the real thing and the Disney version. David Lowenthal, a pioneering figure in heritage studies and one of its most influential writers, asserts that "lack of hard evidence seldom distresses the public at large, who are mostly credulous, undemanding, accustomed to heritage mystique, and often laud the distortions, omissions, and fabrications central to heritage reconstruction."[23]

Rather than this history of falsification—which presumes, to use the terms of philosopher Miguel Tamen, that the preserved object possessed an original context in which it spoke its true intention—I have tried to present the history of the city's historicization in the late twentieth century as itself emerging from a landscape of latent but unformed pasts, assembled and given form by acts of documenting, collecting, reconstructing, and celebrating.[24] I have focused attention on these processes themselves, not in order to establish the authenticity or inauthenticity of the objects involved but to understand how groups of people claimed them through these proprietary gestures. State and commercial forms of the past were just clusters of appropriations among many. The local activist and avant-gardist forms of archiving the vernacular city's artifacts worked dialectically—sometimes openly oppositional, sometimes interdependent—with popular media, consumer capitalism, and state institutions to develop an iconography of features that would coalesce, at least temporarily, into the city's "heritage." It had been clear since the late 1960s that no public gesture existed free of mass mediation. Whether in the position of local community activist or of historian, ethnographer, or "observationist," protagonists resisted commodification but also recognized the paradoxes of mass society, and either playfully or earnestly participated in the processes of mediation that made the local meaningful to larger audiences. At the same time, the many letter writers adding details and new stories to the oral historical archive of *Yanesen* magazine, the journalists and local fans who sought to determine the story that lay behind a street observationist "property" or to identify new properties, and the museumgoers who rejected curators' representations of the past when those representations conflicted with their own memories all revealed that the audiences for Tokyo heritage were anything but credulous and undemanding. On the contrary, many Tokyoites outside the circles of people actively constituting and curating that heritage insisted on participating and wanted to see that the story was gotten right in accordance with their own ideas of the vernacular past.

The large role of popular memory in Tokyo's historicization raises a related issue at the heart of postmodern cultural critique, that of nostalgia. Frederic Jameson famously identified nostalgic pastiche as a key feature of postmodernism. He distinguished this postmodern nostalgia from "properly modernist nostalgia" by its incompatibility with "genuine historicity."[25] Writing of nostalgia in late twentieth-century Japan, Marilyn Ivy describes a pervasive condition of "self-obsession" and "longing" for a realm of marginal and disappearing cultural objects, the "fetishes" of modernity, which she describes as "never allowed to disappear, [but] kept hovering, with anxiety and dread, on the edge of absence."[26] This social psychological reading depends ultimately on the figure of the social body or mass subject—whether that subject is called "the Japanese nation," the masses, or, to use a term that gained currency in Japan in the 1970s, the "middle mass" (*chūkan taishū*). Diagnosing nostalgia from the evidence of artifacts or events projects this internal condition onto the mass subject. Nostalgia in its original sense, as an affliction of the mind, then implicitly casts the mass subject as passive, suffering emotional paralysis between past and future, unable to accept present reality. Since the condition is a mental one, the subject remains disembodied. If there is redemption from this internal malaise—a way out, as it were—for the mass subject, it must lie first in the subject's recognition of its own predicament (what an earlier Marxism would have called class consciousness) and determination to overcome the illusions fabricated for it by commodity capitalism.

This critique of nostalgia continues to be potent because it continues to be possible—and politically productive—to imagine the masses in various forms as a subject. Yet as Ivy and many others have noted, it was precisely the coherent existence of the masses that was thrown into question in the late 1960s. From the early 1970s on, what had appeared to exist in the form of a social body until the 1960s began to disinte-grate.[27] In countless places and situations, national politics gave way to local micropolitics. Preservationism in Japan emerged as a political force in this milieu. For preservationists, as for many kinds of local activists, politics persisted but ceased to be about the mass subject or the nation-state. Preservationist activities differed at the same time from the local environmental movements of the 1960s and 1970s because protagonists rarely targeted the state and made no claim on the basis of what was due to them as citizens. Instead, local historians, street obser-vationists, and museum curators placed utopian faith in everyday spaces believed to have preceded the modern state-society dyad, the literal and figurative cul-de-sacs that Yoshimoto Takaaki described in 1969, where "both the good and the evil of modernity have passed right over . . . without leaving a scratch."

Protagonists in each of the cases in this book rejected the label "nos-talgist." This does not mean that they must be taken at their word, or that they should be seen as intellectual free actors, unaffected by the cultural or ideological formations around them. It indicates simply that they recognized and sought to distance themselves from the psychologi-cal characterization that the term "nostalgia" implied, which was inim-ical to an ethos of progressive collective action. The recent memory of the spaces of mass politics, and particularly of the multivalent political space of the public square, animated their belief in collectivity. Groups of collectors, historians, and preservationists were as engaged in com-posing the past as protesters in Shinjuku in 1969 had been in composing the present. Just as the collapse of industrial society and the global envi-ronmental crisis made it clear that no pure domain of Nature exists discrete from the domain of human artifice, the transition from a pro-gressive vision of Society as a collective body on a path toward a unitary political destination to an ironic vision of human collectivities as assem-blages of fragmented motives and desires made evident that the terms of the social must always be composed anew.[28]

HISTORIOGRAPHY AND POLITICS

If "Society" with a capital S had become elusive, there were instead "societies." These gatherings or networks of people concerned with particular places or things may be called interpretive communities, or, in Tamen's felicitous phrase, "friends of interpretable objects." *Yanesen* activists, editors, writers, and readers gathered traces of the past to create a historical identity for a cluster of streets previously not identified with one another. In giving meaning to the place they constituted themselves as subjects of its history at the same time. Architects, artists, and their fans isolated particular spaces, paths, structures, and physical remains from the entropic totality of the city and made them discrete things, which then appeared to tell small histories themselves. Edo-Tokyo historians, curators, exhibit designers, and museumgoers assembled around the meaning of an alley as an embodiment of local community, a table as the embodiment of the community of a household, or the mass-produced commodity of a generation earlier as the embodiment of collective memory. That the work of the interpretive community was more important than anything intrinsic to the object is clear from the fact that existing canons of value imputed little significance to these objects of interpretation before "societies of friends" formed around them.

The empirical work of gathering stories and objects defended these interpretive communities against charges of dilettantism or nostalgia. The ethos of empiricism operated in *Yanesen* magazine's history, told in the voices of people who lived it; in street observation's insistence on material evidence, recorded unaltered; and in the everyday life museum exhibit's meticulous reconstructions of physical details. Although nurtured in part by the people's history that flourished in the academy and among local amateurs in the 1960s, these new vernacular historiographies were distinct from that mode of history in their embrace of empiricism for its own sake and their refusal to engage directly in debate over historical abstractions such as modernization, class, capital, or the emperor system.

Museum exhibits of everyday life offered the final venue for empirical practice, where vernacular historiography pursued in the streets could reconnect to the classical tradition of empirical historiography dating back to the nineteenth century, which attempted to reconstruct the past whole, "as it was," as if the recording of history were akin to taxidermy, stretching the skin of the past over a new frame to make it appear completely lifelike.[29] In the minds of participating historians and curators at the Edo-Tokyo Museum and elsewhere, recovering and preserving the history of everyday life differentiated their intellectual project from a state-centered conservative historiography built around great men and the triumph of modernization, while the avoidance of theory vouchsafed them against charges of ideological bias.

The essential materiality of places and things is what made gathering around them possible for broader publics in an era when growing numbers of people perceived assembly in the name of social and political abstractions as suspect or futile. Vernacular empiricism participated in a reaction against processes of abstraction across all fields of urban experience: not only the abstracting effects of the mass media, the market, international capital, or government rhetoric of rationalization, but the abstraction of democracy itself. The democratic public as an abstraction lost its utopian appeal when it ceased to be manifested in the concrete bodily politics of mass rallies and protests. This happened at the same time that spaces of the city seemed increasingly detached from their locality and materiality by television and other mass media. Beyond the era of the democratic public lay the new democracy of the consumer, promised by deft marketers and repeated with variations by a range of pundits, followed by a consumerist crescendo in rampant real estate speculation, with its concomitant cultural ripple effects, in the city of the 1980s. In an era when theories of commodification yielded to the commodification of theory, *reality* offered a means of checking out. When postmodern theorist Asada Akira was lecturing sell-out crowds at a department store on escaping contemporary mass society, collecting material minutiae provided a way of staking out an intellectual position that seemed to claim greater integrity. Yet unlike the writing of reclusive antimodernist literati, vernacular empiricism did not stand apart from contemporary society: it was practiced collectively, seeking to form new publics. Thus it found itself engaged as much as everything else with the mass media that exploited and amplified it.

TROUBLESOME HISTORIES AND OCCLUDED OBJECTS

Bringing certain types of objects to the foreground occludes other objects. Historicizing Tokyo in terms of everyday spaces, locality, minutiae, and margins made it difficult to incorporate the macroscopic view of Tokyo as national and imperial capital, for example. It was precisely this role as center of modern state power and of state-led modernization that Ogi Shinzō and other scholars of Edo-Tokyo studies wished to counter with their vision of the city of the "common people" (*shomin*). In another era—particularly before 1945—community activists, historians, and museum curators in marginal locations would have sought to stress connections between their locality and the nation-state or the imperial house. In the countryside of the early twentieth century, for example, proud local boosterists erected monuments wherever the Meiji emperor had stayed. In contrast, late twentieth-century Edo-Tokyo everyday life history conceived a national capital without the nation-state.

Nowhere was the occlusion clearer than in the case of the 7.4-square-kilometer grounds of the Imperial Palace itself, which Roland Barthes famously called the city's "empty center." In the opening of his 1986 essay, "I Discovered the Imperial Palace," street observationist Fujimori Terunobu recognized this dilemma for studies of the city: "If you plough through the mountain of recent writing about Tokyo, what tumbles out is the humanism of the back alleys, the semiotics of the neon signs, the theories of the Yamanote middle classes, the rivers and the puddles. No matter how much you dig, there's no sign of the Imperial Palace." The essay went on to describe the author taking on the palace plaza in a fight and almost being defeated by it. "Postwar democracy was knocked reeling" by a miasma rising from the moat, Fujimori wrote, equating himself ironically with a now-vanquished national social body. The essay concluded in an epiphany, when Fujimori reported finding that someone was maintaining a clandestine vegetable patch on the edge of the moat. Redemption in this oppressive place thus came in the discovery of an undetected guerrilla action.[30] Everyday life historians and activists had nothing in their arsenal for doing direct battle with the emperor or the palace. The only choice was insurgency, and in its most marginal forms.

The other topic with a troubled place in the historicization of everyday Tokyo was the firebombing of the city in March 1945. This was not because it was absent. Probably no other experience was retold to oral historians more frequently than that of witnessing or escaping the massive conflagration that engulfed the city on the night of March 9, 1945 (survivors who witnessed it from a safe distance often described it as awe inspiring or beautiful). This traumatic irruption in the everyday world of Shitamachi residents, which took roughly one hundred thousand lives in the course of two hours, posed a problem, however, for municipal commemoration, revealing Tokyo's awkward position between municipality and national capital. The families of many victims held a grievance against the imperial government for having brought the calamity upon them, or at least for having left them exposed to it. Investigative work by journalist Matsuura Sōzō and others revealed that authorities had put the safety and comfort of the emperor over the safety of the mass of Tokyo's citizens, and that air raid warnings had even been delayed as a consequence.[31] After the war, the national government preferred to put the firebombing in the past, emphasizing the

FIGURE 17. Painting by Onozawa San'ichi at the Tokyo Firebombing Museum. Wearing the fireproof hoods that were distributed to civilians during the war, the spirits of children killed in the firebombing peer down on the Sumida River of the present day. Philippe Starck's Asahi Beer Hall, an icon of bubble-era architecture, occupies the center of the canvas. Courtesy Onozawa Toshiko and the Tōkyō daikūshū sensai shiryō sentaa.

nation's and the city's renewal. In 1964, Emperor Hirohito bestowed the Order of the Rising Sun upon General Curtis LeMay, who had directed the bombing of Tokyo and other cities, for his contribution to the postwar revival of Japan's air force. Japan's remilitarization under American tutelage and the continued presence of Hirohito on the throne thus made any demand for commemoration of the firebombing victims an antigovernment and potentially anti-emperor position, associating it with the political Left.[32]

Until 1970, the metropolitan government followed national policy, avoiding commemoration. In that year, progressive governor Minobe Ryōkichi gave financial support to a project initiated by writer and firebombing survivor Saotome Katsumoto to collect survivors' testimony and materials related to the bombing. For decades after this Saotome sought the construction of a municipal museum of the bombing. A city council resolution in 1990 established a planning committee for what was provisionally called the Tokyo Metropolitan Peace Memorial Museum, built around the commemoration of the firebombing, but this was ultimately derailed by politicians on the right and national bureaucrats. Instead of establishing an independent museum, the metropolitan government incorporated plans for a firebombing exhibit into the Edo-Tokyo Museum. In 2000, government officials told Saotome that they would charge him for continued storage of materials he had collected as part of the testimonial project. Governor Ishihara Shintarō froze plans for the peace museum at the same time. Finally, in 2002, Saotome managed to build a museum dedicated to the firebombing with private support (see figure 17). The metropolitan government's ambivalence and the lack of national endorsement kept commemoration of the firebombing on the margins of the city's usable past, in which imperial memory had been segregated from everyday memory as much as possible.[33]

RECYCLING THE PAST AFTER THE ECONOMIC BUBBLE

Everyday spaces and histories could offer useful material for municipal and national government when adopted selectively, as the metropolitan government's lavish investment in the Edo-Tokyo Museum shows. The museum and the growing number of similar places to learn about the city's history created demand for knowledgeable docents and tour guides. In 2006, an organization called the Edo Culture and History Certification Association (Edo Bunka Rekishi Kentei Kyōkai), sponsored by ward government offices, museums, and businesses in the tourist industry, began offering tests and certification for amateurs seeking to demonstrate their expertise on Edo. Test questions emphasized details of everyday life, such as the rent for a backstreet tenement in the early nineteenth century or the name of the hairstyle worn by young men working at the old Nihonbashi fish market.[34] The organization advertised "Enjoy Edo" (Edogaku, or "Edoraku") seminars for history buffs and official textbooks compiled by the Edo-Tokyo Museum for test preparation.

Consumer capitalism, too, found uses for the vernacular past. Aided by marketers and popular media, preservationists in the 1980s had succeeded in winning the affections of a large enough public that Shitamachi streetscapes were now worth commodifying as leisure space. The search for historical traces in Tokyo had yielded the vocabulary of a packageable style, which was recycled in commercially built theme parks as well as in public museums and film sets. The first of these was the Shin-Yokohama

Ramen Museum, which featured a recreated life-size Shitamachi neighborhood set circa 1958, displaying all the features that redevelopment was eliminating from the real city. The details of this one-street working-class town were reproduced on the basis of studies in existing Shitamachi neighborhoods, then carefully rusticated.

The same formula was repeated in several variations by others. The Namuko entertainment firm produced a series of indoor theme parks around the Tokyo region with retro Japanese or Asian themes, all using low lighting and faux finishes to suggest age and a measure of disrepair. A chain of restaurant malls called Yataimura replicated a nighttime streetscape lined with traditional food vendors' carts. Visitors were invited to imagine that they were in a bustling old downtown district at festival time. In these "performancescapes" (as they were known in the trade), gestures toward the past were partly ironic, targeting the appetites of young consumers seeking an exotic experience more than the romantic sensibilities of older nostalgists remembering their own past. Yet the historically precise reconstructions—from the viewer's perspective little different from everyday life exhibits in museums—revealed the same determination to hold on to the vernacular past in as lifelike a form as possible for its alterity, suggesting that the distance between primary nostalgia for places directly experienced and vicarious nostalgia for places only imagined was not great.

The overlooked and marginal features of the vernacular city, first explored by Kon Wajirō in the 1920s, then rediscovered in the 1970s and championed by Akasegawa Genpei, Fujimori Terunobu, and members of the Street Observation Studies Society in the 1980s, filtered back into architectural design in the 1990s. Design team Tsukamoto Yoshiharu and Kaijima Momoyo, who founded Atelier Bow-Wow in 1992, spent the decade of the 1990s collecting examples of what they called "no-good architecture" (*dame kenchiku*) in Tokyo. The buildings, which they documented with photographs and isometric drawings, housed improbable combinations of functions, such as a spaghetti shop and a batting practice center, reflecting the anomalies that can arise in the absence of master planning. Publication of their discoveries in the 2000 book *Made in Tokyo* was followed by another collection, this time of tiny Tokyo buildings on residual lots, published in 2001 as *Pet Architecture Guidebook*. The objects and photographic style recalled street observation, but rather than emphasizing purposelessness, Tsukamoto and Kaijima explicitly sought lessons for urban design in them. The two built a practice based on urban research, gallery shows, and house designs for small lots. In the English-language mono-graph *Behaviorology,* which surveyed their work up to 2010, Tsuka-moto wrote of decoding a "streetscape order" that emerged through repetition and accumulation, and of studying "micro public spaces," formed by the "spirals, eddies and flows where people converge and disperse." Tsukamoto's language, and Bow-Wow's work as a whole, reflected the antiplan disposition and embrace of the spontaneous that had come to define much of Tokyo urban theory.[35] Fujimori contrib-uted an essay to the monograph, placing Atelier Bow-Wow in a lineage extending back to Kon and to street observation.[36]

Tsukamoto was one of two featured designers for the Japanese pavil-ion at the Venice Biennale in 2010, organized under the direction of Yokohama-based architect Kitayama Kō. 2010 marked the fiftieth anniversary of Metabolism, and Kitayama made this the theme, titling the exhibit "Tokyo Metabolizing: Field of Autonomous Self-Regenerat-ing Grain." Exhibit materials expressed a critical view of the Metabolist group, however. Their "megalomaniac vision" had not been realized, Kitayama wrote, but the concept itself still had validity, since the city had continued to grow and change organically. Now, in place of an architecture embodying what he called the "ubiquitous strong force of capital," Tokyo was producing an architecture derived from the "quiet accumulation of everyday life features" that embodied the "weak force" of "a thoroughgoing democracy."[37] Metabolism was thus resuscitated as a concept for the vernacular city without the overarching vision of the architect. Japan's architectural vanguard, whose contribution to world architecture in the 1960s had been megastructure-based master plans for the city of the future, now proposed the opposite: the urban antimonument, which was small, commonplace, serendipitous, and even absurd.

The resurgence of Tokyo's vernacular past had an impact on city plan-ning policy as well. Tokyo's Urban Vistas Ordinance was revised in 2006, incorporating provisions for municipal designation of historical struc-tures that enhanced the streetscape and "local character" (*chiiki no kosei*) but were not covered by national or municipal cultural property designations. Citizen mobilizations in the name of "town mak-ing" (*machizukuri*) had become more tightly integrated with local and municipal planning during the 1980s and 1990s, and were more often devoted to capitalizing on elements of local history. The Center for Local Disaster Prevention and Town Planning (Chiiki Bōsai Machizukuri Sen-taa), a metropolitan government–sponsored office, began publishing the magazine *Machinami* (Townscape) after the Kobe earthquake in 1995. The magazine regularly featured preservation issues. In 2009, the center also became the conduit for grants from the Tokyo Historical Town Planning Fund (Tōkyō Rekishi Machizukuri Fando), which were awarded for repair and maintenance of buildings designated under the Urban Vistas Ordinance.[38]

Even narrow alleys, formerly the city planner's prime evidence of Tokyo's continued backwardness, came to be seen as cultural heritage in official circles. Revision of the national building code in 1998 permitted local authorities to consider exceptions to the four-meter minimum street width that had been universally applied whenever owners sought to rebuild.[39] In Tsukishima, a district of working-class *nagaya* tenements located in central Tokyo's Chūō Ward, the local planning office developed a system for encouraging residents to rebuild in fireproof materials while preserving direct frontage on alleys that were 2.7 meters wide, thus maintaining the scale of the early twentieth-century streetscape. Chūō Ward planners redrew planning maps around the shared alley space between facing rows of houses rather than around the buildings on a single urban block. Focusing on the scale of the common alley space while permitting rebuilding, the planners sought to preserve a stable resident population and what they termed the "Shitamachi feeling [*jōchō*] created by the alley and the *nagaya* houses facing it."[40] The ultimate mandate of planning for old downtown neighborhoods remained the replacement of wooden buildings with fireproof ones, but the Disaster Prevention Center's new agenda was to ease the rules for low-rise private reconstruction while promoting the preservation of local character. This was carried out under what was still called "adjustment of dense wood-built districts," which had formerly been a euphemism for slum clearance.

POST-BUBBLE RESTRUCTURING

Despite these trends toward reappraisal of the vernacular streetscape, events in the 1990s made clear that what had occurred during the bubble was a permanent shift in the management and occupancy of urban space. Beginning in the 1980s, large areas of downtown Tokyo had passed into the hands of development companies. Developers became the key players in an extended chain of relationships determining what got built where. Many of the sites they now came to build on and trade had been owner-occupied until the bubble, so a shift away from old shopkeeping households to corporate tenants and condominium owners often accompanied redevelopment. The buildings designed for central areas of Tokyo in this regime targeted a new type of occupant who embodied mobile international wealth. Corporate tenants for rental office space and prospective buyers for residential condominiums alike were presumed to have no particular local connections or needs. And in contrast to the state role in facilitating homeownership until the 1970s, in post-bubble Tokyo, the state allied with real estate companies, abandoning the former goal of promoting stable residence in favor of encouraging high-rise construction for maximum revenues. Underlying this policy shift was the fact that, from the time of the bubble, the politics of land use in Tokyo had come to be determined not simply by state welfare or economic development objectives but by pressures in the international system, to which national and municipal authorities responded through progressive relaxation of urban planning controls and encouragement of new private construction.[41]

Rather than treating the emerging post-bubble glut on the real estate market as an opportunity to channel new development toward improving the livability of existing neighborhoods and building stock, the national government continued to treat construction in Tokyo as an engine of growth. In a series of steps taken across the decade and culminating in the Urban Revitalization Law (Toshi Saisei Hō) of 2002, planning laws were revised to encourage large private development projects with far higher floor area ratios than previously seen in Japanese cities, giving special bonuses for projects combining multiple lots, permitting liberal trade in air rights, and streamlining the approval process to speed construction and effectively exclude the voices of surrounding residents.[42] In direct contrast to local initiatives in many Tokyo wards, these moves at the national level consolidated and perpetuated the building environment that had taken shape in the bubble years, but with preference given to the handful of large developers that had survived the bubble's burst.

REDEMPTION OF THE URBAN COMMONS

In this inhospitable climate for local initiative, Tokyoites in the late twentieth century turned to the traces of the past and asked them to speak of a time when the city was held in common by its citizens. Thus the preservationist activities of the 1970s and 1980s carried forward the political ideals of occupants of the public square in the 1960s, for whom, conversely, the public square was not simply a venue for politics but itself an interpretable object possessing inherent meaning. Like both mass politics and mass culture critique, preservationism imagined a social body, but it did so without claiming for it a transcendent spiritual unity. Instead, it sought solidarities in urban habitation and found the affirmation of those solidarities in the city's material forms and phenomenology. Neither before nor after 1969 did the objects of meaning belong to a stable realm of collective memory formed over generations, however, because the Tokyo landscape as a whole was too unstable, and because most of the societies of friends forming around material things and places of the past bore a mediated connection to their objects rather than the privileged connection of long-term occupancy or proprietorship.[43] In this sense, too, the memory projects of the 1970s and 1980s resembled the claims to the public square of the late 1960s, since they invented their object in the act of claiming it.

Tokyo's historicization was as much a product of citizen politics as of leisure industry expansion, municipal boosterism, or urban branding. This lineage of activism did not emerge from radical politics. Even the occupation of Shinjuku was a relatively tame insurgency within the context of public actions of the time, an effort to inject political meaning into a banal everyday context, guided by the aspiration to engage fellow citizens in discussion or song rather than to overthrow the political system. Yet, although local, usually unpolemical, sometimes ironic in style and sometimes co-optable, the movements and philosophies of everyday life in this book represented not the abandonment of public concerns in favor of private ones, but the opening of new micropublics and political spaces. As mass politics receded and leisure and consumption sites burgeoned after the early 1970s, many youth in Tokyo came to treat Tokyo's public spaces as playgrounds rather than as venues for political expression. Yet to look no further than the end of student radicalism and democratic mass movements and the subsequent fragmentation of the public would be to leave unrealized the project of understanding and pursuing the politics of the everyday put forward by philosophers from Henri LeFebvre to Michel de Certeau to Yoshimoto Takaaki, as well as by the members of Beheiren and other Japanese organizations of the 1960s. Community, commons, and heritage mobilized people and led them toward new kinds of spaces.

Like democratic activists and urban critics in the 1960s and 1970s, preservationists and Edo-Tokyo historians in the 1980s and 1990s shared a sense that the modern state, capitalism, and postindustrial bureaucratic society had diminished the capacity of urban residents to claim and shape the city for themselves, and they responded by looking to the vestiges of the past to articulate their present concerns. Local preservationists mapped neighborhood streets to confirm communal ties and identities, while urban explorers treated the same streets as a primordial commons open to individual and collective claims. Museum professionals sought to narrate community through artifacts and reconstructed scenes of home life in a simpler time. All these appropriations from the past were themselves reappropriated, sometimes toward personal ends and sometimes toward the ends of capital and the state. The distinction between communal and common space had gone largely unrecognized in the politics of the public square in the 1960s, because at the time the public as the community of all citizens appeared a natural and self-evident democratic right. In identifying new local nodes of communal interest, interstitial sites of meaning, and objects to appropriate, the champions of vernacular urbanism after 1969 claimed the city as citizens' property, but without the abstract public as its universal basis.

When placed beside each other, the Renaissance Florentine piazza, with which I began chapter 1, and the mid-twentieth century Japanese family dining table, with which I ended my last chapter, stand in stark contrast: an image of active, self-governing citizenry on the one hand and one of a retreat into privacy—suggesting an interiorized national subjectivity—on the other. There were multiple signs in the first decade of the twenty-first century that the collective claims to the urban commons I have described were coming to a close, beginning with the enclosure of expressions of the vernacular past in the museum itself. *Yanesen* magazine ended its twenty-five-year run in 2009, as the community that had been fostered in the virtual space of a magazine gravitated increasingly into digital media, eliminating the person-to-person transactions involved in printing and distribution that had tied the magazine to real space and the magazine community to its neighborhood. And the Vistas Protection Law of 2004 established new institutions channeling the energies of a range of preservationists and "street observationists" toward officially sanctioned outcomes. Yet this sequence of episodes and their denouements should not be read as an ineluctable or teleological process. Piazzas and dining tables, along with alleyways, tenement row houses, and the wide range of other artifacts and spaces discussed in this book, occupied a common field of historical objects retrieved to express contemporary ideals of urban identity and belonging. Since history is cumulative and its possibilities latent, as those ideals change, nothing puts any one object in the storehouse of the past entirely beyond the reach of those who would reclaim it.

J.B. Jackson has written that in preserving ordinary things and landscapes, people enact a ritual of resurrection. The objects of everyday use must first be lost or forgotten, then recovered, almost as if they belonged to an "ancient myth of birth, death and redemption."[44] The process creates a break, and the break allows the object's rediscovery. The same process also enables the object to move from the particular to the general, from private property to common property, in order to speak for common memory of the lost time of the past. Regardless of whether the traces of the past take on national monumental significance or bind only a small group of adherents, their passage into common property inscribes a history. In the most recent episode of this ongoing process of recycling, some history museums in Japan began abandoning public history itself for private memory. Yet time plows forward, burying histories and throwing up new ruins in its wake. New groups of people will gather around surviving places and things, making them tell new stories of loss and redemption, and creating new societies of friends.

Notes

INTRODUCTION

1. Andreas Huyssen, *Present Pasts: Urban Palimpsests and the Politics of Memory* (Stanford, CA: Stanford University Press, 2003), 1.

2. Rather than a reading of the city, therefore, I am presenting a genealogy of particular readings and the movements and activities associated with them. A number of interpretations of Tokyo exist in English, including Peter Popham, *Tokyo: City at the End of the World* (New York: Kodansha International, 1985); Donald Richie, *Tokyo: Megacity* (Rutland, VT: Tuttle, 2010); Paul Waley's collection of historical essays, *Tokyo: City of Stories* (New York: Weatherhill, 1991); Edward Seidensticker's two-volume history, *Low City, High City: Tokyo from Edo to the Earthquake* (Cambridge, MA: Harvard University Press, 1985) and *Tokyo Rising: The City since the Great Earthquake* (Cambridge, MA: Harvard University Press, 1990); and Roman Cybriwsky's study, *Tokyo: The Shogun's City at the Twenty-First Century* (Chichester, NY: J. Wiley and Sons, 1998).

3. For a study treating modern high-rise office buildings as vernacular architecture, see Carol Willis, *Form Follows Finance: Skyscrapers and Skylines in New York and Chicago* (Princeton, NJ: Princeton Architectural Press, 1995). For a discussion of the problem of mass culture in relation to the vernacular in the work of Robert Venturi and Denise Scott Brown, see Deborah Fausch, "Ugly and Ordinary: The Representation of the Everyday," in *Architecture of the Everyday,* edited by Steven Harris and Deborah Berke (Princeton, NJ: Princeton Architectural Press, 1997), 75–106.

4. For a historical discussion of some of the important features of Tokyo's vernacular landscape, see Hidenobu Jinnai, *Tokyo: A Spatial Anthropology*, translated by Kimiko Nishimura (Berkeley: University of California Press, 1995). See also the brief architectural studies and meditations on Tokyo's vernacular

landscape in *small Tokyo: Measuring the Non-Measurable*, edited by Darko Radovic and Davisi Boontharm (Tokyo: flick studio, 2012).

5. Huyssen, *Present Pasts*, 38–40.

6. Alois Riegl, "The Modern Cult of Monuments: Its Character and Origin," translated by K. W. Forster and D. Ghirardo, *Oppositions* 25 (1982): 20–51.

7. Ogino Masaharu, "Bunka isan e no shakaigakuteki apurōchi," in *Bunka isan no shakaigaku: Rūburu bijutsukan kara genbaku dōmu made* (Tokyo: Shin'yōsha, 2002), 11–14.

8. Oda Mitsuo, *Kōgai no tanjō to shi* (Tokyo: Seikyūsha, 1997), 29 (chart).

9. Yosuke Hirayama, "Reshaping the Housing System: Home Ownership as a Catalyst for Social Transformation," in *Housing and Social Transition in Japan,* edited by Yosuke Hirayama and Richard Ronald (London: Routledge, 2007), 15; Oda, *Kōgai no tanjō to shi,* 33.

10. See Simon Partner, *Assembled in Japan: Electrical Goods and the Making of the Japanese Consumer* (Berkeley: University of California Press, 1999); Laura Neitzel, "Living Modern: *Danchi* Housing and Postwar Japan" (PhD dissertation, Columbia University, 2003).

11. For a review of some of the theoretical framings of public and private in political and sociological literature that shows the limits of the dichotomous model, see Jeff Weintraub, "The Theory and Politics of the Public/Private Distinction," in *Public and Private in Thought and Practice: Perspectives on a Grand Dichotomy,* edited by Jeff Weintraub and Krishan Kumar (Chicago: University of Chicago Press, 1997), 1–42. My purpose here is to convey that the spatial and social duality of the democratic national public and nuclear-family privacy was adequate to a particular era, then found wanting—a point echoed by the work of Nishikawa Yūko, Ochiai Emiko, and others.

12. Yoshimi Shun'ya, *Posuto sengo shakai* (Tokyo: Iwanami shoten, 2009), 28–29.

13. Yasumaru Yoshio, "Sengo shisōshi no naka no 'minshū' to 'taishū,'" in *Reisen taisei to shihon no bunka: 1955 nen igo,* edited by Yoshimi Shun'ya et al. (Tokyo: Iwanami shoten, 2002), 87.

14. The wartime state, of course, made no such guarantee, conscripting soldiers and factory labor, then household goods, for the needs of the military.

15. Simon Avenell, *Making Japanese Citizens: Civil Society and the Mythology of the Shimin in Postwar Japan* (Berkeley: University of California Press, 2010), 13.

16. Tada Michitaro, "The Glory and Misery of 'My Home,'" in *Authority and the Individual in Japan: Citizen Protest in Historical Perspective,* edited by Victor Koschmann (Tokyo: University of Tokyo Press, 1978), 207–217; Sepp Linhart, "From Industrial to Postindustrial Society: Changes in Japanese Leisure-Related Values and Behavior," *Journal of Japanese Studies* 14, no. 2 (Summer 1988): 287.

17. Oda, *Kōgai no tanjō to shi,* 43.

18. Hirayama, "Reshaping the Housing System," 24.

19. Sukenari Yasushi, "Nichijō seikatsu hihan no rokujū-nanajū nendai," in

Karuchuraru poritikkusu 1960/70, edited by Kitada Akihiro, Nogami Gen, and Mizutamari Mayumi (Tokyo: Serika shobō, 2005), 25.

20. This suburbanization process is sketched in Oda, *Kōgai no tanjō to shi*, 5–61.

21. Kurokawa Noriaki, "Oh! Saibōgu no okite: Kapuseru sengen 1969," *SD: Space Design* 52 (March 1969): 50.

22. This characterization applies mainly to the visionary projects that remained on paper. Individual members of the group, particularly Ōtaka Masato and Maki Fumihiko, engaged in community-based planning projects. On Metabolism, see Zhongjie Lin, *Kenzo Tange and the Metabolist Movement: Urban Utopias of Modern Japan* (London: Routledge, 2010); Cherie Wendelken, "Putting Metabolism Back in Place: The Making of a Radically Decontextualized Architecture in Japan," in *Anxious Modernisms: Experimentation in Postwar Architectural Culture*, edited by Sarah Goldhagen and Réjean Legault (Cambridge, MA: MIT Press, 2002), 279–299.

23. Emiko Ochiai, *The Japanese Family System in Transition: A Sociological Analysis of Family Change in Postwar Japan*, translated by Geraldine Harcourt (Tokyo: LTCB International Library Foundation, 1994); Miura Atsushi, *"Kazoku" to "kōfuku" no sengoshi: Kōgai no yume to jitsugen* (Tokyo: Kōdansha, 1999).

24. Ueno Junko, "Jūtakuchi no teemaka to fudōsan kōkoku: 1980 nendai ni okeru daikibo takuchi kaihatsu no tenkai," *Kantō toshi gakkai nenpō* 5 (2003): 25–36.

25. Matsubara Hiroshi, *Fudōsan shihon to toshi kaihatsu* (Tokyo: Mineruba shobō, 1988), 139. See also Mike Douglass, "The 'New' Tokyo Story: Restructuring Space and the Struggle for Place in a World City," in *Japanese Cities in the World Economy*, edited by Kuniko Fujita and Richard Child Hill (Philadelphia: Temple University Press, 1993), 83–119.

26. Theorists of postmodernity have associated the diminished status of radical politics and mass movements after the 1960s with the collapse of grand narratives of progress and human liberation. For a summary and analysis of this shift focusing on the work of Lyotard and Jameson, see Perry Anderson, *The Origins of Postmodernity* (London: Verso, 1998). For Japan, see essays in *Postmodernism and Japan*, edited by Masao Miyoshi and Harry D. Harootunian (Durham, NC: Duke University Press, 1989).

27. This is the logic underlying David Harvey's discussion of "bread and circuses" in the postmodern city, for example. See Harvey, *The Condition of Postmodernity: An Enquiry into the Origins of Cultural Change* (Oxford: Blackwell, 1989), 88–91.

28. Simon Avenell proposes two phases of citizen politics after the mid-1970s, the "new civic movements" period, from 1975 to 1989, and the "rise of civil society," after 1990. Avenell, *Making Japanese Citizens*, 240–245. Most scholarship on Japanese mass politics in the late 1960s has focused on campus movements in 1968 and 1969 in a narrative that ends with the self-destruction of the radical Left at Asama in 1972.

29. On the citizen protest groups that emerged from the Anpo protests, see Wesley Sasaki-Uemura, *Organizing the Spontaneous: Citizen Protest in*

Postwar Japan (Honolulu: University of Hawaii Press, 2001). On residents' movements for sunlight rights, see Margaret McKean, *Environmental Protest and Citizen Politics in Japan* (Berkeley: University of California Press, 1981), 101–125.

30. Raphael Samuel suggests that the growth of "conservationist sentiment" in England beginning in the 1960s may be related to the increase in private homeownership. It seems reasonable to suppose that the long-term investment entailed in buying a house would dispose people to look with greater interest on historic houses and interiors. The same thing may have happened in Japan. Yet in contrast to the English case, the generation that came to Tokyo and stepped onto the "housing ladder" in the same period often experienced the upheaval of mass migration and urban redevelopment in the same process, making alienation from traditional community as much a part of the perception of homeownership as the achievement of social and personal stability through acquisition of property. It further reveals the contrast of these urban experiences that much of the new homeownership Samuel describes in English cities occurred through the retrofitting of old houses and gentrification of old neighborhoods, whereas these phenomena were practically unknown in Japan until the late 1990s. Samuel, *Theatres of Memory,* vol. 1, *Past and Present in Contemporary Culture* (London: Verso, 1994), 237.

31. Gage Averill, "Global Imaginings," in *Making and Selling Culture,* edited by Richard Ohmann (Hanover, NH: University Press of New England/ Wesleyan University Press, 1996), 215.

32. Tsuru Shigeto, *Japan's Capitalism: Creative Defeat and Beyond* (New York: Cambridge University Press, 1993), 181–185, 192–199.

33. Miyamoto Ken'ichi records that one of the slogans at the first Earth Day, held in 1970, was "no more Tokyos." Miyamoto, "Tokyo to Edo no tanima: Kokusai toshiron no kyojitsu," *Sekai* 490 (July 1986): 24. For descriptions of the transformation of the two western Tokyo hubs of Shinjuku and Shibuya in the 1970s, see Roman Cybriwsky, *Tokyo: The Changing Profile of an Urban Giant* (Boston: G. K. Hall, 1991), 156–170.

34. "Kaigai ryokō kyakusū no suii," data from Kokudo kōtsūshō sōgō seisakukyoku kankō bu, *Kankō hakusho,* represented in graph form at "Shakai jitsujō deeta zuroku," www2.ttcn.ne.jp/honkawa/6900.html.

35. See, for example, "Tōkyō esunikku densetsu: Ethnic Tokyo," edited by Jinnai Hidenobu et al., special issue, *Process Architecture* 72 (1987).

36. Donald MacKenzie, "Models of Markets: Finance Theory and the Historical Sociology of Arbitrage," *Revue d'histoire des sciences* 57, no. 2 (January 2004): 414–418. Jameson and other theorists have read this development in finance as creating a realm of pure representation, paralleling cultural developments associated with postmodernism. Frederic Jameson, "Culture and Finance Capital," in *The Cultural Turn: Selected Writings on the Postmodern, 1983–1998* (London: Verso, 1998), 136–161; Jean-Joseph Goux, "Ideality, Symbolicity, and Reality in Postmodern Capitalism," in *Postmodernism, Economics and Knowledge,* edited by Stephen Cullenberg, Jack Amariglio, and David F. Ruccio (London: Routledge, 2001), 166–181; Mark Taylor, *Confidence Games: Money and Markets in a World without Redemption* (Chicago: University of Chicago Press, 2004).

37. For an analysis of this streamlining process and its social effects, see Saskia Sassen, *The Global City: New York, London, Tokyo,* 2nd ed. (Princeton, NJ: Princeton University Press, 2001).

38. Belá G. Lipták, *Municipal Waste Disposal in the 1990s* (Radnor, PA: Chilton, 1991), 328; Harvey, *The Condition of Postmodernity,* 331.

39. Roman Cybriwsky, *Tokyo: The Changing Profile of an Urban Giant* (Boston: G.K. Hall, 1991), 110, 111 (table).

40. John Logan and Harvey Molotch, *Urban Fortunes: The Political Economy of Place* (Berkeley: University of California Press, 1987), 32. On the growth coalition in 1980s Tokyo, see Machimura Takashi, *"Sekai toshi" Tōkyō no kōzō tenkan: Toshi risutorakuchuaringu no shakaigaku* (Tokyo: Tōkyō daigaku shuppankai, 1994), 103–140. My discussion here draws substantially from Machimura.

41. K. Hayakawa and Y. Hirayama, "The Impact of the Minkatsu Policy on Japanese Housing and Land Use," *Environment and Planning D: Society and Space* 9, no. 2 (June 1991): 157. For a discussion of the broader context of planning in the 1980s, see André Sorensen, *The Making of Urban Japan: Cities and Planning from Edo to the Twenty-first Century* (New York: Routledge, 2002), 256–287. See also Mike Douglass, "The 'New' Tokyo Story," 83–119.

42. Ōtsuka Yūji, "Chika kōtō 'Nakasone minkatsu' no kyokō o tsuku," *Chūō kōron* 102, no. 1 (January 1987): 158–159.

43. Saito Asato, "Global City in Developmental State: Urban Restructuring in Tokyo," in *Planning in a Global Era,* edited by Andy Thornley and Yvonne Rydin (Aldershot, UK: Ashgate, 2002), 27–46.

44. Michael Hebbert and Norihiro Nakai, "Deregulation of Japanese Planning in the Nakasone Era," *Town Planning Review* 59, no. 4 (October 1988): 385.

45. Yukio Noguchi, "The 'Bubble' and Economic Policies in the 1980s," *Journal of Japanese Studies* 20, no. 2 (Summer 1994): 291–329.

46. Ibid., 292.

47. Ibid., 304.

48. Reiko Habe Ebansu and Ōno Teruyuki, *Toshi kaihatsu o kangaeru* (Tokyo: Iwanami shoten, 1992), 111.

49. Sō Kenmei, "Tochi no yūkō riyō: Kō to shi no kankei o chūshin to shite," *Hokudai hōgaku kenkyūka juniaa risaachi jaanaru* 5 (November 1998): 33–65. Sō examines six such cases.

50. Toki Hiroshi, *Tōkyō mondai no seijigaku,* 2nd ed. (Tokyo: Nihon hyōronsha, 2003), 103.

51. Takashi Machimura, "Symbolic Use of Globalization in Urban Politics in Tokyo," *International Journal of Urban and Regional Research* 22, no. 2 (1998): 183–194. The full slogan was "My town Tokyo: A town we can call home *(furusato)."*

52. For an interpretation of the longer history of local identity in relation to the modern nation in Japan, see Hoyt Long, *On Uneven Ground: Miyazawa Kenji and the Making of Place in Modern Japan* (Stanford, CA: Stanford University Press, 2011).

53. For an analysis of the Ōhira report, see Harry D. Harootunian, "Visible Discourses, Invisible Ideologies," in *Postmodernism and Japan,* edited by

Masao Miyoshi and Harry D. Harootunian (Durham, NC: Duke University Press, 1989), 78–90.

54. Michael Hardt and Antonio Negri, *Empire* (Cambridge, MA: Harvard University Press, 2000), 293.

55. For a discussion of the way the folk craft movement articulated between local and national cultural goals, see Kim Brandt, *Kingdom of Beauty: Mingei and the Politics of Folk Art in Imperial Japan* (Durham, NC: Duke University Press, 2007), 135–155. On the sublation of local culture into the nation in the founding work of folklorist Yanagita Kunio, see Harry D. Harootunian, "Figuring the Folk: History, Poetics, and Representation," in *Mirror of Modernity: Invented Traditions in Modern Japan,* edited by Stephen Vlastos (Berkeley: University of California Press, 1998), 144–159.

56. *Edo Tōkyō hakubutsukan kensetsu no ayumi: Kensetsu to kaihatsu junbi no kiroku* (Tokyo: Edo Tōkyō rekishi bunka zaidan, 1997), 81.

57. On cultural administration in the Tokyo Metropolitan Government, see Mikako Iwatake, "Tokyo Renaissance: Constructing a Postmodern Identity for Contemporary Japan" (PhD dissertation, University of Pennsylvania, 1993), 92–96. For an analysis of the workings of cultural administration in local place making, see Jennifer Robertson, *Native and Newcomer: Making and Remaking a Japanese City* (Berkeley: University of California Press, 1991). Local revitalization plans developed in the 1970s for Tōno, in northeastern Japan, reveal a similar idealistic rhetoric. See Marilyn Ivy, *Discourses of the Vanishing: Modernity, Phantasm, Japan* (Chicago: University of Chicago Press, 1995), 103–117. For an institutional history of cultural administration offices, see Mori Hajime, "Bunka gyōsei no ayumi," in *Bunka gyōsei to machizukuri,* edited by Tamura Akira and Mori Hajime (Tokyo: Jiji tsūshinsha, 1983), 271–294.

58. Concurrently, as Theodore Bestor has shown, members of the shopkeeping "old middle class" used evocations of traditional community as a strategy to maintain local control amid an increasingly white-collar urban population. Bestor, *Neighborhood Tokyo* (Stanford CA: Stanford University Press, 1989), 262–268.

59. Oda, *Kōgai no tanjō to shi,* 239.

60. Richard Torrance, "*Otoko wa tsurai yo*: Nostalgia or Parodic Realism?" in *Word and Image in Japanese Cinema,* edited by Dennis Washburn and Carole Cavanaugh (Cambridge: Cambridge University Press, 2001), 226–249. Torrance notes that the protagonist was portrayed as an anachronism already in 1971. In a scene parodying the contemporary boom in folklore studies among young people, he gives his famous sales patter to a group of college students with a tape recorder (Torrance, 239).

61. See Theodore C. Bestor, "The Shitamachi Revival," *Transactions of the Asiatic Society of Japan,* 4th series, vol. 5 (1990): 71–86.

62. I take the term "heterotopia" from Michel Foucault's "Of Other Spaces" (1984), available online in translation by Jay Miskowiec at http://foucault.info /documents/heteroTopia/foucault.heteroTopia.en.html. For further perspectives on exoticism and heritage, see Dean MacCannell, *The Tourist: A New Theory of the Leisure Class,* rev. ed. (New York: Schocken Books, 1989); David Lowenthal, *The Past Is a Foreign Country* (Cambridge: Cambridge University Press, 1985).

63. See Henry D. Smith II, "Tokyo as an Idea: An Exploration of Japanese Urban Thought until 1945," *Journal of Japanese Studies* 4, no. 1 (Winter 1978): 45–80; Carol Gluck, "The Invention of Edo," in *Mirror of Modernity: Invented Traditions in Modern Japan,* edited by Stephen Vlastos (Berkeley: University of California Press, 1998), 262–284. Mikako Iwatake discusses the nineteenth- and twentieth-century centennial events marking Edo's founding in "From Shogunal City to a Life City: Tokyo between Two Fin-de-Siècles" in *Japanese Capitals in Historical Perspective: Place, Power and Memory in Kyoto, Edo and Tokyo,* edited by Paul Waley and Nicholas Fieve (London: RoutledgeCurzon, 2003), 233–256.

64. I am indebted to Henry Smith for this point.

65. Augustin Berque, *Japan: Cities and Social Bonds,* translated by Chris Turner (1993; Northamptonshire, UK: Pilkington Press, 1997), 98.

66. Svetlana Boym, *The Future of Nostalgia* (New York: Basic Books, 2001), 49–51. Boym draws the distinction between "restorative" national nostalgia and "reflective" personal nostalgia. I choose the word *redemptive* because mobilization of nostalgia in the name of the nation or another political community often proposes to redeem people in abstract spiritual terms rather than restoring anything material. For instances of a "reflective" and obsessively local Tokyo literature indebted to Nagai Kafū, see Tomita Hitoshi, *Jūsho to hizuke no aru Tōkyō fūkei* (Tokyo: Shinjuku shobō, 1989); Kobayashi Nobuhiko and Araki Nobuyoshi, *Shisetsu Tōkyō hanjōki* (Tokyo: Chūō kōronsha, 1984); Sakazaki Shigemori, *Tōkyōbon yūranki* (Tokyo: Shōbunsha, 2002).

67. It bears noting that most writing about memory and the city that we read in English was penned in cities built of brick and stone. In writing, as in material forms, it seems reasonable to expect a different language of memory depending on the physical environment of the remembering.

1. HIROBA

1. Hani Gorō, *Mikeruanjero* (Tokyo: Iwanami shoten, 1939), 3.

2. Hani Gorō, *Toshi* (Tokyo: Iwanami shoten, 1949), 63–64. Hani's phrase appears in his translation of a passage from a text by German legal historian Georg Ludwig von Maurer.

3. Sugimura Nobuji, "Toshi ni okeru hiroba no kinō: Yōroppa narabi ni sono shokuminchi ni tsuite," *Toshi mondai* 47, no. 4 (April 1956): 71.

4. Yoshizaka Takamasa and Tonuma Kōichi, *Toshiron, jūtaku mondai (Kenchikugaku taikei 2)* (Tokyo: Shōkokusha, 1960), 202–204. A leading figure in Japanese modernism, Yoshizaka had studied under Le Corbusier and was a professor of architecture at Waseda University. Tonuma was a Waseda student at the time the book was published.

5. See, for example, Miyauchi Yasushi, "Hiroba wa dare no mono ka," *Asahi shinbun,* May 28, 1969: 7.

6. Hoyt Long, "Performing the Village Square in Interwar Japan: Toward a Hidden History of Public Space," *Journal of Asian Studies* 70, no. 3 (August 2011): 763. For a historical and spatial analysis of a modern *hiroba* profoundly tied to national monumentality, see Wu Hung, *Remaking Beijing: Tiananmen*

Square and the Creation of a Political Space (Chicago: University of Chicago Press, 2005), 15–50.

7. See Jinnai Hidenobu, *Tokyo: A Spatial Anthropology,* translated by Kimiko Nishimura (Berkeley: University of California Press, 1995), 78–82. For an analysis of the process of commoner appropriation of fire breaks, see James McClain, "Edobashi: Power, Space and Popular Culture in Edo," in *Edo and Paris: Urban Life and the State in the Early Modern Era,* edited by James McClain, John Merriman, and Ugawa Kaoru (Ithaca, NY: Cornell University Press, 1997), 105–131.

8. For a discussion of the fate of these and other contemporaneous plans, see Fujimori Terunobu, *Meiji no Tōkyō keikaku* (Tokyo: Iwanami shoten, 1990), 259–304.

9. Koshizawa Akira, *Tōkyō toshi keikaku monogatari* (Tokyo: Nihon keizai hyōronsha, 1991), 35; Narita Ryūichi, "Teito fukkō o meguru toshiron no kōki to henshitsu," in *Tenkanki no rekishigaku,* edited by Tōkyō rekishi kagaku kenkyūkai (Tokyo: Gōdō shuppan, 1979), 214–217.

10. Prior to the construction of Hibiya Park, public parks had been built on land formerly held by temples and shrines. Hibiya Park was the first public park for which land was allocated by the national government and the landscape created anew.

11. On political uses of Hibiya Park, see Andrew Gordon, *Labor and Imperial Democracy in Prewar Japan* (Berkeley: University of California Press, 1991), 42–50. As Isoda Kōichi notes, flanked by offices of the Ministry of Justice and the Police, Hibiya Park evoked a provisional "freedom under surveillance." See Isoda Kōichi, "Rokumeikan no keifu," in *Isoda Kōichi chosakushū,* vol. 5 (Tokyo: Ozawa shoten, 1991), 221–222.

12. Hara Takeshi, *Kōkyo mae hiroba* (Tokyo: Kōbunsha, 2003), 114. For a discussion of the range of activities surrounding this celebration, see Kenneth Ruoff, *Imperial Japan at Its Zenith: The Wartime Celebration of the Empire's 2,600th Anniversary* (Ithaca, NY: Cornell University Press, 2010).

13. On the imperial gaze and earlier uses of the plaza, see Takashi Fujitani, *Splendid Monarchy: Power and Pageantry in Modern Japan* (Berkeley: University of California Press, 1996), 128–145. Hara Takeshi argues that the role of the emperor in events in the plaza became conspicuous only in the 1930s.

14. Hara, *Kōkyo mae hiroba,* 141.

15. George R. Packard, *Protest in Tokyo: The Security Treaty Crisis of 1960* (Princeton, NJ: Princeton University Press, 1966), 262.

16. On face-to-face communication as the foundation of Habermas's conception of the public sphere, see Nicholas Garnham, "The Media and the Public Sphere," in *Habermas and the Public Sphere,* edited by Craig Calhoun (Cambridge, MA: MIT Press, 1992), 359–376.

17. *Minikomishi* activism can in turn be traced back to the "circle" movement of the 1950s. See Wesley Sasaki-Uemura, *Organizing the Spontaneous: Citizen Protest in Postwar Japan* (Honolulu: University of Hawaii Press, 2001), 26–29; Tsurumi Kazuko, *Social Change and the Individual: Japan before and after Defeat in World War II* (Princeton, NJ: Princeton University Press, 1970), 213–303.

18. Wesley Sasaki-Uemura, "Competing Publics: Citizens' Groups, Mass Media, and the State in the 1960s," *positions: east asia cultures critique* 10, no. 1 (2002): 95.

19. "Nihon no toshi kūkan," edited by Itō Teiji, special issue, *Kenchiku bunka* 18, no. 206 (December 1963): 47–152. Articles included English translation of titles and abstracts.

20. Toyokawa Saikaku, "Nijū seiki Nihon kenchiku no 'yorokobashiki chishiki'," *10+1* 50 (March 2008): 88; Kikuchi Makoto, "Kūkan no kaihatsu, kankyō no seigyō," *10+1* 50 (March 2008): 96.

21. "Kaiwai: Activity Space," in "Nihon no toshi kūkan," 68. This dynamic conception echoes Peter Linebaugh's conception of commons as practice rather than resource. Linebaugh, *The Magna Carta Manifesto: Liberties and Commons for All* (Berkeley: University of California Press, 2008), 279.

22. "Nihon no toshi kūkan," 71.

23. Ibid., 138.

24. The issue also introduced other spatial concept terms that would subsequently become ubiquitous in Japanese design discourse, such as the notion of *ma,* or interstitial space. For further elaboration of this concept, see Arata Isozaki, *Ma: Space-Time in Japan* (New York: Cooper Hewitt Museum, 1979).

25. For an analysis of ways in which ideas of commons signify a political retreat, see Elizabeth Blackmar, "Appropriating 'the Commons': The Tragedy of Property Rights Discourse," in *The Politics of Public Space,* edited by Seth Low and Neil Smith (New York: Routledge, 2006), 49–80.

26. For a history of Shinjuku Station and its literary representations, see Alisa Freedman, *Tokyo in Transit: Japanese Culture on the Rails and Roads* (Stanford, CA: Stanford University Press, 2011).

27. The incident was documented on film by director Ōuchida Keiya and titled *Chika hiroba.* For an analysis of the incident and the film, see Peter Eckersall, "The Emotional Geography of Shinjuku," *Japanese Studies* 31, no. 3 (December 2011): 333–343.

28. Thomas Havens, *Fire across the Sea: The Vietnam War and Japan, 1965–1975* (Princeton, NJ: Princeton University Press, 1987), 169–170.

29. Rikki Kersten, "The Intellectual Culture of Postwar Japan and the 1968–69 University of Tokyo Struggles: Repositioning the Self in Postwar Thought," *Social Science Japan Journal* 12, no. 2 (2009): 227–245.

30. Hani Gorō, *Toshi no ronri: Rekishiteki jōken, gendai no tōsō* (Tokyo: Keisō shobō, 1968), 52.

31. Quoted in Peter Starr, *Commemorating Trauma: The Paris Commune and Its Cultural Aftermath* (New York: Fordham University Press, 2006), 28.

32. Sasaki-Uemura, *Organizing the Spontaneous,* 206–208. As William Marotti has shown, Beheiren's nonviolent protests drew media attention in part because both student violence and police brutality toward citizens and journalists in 1968 had dramatized the confrontation between the antiwar movement and the state. Violence in 1968 thus set the stage for nonviolence in 1969. See Marotti, "Japan 1968: The Performance of Violence and the Theater of Protest," *American Historical Review* 114, no. 1 (February 2009): 129. For more

specifics on Beheiren structure, personnel, and backgrounds, see Havens, *Fire across the Sea,* 54–57.

33. Yumiko Iida, *Rethinking Identity in Modern Japan: Nationalism as Aesthetics* (London: Routledge 2002), 122.

34. First printed in *Bungei shunjū,* August 1969, and reprinted in *Shiryō beheiren undō,* edited by Betonamu ni heiwa o shimin rengō, vol. 2 (Tokyo: Kawade shobō shinsha, 1974), 96–97.

35. The estimate of one million appears in "Enzetsu, kanpa katsudō issō: Kon'ya jitsuryoku kōshi shite Shinjuku nishiguchi hiroba kara," *Asahi shinbun,* May 14, 1969: 11. The *Asahi* later reported the station master's estimate of between five hundred thousand and over one million passengers passing through the west exit daily. "Hiroba ka tsūro ka: kamitsu toshi no nageki," *Asahi shinbun,* July 24, 1969: 16. The 1970 *Guinness Book of World Records* reported that based on statistics from October 1967, the "Tokyo subway service of the Japanese National Railways" was the busiest rail service in the world, and that Tokyo Station was the busiest train station, with 809,660 passengers every twenty-four hours. Norris and Ross McWhirter, *Guinness Book of World Records,* 9th enlarged ed. (New York: Sterling, 1970), 275. The reliability of this data is open to question, however, since the Tokyo subway system was not in fact operated by the JNR. With private commuter lines terminating in Shinjuku in addition to the subways and the JNR lines, it seems likely that the total number of passengers in Shinjuku during a twenty-four-hour period would have exceeded that in Tokyo Station.

36. Sekine Hiroshi, "Shinjuku nishiguchi hiroba no rekishi," *Shisō no kagaku* no. 103 *rinji zōkan* [special supplement] (June 1970): 15; Nyaromeo07 (penname), "Fōku gerira o shitteru kai sono 6," *After the Gold Rush: Tōku made ikunda bokura no sukina ongaku yo* (blog), February 2, 2008, http://ameblo.jp/nyaromeo07/entry-10069705232.html.

37. Konaka Yōtarō, *Watakushi no naka no Betonamu sensō: Beheiren ni kaketa seishun to gunzō* (Tokyo: Sankei shinbunsha shuppankyoku, 1973), 106–107.

38. "Enzetsu, kanpa katsudō issō," 11.

39. "Shinjuku ni utau 3000 nin: Keisatsu wa 'gaman,'" *Asahi shinbun,* May 25, 1969.

40. Sekine, "Shinjuku nishiguchi hiroba no rekishi," 14.

41. Nishinari Norihisa, "Shinjuku nishiguchi hiroba no seiritsu to hiroba ishiki: Nishiguchi hiroba kara nishiguchi tsūro e no meishō henkō mondai o tsūjite," *Toshi keikaku ronbunshū* 40, no. 3 (October 2005): 245.

42. Simon Avenell, *Making Japanese Citizens: Civil Society and the Mythology of the Shimin in Postwar Japan* (Berkeley: University of California Press, 2010), 137–143.

43. Henri LeFebvre, "The Right to the City," in *Writings on Cities,* translated and introduced by Eleonore Kofman and Elizabeth Lebas (Oxford: Blackwell, 1996), 158–159.

44. "Bakuhatsu suru wakasa uzumaku nekki: Utagoe ni aji, hakushu fōku songu shūkai," *Asahi shinbun,* June 22, 1969: 16. On *gewalt* in the Japanese student movements, see Marotti, "Japan 1968," 131.

45. Ken Hirschkop, *Mikhail Bakhtin: An Aesthetic for Democracy* (Oxford: Oxford University Press, 1999), 261.

46. Yotaro Konaka, "Shinjuku: Community of Encounter," *Japan Quarterly* 38, no. 3 (July 1991): 301–310.

47. The ideal of a public "community of encounter" also tied to the experience of many Tokyo youth, for whom the streets of the city represented liberation from the home. Folk guerrilla Yoshioka Shinobu began his account *Who Are the Folk Guerrillas?* with a romantic story representing the new world of ideas in the streets versus the closed world of the home, and proposed that *hiroba* were created by the continually changing experience of the streets. Yoshioka Shinobu, *Fōku gerira to wa nanimono ka* (Tokyo: Jiyū kokuminsha, 1970), 10–12.

48. The station-front plaza that had preceded this one, designed in 1934 and completed in 1941, had also put priority on traffic flow. Yet planners had at the same time spoken of the development of a "civic center" (*shibikku sentaa*) to be built around the West Exit Plaza. See Koshizawa Akira, *Tōkyō toshi keikaku monogatari* (Tokyo: Nihon keizai hyōronsha, 1991), 76–91.

49. Tōkyōto shuto seibikyoku et al., "Shinjuku fukutoshin kaihatsu keikaku ni okeru ekimae hiroba no rittaiteki zōsei," *Kenchiku zasshi* 83, no. 1002 (October 1968), 740.

50. Yamada Masao, "Taishū shakai no tanjō: Shinjuku fukutoshin no kensetsu," *Ekonomisuto* 60, no. 38 (September 14, 1982): 112. Designers and the *Asahi* newspaper referred to the plaza as a "plaza of sun and fountains."

51. "Shinjuku nishi guchi eki hon'oku biru," *Shin kenchiku* 43, no. 3 (March 1968): 186. At the time, Sasaki was a student of Tange Kenzō at Tokyo University.

52. Yangu beheiren C-kun, quoted in "Hiroba ka tsūro ka: Kamitsu toshi no nageki, Shinjuku nishiguchi ronsō," *Asahi shinbun*, July 24, 1969: 16.

53. Quoted in Konaka Yōtarō, *Watakushi no naka no betonamu sensō*, 110.

54. Nishinari Norihisa notes that Hibiya did not serve their purposes because it was a "single-use space."

55. Sekine, "Shinjuku nishiguchi hiroba no rekishi," 17. At some time subsequent to the incident, station signage reverted to the term *hiroba*.

56. They would eventually be found guilty in a municipal court in September 1972 and ordered to pay fines. *Shiryō beheiren undō*, 2: 494.

57. "Shinjuku nishiguchi chika, keishichō de wa 'dōro': 'Utagoe' wa dōkōhō de torishimari," *Asahi shinbun*, July 24, 1969: 11.

58. Sekine, "Shinjuku nishiguchi hiroba no rekishi," 20.

59. Minobe Ryōkichi, *Tochiji jūninen* (Tokyo: Asahi shinbunsha, 1979).

60. Walter L. Ames, *Police and Community in Japan* (Berkeley: University of California Press, 1981), 219–220.

61. "'Hiroba' ga hoshii: Honsha e no tōsho kara," *Asahi shinbun*, July 26, 1969, evening edition: 10.

62. Cited in Sekine, "Shinjuku nishiguchi hiroba no rekishi," 16–17.

63. Ai Maeda, "Urban Theory Today," *Current Anthropology* 28, no. 4, "Supplement: An Anthropological Profile of Japan" (August–October 1987): 101–104F.

64. Itō Teiji et al., "Nihon no hiroba," *Kenchiku bunka* 298 (August 1971): 75–170. I have chosen to leave the word *hiroba* untranslated here to follow the

apparent intent of the editors. In the English table of contents accompanying the special issue, the title is "A Special Issue for Hiroba (Man-Made Open Space Served for [sic] Mutual Communication in Japan)."

65. Ibid., 76.

66. "Hiroba to wa nani ka," *Kenchiku bunka* 298 (August 1971): 76.

67. Itō and his colleagues were not alone in finding *hiroba* in places other than planned public plazas. The term was sufficiently elastic and appealing that one of the designers of the city's first high-rise luxury hotel, which was completed just outside the Shinjuku West Exit in 1970, claimed that the hotel itself was a *hiroba*. Murao Narufumi, "Keiō puraza hoteru: Chōkōsō toshi hoteru to shite no imi to shomondai," *Shin kenchiku* 46, no. 7 (July 1971): 191.

68. Itō's reading of the concept of *hiroba* also calls to mind Hannah Arendt's "associational" definition of a public as formed by people gathering in any place in which "freedom can appear." See Seyla Benhabib, "Models of Public Space: Hannah Arendt, the Liberal Tradition, and Jürgen Habermas," in *Habermas and the Public Sphere,* edited by Craig Calhoun (Cambridge, MA: MIT Press, 1992), 78.

69. Itō et al, "Nihon no hiroba," 77.

70. See, for example, Hattori Keijirō, *Toshi to sakariba: Shōgyō ritchiron josetsu* (Tokyo: Dōyūkan, 1977); and *Sakariba: Ningen yokubō no genten* (Tokyo: Kajima shuppankai, 1981). For an overview of a range of other *sakariba*-related studies, particularly in the field of architecture, see Zaino Hiroshi, *Kaiwai* (Tokyo: SD Sensho, 1978), 12–32. For a sociological analysis of Tokyo's changing *sakariba* in the twentieth century, see Yoshimi Shun'ya, *Toshi no doramatu- rugii: Tōkyō sakariba no shakaishi* (Tokyo: Kōbundō, 1987).

71. Kersten, "The Intellectual Culture of Postwar Japan and the 1968–69 University of Tokyo Struggles," 233–234.

72. Yoshimoto Takaaki, "Toshi wa naze toshi de aru ka," *Toshi* 1, no. 1 (December 1969): 23–34.

73. Okuno Takeo, *Bungaku ni okeru genfūkei: Harappa dōkutsu gensō* (Tokyo: Shūeisha, 1972), 26.

74. Okuno defined *genfūkei* as "time-spaces [jikūkan] and the images symbolizing them, inseparable from the weight of blood relations and neighborhood relations, that lodge in the unconscious as spaces of self-formation shaped in childhood or youth, and unconsciously define a writer's literature." Okuno, *Bungaku ni okeru genfūkei,* 45. The *Asahi shinbun* ran a series titled "Shōsetsu no genfūkei" (Originary landscapes of the novel) beginning in August 1971. The title may have been inspired by Okuno, who had begun serializing the essays that would become *Bungaku ni okeru genfūkei* in the journal *Subaru* in October 1970. The word had not been used in the newspaper previously. There is no entry for *genfūkei* in the 1974 second edition of the standard Japanese dictionary *Kōjien*. The term appears in the 1991 third edition.

75. Instead of designing megastructures or citizens' plazas, some architects after the late 1960s, including former Metabolist Maki Fumihiko, turned instead to studying and seeking to realize the kinds of space of everyday activity and encounter first suggested by the concept of *kaiwai*. See Maki Fumihiko et al., *Miegakure suru toshi* (Tokyo: SD Sensho, 1980).

76. Kawazoe Noboru, *Tōkyō no genfūkei: Toshi to den'en no kōryū* (Tokyo: NHK Books, 1979), 214–225.

77. Hasegawa Takashi, *Toshi kairō: Aruiwa kenchiku no chūseishugi* (Tokyo: Sagami shobō, 1975), 65–67.

78. For a colorful evocation of this *hiroba* amnesia, see Fujimori Terunobu, "Kōkyo ga mitsukatta," in *Kenchiku tantei no bōken* (Tokyo: Chikuma shobō, 1986), 135–168. See also chapter 5 of this book for further discussion.

79. See Jinnai Hidenobu, *Mizu no Tōkyō* (Tokyo: Iwanami shoten, 1993), 88–89; Suzuki Masao, *Edo-Tōkyō no kawa to mizube no jiten* (Tokyo: Kashiwa shobō, 2003), 439–443.

80. On the spread of television in the 1960s, see Hidetoshi Kato, "Japan," in *Television: An International History*, edited by Anthony Smith and Richard Paterson (Oxford: Oxford University Press, 1998), 169–181.

81. Tamura Norio, *Hiroba no shisō* (Tokyo: Bunwa shobō, 1976), 177–178.

82. Taki Kōji et al., "Toshi 3: Toshi wa mienai, sono ni," *Asahi jaanaru* 15, no. 12 (March 30, 1973): 83.

83. Funo Shūji, *Sengo kenchiku no shūen: Seikimatsu kenchiku ron nōto* (1981; Tokyo: Renga shobō shinsha, 1995), 208–209.

84. Tamura, *Hiroba no shisō,* 179–181. The group sent a public letter of protest to Governor Minobe urging him to recognize "pedestrian paradises" as *hiroba* for free communication among the citizens of Tokyo, and they received a reply that their activities should be permitted by the police, but his words seem to have gone unheeded.

85. Tamura, *Hiroba no shisō,* 177–179.

86. Miki Hasegawa, *We Are Not Garbage: The Homeless Movement in Tokyo, 1994–2002* (New York: Routledge, 2006), 13–15, 84–96; Shinjuku renraku kai, ed., *Shinjuku danbōru mura tatakai no kiroku* (Tokyo: Gendai kikakushitsu, 1997).

87. Sharon Hayashi and Anne McKnight, "Good-bye Kitty, Hello War: The Tactics of Spectacle and New Youth Movements in Urban Japan," *positions: east asia cultures critique* 13, no. 1 (Spring 2005): 87–113. For a discussion of other groups using public space in playful forms of protest, see Carl Cassegård, "Play and Empowerment: The Role of Alternative Space in Social Movements," *Electronic Journal of Contemporary Japanese Studies* 12, no. 1 (May 21, 2012), www.japanesestudies.org.uk/ejcjs/vol12/iss1/cassegard.html.

2. YANESEN

1. One *chō* in modern Tokyo is an area of several blocks given a name and administrative status. In 1985, Taitō Ward was made up of thirty-four named *chō* (with multiple numbered subunits) and housed a total population of roughly 178,000. The nineteen named *chō* of Bunkyō Ward had a total population of roughly 196,000. Tōkyōto sōmukyoku tōkeibu, ed., *Tōkyōto tōkei nenkan Shōwa 61 nen* (Tokyo: Tōkyōto, 1986), 28–29. Available at www.toukei.metro.tokyo.jp/tnenkan/tn-index.htm.

2. Mori Mayumi, *Yanaka suketchibukku: Kokoro yasashii toshi kūkan* (Tokyo: Eruko, 1985), 18–21; Aida Hanji, *Yanaka sōwa* (Tokyo: Meiji shoin,

1961), 3–7, 43. See also Paul Waley, "Who Cares about the Past in Today's Tokyo?" in *Urban Spaces in Japan: Cultural and Social Perspectives,* edited by Christoph Brumann and Evelyn Schulz (New York: Routledge, 2012), 148–166.

3. The story of Kasamori Osen, a waitress at the Kagiya teahouse made famous by print artist Suzuki Harunobu, takes up three chapters in Aida's *Yanaka sōwa:* one on Osen herself, one on the shrine dedicated to her memory, and one on plays and stories about her. This emphasis on an Edo story involving some celebrated figure (particularly a courtesan or a beautiful teahouse girl) and associated *lieux de memoires* characterizes a tradition of male Edo-Tokyo writers extending from the eighteenth century to the 1970s.

4. Aida, *Yanaka sōwa,* 145–146.

5. Mori Mayumi, *Fushigi no machi Nezu: Hissori to shita toshi kūkan* (Tokyo: Yamate shobō shinsha, 1992), 55–71.

6. For population and industry in late nineteenth- and early twentieth-century Nezu, see Bunkyō kuyakusho ed., *Bunkyō kushi dai 3 kan* (Tokyo: Bunkyō kuyakusho, 1967), 472–480, 636–731.

7. The discovery was made in an interview with the proprietor, reported in a *Yanesen* special issue on the Nezu prostitution district.

8. Mori Mayumi, *Dakishimeru Tōkyō* (Tokyo: Kōdansha, 1993), 74–75.

9. Reprinted in Yanesen kōbō, *Besuto obu Yanesen: Machi no aakaibusu* (Tokyo: Aki shobō, 2009), 1–2.

10. Robin LeBlanc, *Bicycle Citizens: The Political World of the Japanese Housewife* (Berkeley: University of California Press, 1999).

11. Mori Mayumi, "Owari ni," in *Besuto obu Yanesen: Machi no aakaibusu,* by Yanesen kōbō, (Tokyo: Aki shobō, 2009), 347.

12. Takeuchi Makoto, "Shitamachi," in *Edo-Tōkyōgaku jiten,* edited by Ogi Shinzō et al. (Tokyo: Sanseidō, 1987), 97–98.

13. Ibid., 97–98. See also Takeuchi, "Edo no chiiki kōzō to jūmin ishiki," in *Kōza Nihon no hōken toshi 2,* edited by Toyoda Takeshi, Harada Tomohiko, and Yamori Kazuhiko (Tokyo: Bun'ichi sōgō shuppan, 1983), 302–313.

14. Theodore Bestor, "The Shitamachi Revival," *Transactions of the Asiatic Society of Japan,* 4th ser., 5 (1990): 74.

15. See, for example, the series published in the *Asahi shinbun* from August through December 1977, and republished as Asahi shinbunsha honsha shakaibu, *Shitamachi* (Tokyo: Asahi shinbunsha, 1978). The *Mainichi shinbun* ran a similar series in 1985. For an early reference to a Shitamachi "boom," see "'Yoki jidai' e no kaiko de būmu ni: Shitamachi o shiru hon," *Shūkan sankei,* August 3, 1978: 82. The first English guidebook to the area was Enbutsu Sumiko, *Discover Shitamachi: A Walking Guide to the Other Tokyo* (Tokyo: Shitamachi Times, 1984).

16. Takeuchi, "Shitamachi," 98.

17. *Burū gaido pakku: Shitamachi* (Tokyo: Jitsugyō no Nihonsha, 1987), 64–66. Yanesen had appeared as part of Shitamachi in a few popular magazine features earlier. See, for example, "Edo Shitamachi," *Anguru,* January 1979: 9–13. This profile of local shops included a section covering Yanaka, Nezu, and Sendagi. Literary and cultural critic Isoda Kōichi noted in 1985 that the Yanaka, Hongo, and Yushima neighborhoods were being identified as a "new Shitamachi"

because they retained some of the character of prewar Tokyo. Isoda Kōichi, "Nosutarujia no Tōkyō: Mō hitotsu no Shitamachi," in *Isoda Kōichi chosakushū*, vol. 5 (Tokyo: Ozawa shoten, 1991), 360.

18. Mori Mayumi, *Tōkyō isan: Hozon kara saisei, katsuyō e* (Tokyo: Iwanami shoten, 2003), 85.

19. See Kurasawa Susumu, *Komyunitiron* (Tokyo: Hōsō daigaku kyōiku shinkōkai, 2002), 9–29.

20. Ibid., 30–43; Theodore Bestor, *Neighborhood Tokyo* (Stanford, CA: Stanford University Press, 1989), 70. For an extended study of the *chōnaikai* and reappraisal of its social origins, see Tamano Kazushi, *Kindai Nihon no toshika to chōnaikai no seiritsu* (Tokyo: Kōjinsha, 1993). On the *chōnaikai* in the early twentieth century, see Sally Ann Hastings, *Neighborhood and Nation in Tokyo, 1905–1937* (Pittsburgh: University of Pittsburgh Press, 1995), 69–85.

21. Egami Wataru, quoted in Kurasawa, *Komyunitiron*, 19–22.

22. Miyazawa Hiroshi, "Komyuniti ni tsuite," in *Komyuniti dokuhon*, edited by Chihō jichi seido kenkyūkai (Tokyo: Teikoku chihō gyōsei gakkai, 1973), 3.

23. Shun'ichi J. Watanabe, "Toshi Keikaku vs. Machizukuri: Emerging Paradigm of Civil Society in Japan, 1950–1980," in *Living Cities in Japan: Citizens' Movements, Machizukuri and Local Environments*, edited by André Sorensen and Carolin Funck (London: Routledge, 2007), 39–55; Hiroshi Nunokawa, "Machizukuri and Historical Awareness in the Old Town of Kobe," in the same volume, 172–186. A useful review of *machizukuri* and *komyuniti* writing and government programs in the 1970s and 1980s is provided in Yoneno Fumitake, "Machizukuri to media no kankeishi," *Zōkei fukkangō* 37 (August 2003): 14–17.

24. For a discussion of different agents and competing visions in the context of a particular *machizukuri* project in central Tokyo, see Machimura Takashi, *"Sekai toshi" Tōkyō no kōzō tenkan* (Tokyo: Tōkyō daigaku shuppankai, 1994), 209–235.

25. *Yanesen* editors refused, for example, to collaborate with a major newspaper in the campaign to reconstruct the Tennōji pagoda in Yanaka or to involve themselves in the Taitō-Bunkyō Shitamachi Festival. Mori Mayumi, *Tōkyō isan*, 95–97.

26. See Laura Neitzel, "Modern Living: *Danchi* Public Housing Projects and the Reorganization of Urban Space and Everyday Life in Postwar Japan" (PhD dissertation, Columbia University, 2003); Christie Kiefer, "The Danchi-Zoku and the Evolution of the Metropolitan Mind," in *Japan: The Paradox of Progress*, edited by Lewis Austin (New Haven, CT: Yale University Press, 1976), 279–300. For evidence that the social and generational homogeneity of *danchi* actually encouraged community activism, see Emiko Ochiai, *The Japanese Family System in Transition: A Sociological Analysis of Family Change in Postwar Japan* (Tokyo: LTCB International Library Foundation, 1997); and Hara Takeshi, *Takiyama komyūn 1974* (Tokyo: Kōdansha, 2007).

27. See Suzuki Shigebumi, *51C hakusho: Watakushi no kenchiku keikakugaku sengoshi* (Tokyo: Sumai no toshokan shuppankyoku, 2006), 84–144; Yoshitake Yasumi, *Kenchiku keikakugaku e no kokoromi* (Tokyo: Kajima

shuppankai, 1987). For a discussion of *danchi* house plans, see Ann Waswo, *Housing in Postwar Japan: A Social History* (London: Routledge, 2002), 62–85.

28. Suzuki Shigebumi, *"Ie" to "machi,"* (Tokyo: Kajima shuppankai, 1984), 95–97.

29. Suzuki, *51C hakusho,* 258–261.

30. Suzuki, *"Ie" to "machi,"* 96; Suzuki, *51C hakusho,* 175–181.

31. The entanglement of architectural and social questions in the restoration of Tsumago is detailed in Cherie Wendelken-Mortensen, "Living with the Past: Preservation and Development in Japanese Architecture and Town Planning" (PhD dissertation, Massachusetts Institute of Technology, 1994), 183–266.

32. Ibid., 178–180.

33. Uta Hohn, "Townscape Preservation in Japanese Urban Planning," *Town Planning Review* 68, no. 2 (1997): 221.

34. Wendelken-Mortensen, "Living with the Past," 220–223.

35. On residents' charters for townscape preservation, see Masuda Kanefusa and Ueno Kunikazu, "Jūmin ga susumeru machizukuri to machinami hozon kenshō," in *Shin machinami jidai: Machizukuri e no teian,* edited by Zenkoku machinami hozon renmei (Tokyo: Gakugei shuppan, 1999), 88–95.

36. A mix of motives and ideals operated at the local level. For a discussion of contrasting local articulations of the preservation movement's history in Tsumago, see Peter Siegenthaler, "Creation Myths for the Preservation of Tsumago Post-town," *Planning Forum* 9 (2003): 28–45.

37. See Ishikawa Tadaomi, "'Jūmin shutairon' no honshitsu to keifu," in *Shin machinami jidai,* 161–169.

38. As Wendelken-Mortensen notes, it was the sign of a new flexibility about historical value that the term chosen here was "traditional" rather than "historic." Wendelken-Mortensen, "Living with the Past," 175.

39. Hohn, "Townscape Preservation in Japanese Urban Planning," 215.

40. "Mamorō rekishiteki machinami: ippo susumu jūmin undō," *Asahi shinbun,* February 24, 1972: 4. Judging by the frequency of its appearance in the pages of the *Asahi shinbun,* the term *machinami* itself, which roughly corresponds to the English "townscape," entered common parlance in the same years.

41. "'Shitamachi hakubutsukan' ni kakeru yume: Sakka Shirai Kyōji shi, shomin no isan o tsutaetai," *Asahi shinbun,* January 14, 1967: 16. Lacking support from Taitō Ward at the time, Shirai's campaign to build a Shitamachi Museum for the Meiji Centennial failed. Planning for the museum that was eventually completed a decade later is discussed in chapter 4.

42. Mori, *Dakishimeru Tōkyō,* 124.

43. Ibid., 141. The idea of the *kemonomichi,* or "animal trail," would play a role in other movements to rediscover and reimagine Tokyo, including street observation studies, which is discussed in the next chapter.

44. John Urry, *The Tourist Gaze,* 2nd ed. (London: Sage Publications, 2002) 1–3. The term "exoticism" is often used with a pejorative sense, but as expressed in the ruminative writing of Victor Segalen, exoticism roots itself first simply in the pleasure of difference. See Segalen, *Essay on Exoticism: An Aesthetics of Diversity,* translated and edited by Yaël Rachel Schlick (Durham, NC: Duke University Press, 2002).

45. "Ningensei o uriwatasu koto wa dekinai: Hattori Hirohisa-san ni kiku," *Chiiki zasshi: Yanaka, Nezu, Sendagi* 12 (June 1987): 6–14. Holdouts against real estate development like Hattori are not exclusive to Japan: they have been seen in cities everywhere. Nor is the phenomenon restricted to countries where rights of private property are sovereign: there have been many similar cases in China since the 1990s, where such houses are known popularly as "nail houses."

46. The drama of mobsters and speculators continued behind the scenes. In 1991, the president of the real estate company that had tried to force Hattori out of his house was found murdered in the luxurious residence he had built himself for 3.5 billion yen (roughly 30 million U.S. dollars). Mori, *Dakishimeru Tōkyō*, 227.

47. Mori Mayumi, *Yanesen no bōken* (1991; Tokyo: Chikuma bunko, 2002), 217–218.

48. "Ningensei o uriwatasu koto wa dekinai," 8.

49. Edo no aru machi Ueno-Yanesen kenkyūkai, eds., *Shinpen Yanesen roji jiten* (Tokyo: Sumai no toshokan shuppankyoku, 1995), 24. The research group was under the titular leadership of Urai Masaaki, priest at the Ueno temple Kan'eiji. I myself was one of the students participating. For a recent ethnographic study of Yanesen area alleys, see Heide Imai, "Tokyo's Contested Alleyways: The Role of the Roji in Understanding Globalisation, Attachment and the Social Construction of Place" (PhD dissertation, Manchester Metropolitan University, 2009).

50. André Sorensen, *The Making of Urban Japan: Cities and Planning from Edo to the Twenty-First Century* (New York: Routledge, 2002), 314. For a detailed discussion of alley width regulation, see Kobayashi Shigenori, Takamizawa Kunio, and Katō Hitomi, "Kyōai dōro to machizukuri," in *Kyōai dōro to machizukuri,* by Takamizawa Kunio et al. (Tokyo: Chiiki kagaku kenkyūkai, 1996), 3–32.

51. Dean MacCannell, *The Tourist: A New Theory of the Leisure Class,* rev. ed. (New York: Schocken Books, 1989), 91–107.

52. Carol M. Rose, *Property and Persuasion: Essays on the History, Theory, and Rhetoric of Ownership* (Boulder, CO: Westview Press, 1994), 290–294.

53. Edo no aru machi Ueno-Yanesen kenkyūkai, eds., *Shinpen Yanesen roji jiten,* 68, 91.

54. See Mori, *Yanesen no bōken,* 22–24.

55. "Ueno, Yanesen kenchiku rabu kōru," *Chiiki zasshi: Yanaka, Nezu, Sendagi* 13 (September 1987), 18–19.

56. Mori, *Yanesen no bōken,* 106–107.

57. Local campaigns had several noteworthy successes, however, including the preservation of a shop in Yanaka and a house in Sendagi as house museums, restoration and national designation for a music hall in Ueno, reduction in the height of an apartment building in Bunkyō Ward to preserve the last vista of Mount Fuji from street level in central Tokyo, and the cancellation of municipal plans to build a parking lot under Shinobazu Pond. See Mori, *Tōkyō isan.*

58. Yanesen kōbō, *Besuto obu Yanesen,* 235.

59. Interview with Mori Mayumi, January 6, 2005. Despite the ward governments' initial indifference to the magazine and the effort of its editors to rouse interest in the area's past, they subsequently came to compete with *Yanesen*, pouring money into construction of a "stylish retro town" (*haikara retoro taun*) stage set for the "Shitamachi festival" to show their awareness of local history.

60. "Kono michi, zuibun magatteru ne: Aizomegawa sutoriito raifu," *Chiiki zasshi: Yanaka, Nezu, Sendagi* 3 (March 1985): 5.

61. Interview with Mori Mayumi, January 6, 2005.

62. At its peak, circulation was about fifteen thousand copies per issue.

63. Mori Mayumi, comments at the book launch for *Besuto obu Yanesen* held at the Tōkyōdō shoten bookstore in Tokyo on March 12, 2009. Mori also noted that gender and age were factors in the frequent calls they received correcting their reports. Older readers, particularly male ones, would call in a didactic tone to instruct the young female editors.

64. For example, "Yanesen sokochigai, 'saikaihatsu' dokuhon: Hoi no hoi," *Chiiki zasshi: Yanaka, Nezu, Sendagi* 14 (December 1987): 28–29.

65. Eighty-nine-year-old sign painter Kirimura Yasutarō was quoted, for example, as saying, "Every day was fun back then," in "Shichimenzaka roji," *Chiiki zasshi: Yanaka, Nezu, Sendagi* 13 (September 15, 1987): 13.

66. The largest part of *Yanesen*'s readership, in Mori's estimation, comprised people over fifty, with more male readers than female. This demographic profile matches the readership of much of the nostalgic writing about the city. Mori Mayumi, *Yanesen no bōken*, 85.

67. André Sorensen discusses how *machizukuri* groups that grew out of *Yanesen* asserted residents' rights, including a community covenant issued in 2004 by a council that combined representatives of the old neighborhood associations with representatives of local nonprofits. See André Sorensen, "Neighborhood Streets as Meaningful Spaces: Claiming Rights to Shared Spaces in Tokyo," *City and Society* 21, no. 2 (2009): 221–225.

68. Kitahara Toshio, "Seikatsu no ba to shite no toshi," in *Iwanami kōza toshi saisei o kangaeru dai 3 kan: Toshi no kosei to shimin seikatsu*, edited by Ueda Kazuhiro et al. (Tokyo: Iwanami shoten, 2005), 12–20.

69. Itō Shigeru, "Koseitekina machi wa dono yō ni keisei sareru ka," in *Iwanami kōza toshi saisei o kangaeru dai 3 kan: Toshi no kosei to shimin seikatsu*, edited by Ueda Kazuhiro et al. (Tokyo: Iwanami shoten, 2005), 43–45.

70. For a study of artists in the gentrification process, see Sharon Zukin, *Loft Living: Culture and Capital in Urban Change* (Tokyo: Johns Hopkins University Press, 1982).

71. Maeno Masaru, "Toshi no rekishiteki isan kara nani o manabu ka," in *Shin machinami no jidai: Machizukuri e no teian*, edited by Zenkoku machinami hozon renmei (Tokyo: Gakugei shuppansha, 1999), 170–174. For a discussion of Yanaka gakkō, one of the precursors of the Taitō rekishi toshi kenkyūkai, by one of its members, see Shiihara Akiko, "Tsukuru/sodateru: Toki to omoi no mieru machi," in *Shin machinami no jidai*, 107–123. For a broader discussion of these and other *machizukuri* activities in the Yanesen area, see Sorensen, "Neighborhood Streets as Meaningful Spaces," 207–229.

3. DEVIANT PROPERTIES

1. Akasegawa Genpei, quoted in "Kieyuku machinami ni 'gakeppuchi ishiki': Rojō kansatsu gakkai," *Asahi shinbun,* June 12, 1986: 21.

2. Suzuki Takeshi, "Machi ni Tomason o otte," in *Rojō kansatsugaku nyūmon,* edited by Akasegawa Genpei, Fujimori Terunobu, and Minami Shinbō (Tokyo: Chikuma shobō, 1986), 195.

3. Fujimori Terunobu, "Rojō kansatsu no hata no moto ni," in *Rojō kansatsugaku nyūmon,* 9–10.

4. Akasegawa Genpei, "'Zen kankyō toshi' Aaku hiruzu ni Tentokuyu no entotsu no rei ga suberikonde ita," *Chūō kōron* 101, no. 9 (August 1986): 330–331.

5. On the relevance of Hegel's interpretation of property to contemporary social issues, see Margaret Jane Radin, *Reinterpreting Property* (Chicago: University of Chicago Press, 1993), 44–48.

6. A survey of fifteen- to twenty-four-year-olds living in the central wards of Tokyo in 1981 found that 74 percent of them had been born in Tokyo. Sōgō kenkyū kaihatsu kikō, ed., *Wakamono to toshi* (Tokyo: Gakuyō shobō, 1983), 16–17. For a sociological comparison of these generations mapped onto the spaces of Shinjuku and Shibuya, see Yoshimi Shun'ya, *Toshi no doramaturugii: Tōkyō sakariba no shakaishi* (Tokyo: Kōbundō, 1987).

7. Murakami Tomohiko, "Jōhōshiteki sekai no naritachi: The World According to PIA," *Shisō no kagaku,* 7th ser., 5 (February 1985): 74–75.

8. Machimura Takashi, *"Sekai toshi" Tōkyō no kōzō tenkan: Toshi risutorakuchuaringu no shakaigaku* (Tokyo: Tōkyō daigaku shuppankai, 1994), 197–200.

9. On Tokyo Disneyland as an embodiment of the new consumer society of the 1980s, see Yoshimi Shun'ya, "Yūenchi no yūtopia," *Sekai* 528 (June 1989): 293–306. On Shibuya in the 1980s as an enveloping commercial environment, see Kitada Akihiro, *Kōkoku toshi Tōkyō: Sono tanjō to shi* (Tokyo: Kōsaidō shuppan, 2002), 51–107.

10. Yamazaki Kōichi, "Kireina mein sutoriito yori mo machi wa roji ura no hō ga omoshiroi!" *Popeye,* August 10, 1986.

11. On nostalgia marketing and Seibu-Parco, see Marilyn Ivy, *Discourses of the Vanishing: Modernity, Phantasm, Japan* (Chicago: University of Chicago Press, 1995), 54–59. For other examples of B-grade taste, see Jordan Sand, "The Ambivalence of the New Breed: Nostalgic Consumerism in 1980s and 1990s Japan," in *The Ambivalent Consumer: Questioning Consumption in East Asia and the West,* edited by Sheldon Garon and Patricia L. Maclachlan (Ithaca, NY: Cornell University Press, 2006), 85–108.

12. *Bukken,* that is, corresponds more closely to the countable concrete noun "property" as it is used in the real estate industry: "this property, valued at . . ." By the same token, it suggests what legal scholars call the *in rem* character of property: its foundation as a concrete relation between persons and physical things, as opposed to a relation, like a contract, between persons (the "bundle of rights" approach that became common in twentieth-century Anglo-American property law). See Stephen Munzer, *A Theory of Property* (New York: Cambridge University Press, 1990), 72–73; Michael Heller, "The

Boundaries of Private Property," *The Yale Law Journal* 108, no. 6 (April 1999): 1191–1203; Thomas W. Merrill and Henry E. Smith, "What Happened to Property in Law and Economics?" *The Yale Law Journal* 111, no. 2 (November 2001): 357–398.

13. Henri LeFebvre, *The Production of Space,* translated by Donald Nicholson-Smith (Oxford: Blackwell, 1991), 356.

14. Akasegawa Genpei, "'Gotōchi mono' no rojō kansatsu: Seika wa Hachiōji no unagi inu, suzu inu," *Chūō kōron* 102, no. 2 (February 1987): 317.

15. As an art experiment, this puts street observation closer to some of the work of American artist Gordon Matta-Clark. Matta-Clark's project "Fake Estates" used the documentation of residual parcels of land in New York to criticize the system of property rights and its limitations on artistic creativity. See Pamela M. Lee, *Object to Be Destroyed: The Work of Gordon Matta-Clark* (Cambridge, MA: MIT Press, 2001), 98–104. For an example of Street Observation "properties" being treated as part of an individual artistic oeuvre, see the presentation of Akasegawa Genpei in Alexandra Munroe, *Japanese Art since 1945: Scream against the Sky* (New York: H.N. Abrams, 1994), 222.

16. See William A. Marotti, "Simulacra and Subversion in the Everyday: Akasegawa Genpei's 1000-yen Copy, Critical Art, and the State," *Postcolonial Studies* 4, no. 2 (July 2001): 211–239; Reiko Tomii, "State v. (Anti-) Art: *Model 1,000-Yen Note Incident* by Akasegawa Genpei and Company," *positions: east asia cultures critique* 10, no. 1 (Spring 2002): 141–172.

17. Akasegawa Genpei, "Ware ika ni shite rojō kansatsusha to narishi ka," in *Rojō kansatsugaku nyūmon,* 4.

18. Gary Thomasson—"father of the *tomason,*" as Akasegawa dubbed him—was recruited by the Tokyo Giants in 1981 and sent home the following year after repeatedly striking out. See Akasegawa Genpei, *Hyperart: Thomasson,* translated by Matt Fargo (New York: Kaya Press, 2009), 17–18.

19. Akasegawa Genpei, "Toshi no muishiki o miru: Purasu no shisen, mainasu no shisen," *Chūō kōron* 101, no. 14 (December 1986): 201–202.

20. The intentional artlessness of the street observationists' photographs also recalled the style used by photoconceptualist artists. See Rosalind Krauss, "Reinventing the Medium," *Critical Inquiry* 25 (Winter 1999): 295.

21. Akasegawa Genpei, *Zenmen jikyō!* (Tokyo: Shōbunsha, 2001), 341.

22. Senior architecture historians also regarded the young Fujimori's coinage of a catchy term to identify his object of study as impudent. The incident showed how carefully guarded the right to classify and name can be in an academic culture with pretenses to scientific method. In this case, characteristic of Japan's intellectual establishment, naming was seen as a privilege reserved for the older generation.

23. See Fujimori's comments in the group discussion, Fujimori et al., "Geijutsu kara, gakumon e," in *Rojō kansatsugaku nyūmon,* 44–48.

24. Some of these essays are collected in *Kenchiku tanteidan no bōken: Tōkyō hen* (Tokyo: Chikuma shobō, 1986). Fujimori's interest in vernacular urbanism shows affinity with the work of Bernard Rudofsky and Jane Jacobs, both of whom were widely read in Japanese architectural circles as in the United States in the 1960s and 1970s. Rudofsky visited Tokyo's Waseda University in

the early 1960s and subsequently offered his praise for aesthetics in Japanese everyday life in *The Kimono Mind: An Informal Guide to Japan and the Japanese* (Garden City, NY: Doubleday, 1965). Any influence on Fujimori would have been through these and other texts. For an analysis of Rudofsky's place in midcentury architectural modernism, see Felicity Scott, "Bernard Rudofsky: Allegories of Nomadism and Dwelling," in *Anxious Modernisms: Experimentation in Postwar Architectural Culture,* edited by Sarah Williams Goldhagen and Réjean Legault (Montreal: Canadian Centre for Architecture; Cambridge, MA: MIT Press, 2000), 215–238.

25. The phrase "colonization of the everyday" is associated with Guy Debord, although many others have used it. See Michel Trebitsch, "The Moment of Radical Critique," translated by Gregory Elliott, in *Critique of Everyday Life,* by Henri LeFebvre, translated by John Moore, vol. 2, *Foundations for a Sociology of the Everyday* (New York: Verso, 2002), xxii.

26. See David Pinder, "Old Paris is No More: Geographies of Spectacle and Anti-Spectacle," *Antipode* 32, no. 4 (2000): 357–386; Greil Marcus, "The Long Walk of the Situationist International," in *Guy Debord and the Situationist International: Texts and Documents,* edited by Tom McDonough (Cambridge, MA: MIT Press, 2002), 1–20; and Tom McDonough, "Situationist Space," in the same volume, 241–265.

27. According to Guy Debord's definition, in a *dérive,* "one or more persons during a certain period drop their relations, their work and leisure activities, and all their other usual motives for movement and action, and let themselves be drawn by the attractions of the terrain and the encounters they find there." Debord asserts that *dérives involve both* "playful-constructive behavior and awareness of psychogeographical effects." Guy Debord, "Theory of the Dérive" (1958), in *Situationist International Anthology,* edited and translated by Ken Knabb, rev. ed. (Berkeley, CA: Bureau of Public Secrets, 2006), 62.

28. Matsui Takeshi, "Shōhiron būmu: Maaketingu ni okeru posutomodan," *Gendai shisō* 29, no. 14 (November 2001): 124–126.

29. Marilyn Ivy, "Formations of Mass Culture," in *Postwar Japan as History,* edited by Andrew Gordon (Berkeley: University of California Press, 1993), 239–258.

30. See Tsutsumi Seiji, *Shōhi shakai hihan* (Tokyo: Iwanami shoten, 1996).

31. Asada Akira, *Kōzō to chikara: Kigōron o koete* (Tokyo: Keisō shobō, 1983); Takeda Seiji, "Asada Akira: Chikara, tōsō," in *Bessatsu Takarajima 52: Gendai shisō nyūmon II: Nihon hen* (Tokyo: JICC shuppankyoku, 1986), 189–191.

32. Marilyn Ivy, "Critical Texts, Mass Artifacts: The Consumption of Knowledge in Postmodern Japan," in *Postmodernism and Japan,* edited by Masao Miyoshi and Harry D. Harootunian (Durham, NC: Duke University Press, 1989), 21–46.

33. See Asada Akira, "Tōsō suru bunmei," in *Tōsōron: Sukizo kidzu no bōken* (Tokyo: Chikuma shobō, 1984), 2–7; originally published in *Burūtasu,* January 15, 1983.

34. Aramata Hiroshi, Fujimori Terunobu, and Harui Yutaka, *Tōkyō rojō hakubutsushi* (Tokyo: Kajima shuppankai, 1987), 287. As Rosalind Krauss

notes in her analysis of Marcel Broodthaers, any critical theory of culture can be absorbed by the culture industry itself. Rosalind Krauss, *A Voyage on the North Sea: Art in the Age of the Post-Medium Condition* (New York: Thames and Hudson, 2000), 33. Like Akasegawa and Fujimori, Broodthaers chose a mix of natural history and surrealism in his effort to avoid this trap.

35. On modernology, see Miriam Silverberg, "Constructing the Japanese Ethnography of Modernity," *Journal of Asian Studies* 51, no. 1 (1992): 30–54; Harry D. Harootunian, *Overcome by Modernity: History, Culture, and Community in Interwar Japan* (Princeton, NJ: Princeton University Press, 2000), 178–201; Tom Gill, "Kon Wajiro: Modernologist," *Japan Quarterly* 43, no. 2 (1996): 198–207.

36. On the circle movement, see Kazuko Tsurumi, *Social Change and the Individual: Social Change before and after World War II* (Princeton, NJ: Princeton University Press, 1970), 213–303.

37. Amino Yoshihiko, "'Undō to shite no chiiki kenkyū' o megutte," in *Iwanami kōza Nihon tsūshi, bekkan 2: Chiikishi kenkyū no genjō to kadai,* edited by Asao Naohiro et al. (Tokyo: Iwanami Shoten, 1994), 105–113.

38. Shigeru Nakayama, *Science, Technology and Society in Postwar Japan* (London: Kegan Paul International, 1991), 23–26; Simon Avenell, *Making Japanese Citizens: Civil Society and the Mythology of the Shimin in Postwar Japan* (Berkeley: University of California Press, 2010), 162–165.

39. Fujimori, "Rojō kansatsu no hata no moto ni," in *Rojō kansatsugaku nyūmon,* 17.

40. For an instance of an "animal trail" across the old Imperial Palace grounds in Kyoto, see Rojō kansatsu gakkai, *Kyōto omoshiro uotchingu* (Tokyo: Shinchōsha, 1988). In 1990, the magazine *QA* published a special issue inspired by street observation studies and titled "Animal Trails of Tokyo" (*Tōkyō no kemonomichi*). Articles explored the city by walking the course of rivers that had been filled and made into roadways, mapping Shinjuku Station underground, following where the city's garbage went, mapping the locations of natural springs in three wards, and charting the path of destruction cut by Godzilla in the original film and two remakes. "Tōkyō no kemonomichi," *QA* 81 *bessatsu* [special supplement] (November 20, 1990).

41. Fujimori Terunobu, Aramata Hiroshi, and Harui Yutaka, *Tōkyō rojō hakubutsushi* (Tokyo: Kajima shuppankai, 1987), 297.

42. Interview with Fujimori Terunobu, October 22, 2000. See also Fujimori's discussion in his afterword to Kon Wajiro, *Nihon no minka* (Tokyo: Iwanami bunko, 1989), 350–351. On the ideal of the primitive hut in European modernism, see Joseph Rykwert, *On Adam's House in Paradise: The Idea of the Primitive Hut in Architectural History* (Cambridge, MA: MIT Press, 1981).

43. Aramata, "Rojō hakubutsugaku teiyō," in Fujimori, Aramata, and Harui, *Tōkyō rojō hakubutsushi,* 61.

44. Fredric Jameson, *Postmodernism, the Cultural Logic of Late Capitalism* (Durham, NC: Duke University Press, 1991), ix, 34–36.

45. This story of the origins of property was a gendered one in Locke's telling and, of course, in much of the history of property law. It is probably no coincidence that whereas the community movement described in the

previous chapter centered on a group of women—and indeed many of the community movements that emerged in Japan in the 1970s and 1980s were dominated by women—the vision of the city as a commons for individual appropriation discussed here came from a group that was overwhelmingly male in composition.

46. Nishi Kazuo and Hirashima Akihiro, *Shōwa 20-nen Tōkyō chizu* (Tokyo: Chikuma shobō, 1986), 300–301.

47. See, for example, Araki Nobuyoshi, *Tōkyō monogatari* (Tokyo: Heibonsha, 1989). A row of bars built in the aftermath of World War II under the railroad tracks in Shinjuku and colloquially known as "Piss Alley" (Shonben Yokochō) was reborn in the early years of the twenty-first century under the new official name "Memory Lane" (Omoide Yokochō).

48. Watanabe Hidetsuna, *Shinjuku Gorudengai* (Tokyo: Shōbunsha, 1986).

49. For a discussion of Araki's work and the Tokyo streetscape, see Iizawa Kōtarō, *Araki!* (Tokyo: Hakusuisha, 1994), 103–137. By 2006, according to an interview in the *Japan Times,* Araki had published 357 books. C.B. Liddell, "Intimate Photography: Tokyo, Nostalgia and Sex [Nobuyoshi Araki]," *Japan Times,* November 23, 2006.

50. Iizawa Kōtarō, *Araki!*, 28–29, 104, 107. Many of Araki's photographs of Tokyo are also marked by melancholy and a sense of loss—most famously in *Tōkyō wa aki,* shot in 1972–1973, but published in 1984. Araki Nobuyoshi, *Tōkyō wa aki* (Tokyo: Sanseidō, 1984).

51. Akasegawa Genpei, "'Gotōchi mono' no rojō kansatsu: Seika wa Hachiōji no unagi inu, suzu inu," 317.

52. Egawa Kōichi, "Toshi no naka no jiyū no tanoshisa," *Sankei shinbun,* July 14, 1986.

53. "Kieyuku machinami ni 'gakeppuchi ishiki: Rojō kansatsu gakkai daidō danketsu shi hakkaishiki," *Asahi shinbun,* June 6, 1986: 21.

54. See Akasegawa Genpei, "Shizukasa no michi ni shimiiru rojō kansatsu," *Chūō kōron* 102, no. 5 (April 1987): 381.

55. "Kitare rojō kansatsusha," *Hot Dog Press,* July 25, 1986.

56. "Binbō demo daijōbu—konna ni asobechau," *Manga akushon,* August 6, 1986.

57. Nakajima Ramo, "Nichijō no obakasan," in *VOW 2: Zoku machi no henna mono katarogu,* edited by Takarajima (Tokyo: Takarajima, 1989), 31–33; Enokido Ichirō, "Nagashima Kazushige no hōmuran wa yoku tobu hōmuran da," in ibid., 219–222.

58. Christian Dimmer, "Renegotiating Public Space: A Historical Critique of Modern Public Space in Metropolitan Japan and its Contemporary Revaluation" (PhD dissertation, Tokyo University, 2007), 142–144. For another creative enterprise connected to Hayashi Jōji's work, see Shirley MacGregor, *Quilting with Manhole Covers: A Treasury of Unique Designs from the Streets of Japan* (Eugene, OR: Carriage Trade Press, 1999), to which Hayashi contributed a foreword.

59. For a comparable case of multiple levels of appropriation in relation to landscape, see John MacArthur, *The Picturesque: Architecture, Disgust and Other Irregularities* (London: Routledge, 2007), 186.

4. MUSEUMS, HERITAGE, AND EVERYDAY LIFE

1. For a discussion of the museum in the context of Suzuki administration campaigns, see Mikako Iwatake, "Tokyo Renaissance: Constructing a Postmodern Identity for Contemporary Japan" (PhD dissertation, University of Pennsylvania, 1993).

2. Lisa C. Roberts, *From Knowledge to Narrative: Educators and the Changing Museum* (Washington, DC: Smithsonian Institution Press, 1997), 137–152; Hilde S. Hein, *The Museum in Transition: A Philosophical Perspective* (Washington, DC: Smithsonian Institution Press, 2000), 65–68.

3. On ethnographic exhibits at nineteenth-century expositions, see Paul Greenhalgh, *Ephemeral Vistas: The Expositions Universelles, Great Exhibitions, and World's Fairs, 1851–1939* (Manchester, UK: Manchester University Press, 1988); Timothy Mitchell, *Colonizing Egypt* (Berkeley: University of California Press, 1988). On Skansen, see P. Aronsson, "Exhibiting Scandinavian Culture: The National Museums of Denmark and Sweden," in *Popularizing National Pasts, 1800 to the Present*, edited by Stefan Berger, Chris Lorenz, and Billie Melman (New York: Routledge, 2011), 169–195; Mattias Backstrom, "Loading Guns with Patriotic Love: Artur Hazelius' Attempts at Skansen to Remake Swedish Society," in *National Museums: New Studies from around the World*, edited by Simon J. Knell et al. (London: Routledge, 2011), 69–87. For a history of reconstructed folkhouses and related exhibit strategies in Japan, see Aoki Toshiya, "Seikatsu saigen tenji no shikō," *Kanagawa daigaku 21 seiki COE puroguramu: Jinrui bunka kenkyū no tame no himoji shiryō no taikeika nenpō* 4 (March 2007): 55–73.

4. Alan Christy, "Representing the Rural: Place as Method in the Formation of Japanese Native Ethnology, 1910–1945" (Ph.D. dissertation, University of Chicago, 1997), 206; Alan Christy, *A Discipline on Foot: Inventing Japanese Native Ethnography, 1910–1945* (Lanham, MD: Rowman and Littlefield, 2012). Naturalist Edward Sylvester Morse built his collection of Japanese everyday artifacts in Salem, Massachusetts, in the 1880s, providing an important precedent for Shibusawa's collection. The collection was not widely known in Japan until after the Attic Museum, however, and Morse appears not to have influenced Shibusawa.

5. The concept of the "transitional object" is associated with psychoanalyst D. W. Winnicott. On transitional objects as the child's first possessions, see Winnicott, "Transitional Objects and Transitional Phenomena: A Study of the First Not-Me Possession," *International Journal of Psychoanalysis* 34 (1953): 89–97.

6. Alan Christy, "Representing the Rural," 178–179. Shibusawa's focus here contrasted with that of Morse, whose more eclectic interests extended to art and souvenirs of any provenance.

7. Ibid., 356.

8. Umesao Tadao, "Minzokugaku to hakubutsukan," in *Umesao Tadao chosakushū dai 15 kan*, edited by Umesao Tadao and Ishige Naomichi (Tokyo: Chūō kōronsha, 1989), 107.

9. Hilde Hein, *The Museum in Transition*, 69–87.

10. Yokohama shiritsu rekishi hakubutsukan and Kanagawa daigaku Nihon jōmin kenkyūjo, eds., *Yaneura no hakubutsukan: Jitsugyōka Shibusawa Keizō*

ga sodateta tami no gakumon (Yokohama: Yokohama rekishi hakubutsukan, 2002), 23.

11. Ibid., 120–121.

12. On the twenty-six hundredth anniversary and surrounding events, see Kenneth J. Ruoff, *Imperial Japan at Its Zenith: The Wartime Celebration of the Empire's 2,600th Anniversary* (Ithaca, NY: Cornell University Press, 2010); Furukawa Takahisa, *Kōki, banpaku, Orinpikku: Kōshitsu burando to keizai hatten* (Tokyo: Chūkō shinsho, 1998).

13. Umesao Tadao, "Sekai no minzoku shiryō o motomete," in *Umesao Tadao chosakushū dai 15 kan,* edited by Umesao Tadao and Ishige Naomichi (Tokyo: Chūō kōronsha, 1989), 19; Ono Hitoshi, *Media no sōzō: Sono keiei to purodyūsu* (Tokyo: Domesu shuppan, 1998), 34.

14. On Miyamoto Tsuneichi, see Sano Shin'ichi, *Tabi suru kyojin: Miyamoto Tsuneichi to Shibusawa Keizō* (Tokyo: Bungei shunjū, 2009); *Gendai shisō sōtokushū: Miyamoto Tsuneichi, seikatsu e no manazashi,* Gendai shisō rinju zōkan [special supplement] (November 2011). See also Miyamoto Tsuneichi, *The Forgotten Japanese: Encounters with Rural Life and Folklore,* translated by Jeffrey S. Irish (Berkeley, CA: Stone Bridge Press, 2010).

15. Kawazoe Noboru, "Nihon no sumai, shukushaku jūbun no ichi: Kokuritsu minzokugaku hakubutsukan no minka mokei," *TCS* [Total Media Kaihatsu kenkyūjo] (March 1993): 40–44.

16. Kon Wajirō, "Seikatsugaku e no kūsō" (1951) in *Kon Wajirō shū dai 5 kan: Seikatsugaku* (Tokyo: Domesu shuppan, 1971), 16–17. This essay equated *seikatsu* with home life. Kon had also written of the idea of *seikatsugaku* twenty years earlier, at that time using it to refer to the study of fashion and custom, not restricted to the home. See Izumi Kuroishi, "Kon Wajirō: A Quest for the Architecture as a Container of Everyday Life" (PhD dissertation, University of Pennsylvania, 1998), 183–186.

17. Kawazoe Noboru, *Seikatsugaku no teishō* (Tokyo: Domesu shuppan, 1982), 24–27.

18. On the word *seikatsusha,* see Simon Avenell, *Making Japanese Citizens: Civil Society and the Mythology of the Shimin in Postwar Japan* (Berkeley: University of California Press, 2010), 226; on the use of *seikatsusha* in consumer organizations in the 1990s, particularly as a designation for housewives, see Robin LeBlanc, *Bicycle Citizens: The Political World of the Japanese Housewife* (Berkeley: University of California Press, 1999), 139–140, 150; on everyday life issues in the policy of Tokyo governor Minobe Ryōkichi's administration, see Laura Hein, *Reasonable Men, Powerful Words: Political Culture and Expertise in Twentieth-Century Japan* (Berkeley: University of California Press, 2004), 162–211. For a broad historical treatment of the concept of the *seikatsusha,* see Amano Masako, *"Seikatsusha" to wa dare ka: Jiritsuteki shiminzō no keifu* (Tokyo: Chūō kōronsha, 1996).

19. Kawazoe Noboru, "Seikatsugaku no naiyō," *Seikatsugaku kaihō dai 1 kan* (September 30, 1974): 19, 24–25. The term "lifeworld," an expression derived from Husserl's *lebenswelt,* had its literal counterpart in the Japanese *seikatsu sekai.*

20. Harry D. Harootunian, *Overcome by Modernity: History, Culture and Community in Interwar Japan* (Princeton, NJ: Princeton University Press, 2001), 378–390; Kim Brandt, *Kingdom of Beauty: Mingei and the Politics of Folk Art in Imperial Japan* (Durham, NC: Duke University Press, 2007), 195–207.

21. Harootunian, *Overcome by Modernity*, 381–386.

22. There are two others: Nomura and Tanseisha. Each also sponsors annual conferences for presentation of research in the field. Exhibit designers had previously had a limited role in the creative work of museum design, specializing instead in technical aspects such as making vitrines and lighting.

23. Interview with Adachi Tsuneo, Takatsu Decorative Art, January 23, 2007.

24. Ono, *Media no sōzō*, 60–74.

25. Ibid., 77–78.

26. Ibid., 264–272.

27. Interview with Takahashi Hiroshi, Total Media Planning, July 5, 2006.

28. Umesao Tadao, "Minzokugaku to hakubutsukan," 1973.

29. Interview with Takahashi Hiroshi, July 5, 2006. Total Media's packaging of formulas for exhibiting everyday life is reflected also in company advertisements; for examples, see advertisements in *Hakubutsukan kenkyū* 28, nos. 8–12 (August–December 1993). For the growth of museums in postwar Japan, see Masatoshi Konishi, "The Museum and Japanese Studies," *Current Anthropology* 28, no. 4 (August–October, 1987), S96–S101.

30. See also Constantine Vaporis, "Digging for Edo: Archeology and Japan's Premodern Urban Past," *Monumenta Nipponica* 53, no. 1 (Spring 1998): 75–80; Koizumi Hiroshi, *Edo o horu: Kinsei toshi kōkogaku e no shōtai* (Tokyo: Kashiwa shobō, 1983). Koizumi Hiroshi led the excavations at Hitotsubashi High School that resulted in the 1985 report.

31. Koizumi, *Edo o horu;* Horiuchi Hideki, "Haiki no handan, kōi to jōhō: Edo iseki shutsudo tōjiki ni shōsha shite," *Tōhokugaku dai 2 ki,* no. 22 (2010): 132–145.

32. Interview with Takahashi Hiroshi, July 5, 2006.

33. Yanesen activists, for example, competed with the Edo-Tokyo Museum for goods from houses being demolished in the Yanesen neighborhood.

34. This is one strain of what Carol Gluck refers to as "oppositional Edo." Carol Gluck, "The Invention of Edo," in *Mirror of Modernity: Invented Traditions of Modern Japan,* edited by Stephen Vlastos (Berkeley: University of California Press, 1998), 270–271.

35. Takeuchi Makoto, "Nishiyama bunka shigaku no futatsu no mine," afterword in *Aru bunjin rekishika no kiseki,* by Nishiyama Matsunosuke (Tokyo: Yoshikawa kōbunkan, 2000), 196–209.

36. Ogi Shinzō, *Edo-Tōkyōgaku kotohajime* (Tokyo: Chikuma shobō, 1991), 3.

37. Ogi Shinzō, *Tōkei shomin seikatsushi kenkyū* (Tokyo: Nihon hōsō shuppan kyōkai, 1979). *Tōkei,* an alternate reading of the city's name used in the 1870s and 1880s, served Ogi as a metaphor for an in-between period when Edo traditions still dominated Tokyo culture.

38. On the "new family," see Emiko Ochiai, *The Japanese Family System in Transition* (Tokyo: LTCB International Library Foundation, 1997), 104–111; for data and a general characterization of newspaper reports on *wan-rūmu manshon,* see Mase Yōsuke et al., "Shinbun kiji ni miru wan-rūmu manshon mondai no hensen ni kansuru kōsatsu," *Nihon kenchiku gakkai taikai gakujutsu kōen kōgaishū (Chūgoku)* (September 2008): 251–252.

39. Nuclear households were not unusual in the Edo backstreets, since the tenement units could accommodate only a few people. Households were unstable, however. See Robert J. Smith, "Small Families, Small Households, and Residential Instability: Town and City in 'Pre-modern' Japan," in *Household and Family in Past Time,* edited by Peter Laslett and Richard Wall (Cambridge: Cambridge University Press, 1972), 429–472.

40. Barbara Kirshenblatt-Gimblett, "Objects of Ethnography," in *Exhibiting Cultures: The Poetics and Politics of Museum Display,* edited by Ivan Karp and Steven D. Lavine (Washington, DC: Smithsonian Institution, 1990), 388.

41. Kikutake Kiyonori, *Hakubutsukan no mirai* (Tokyo: Kashima shuppankai, 1993), 9–10.

42. The same nationalism governed Kikutake's design. The museum's exterior form, he asserted, was intended to "crystallize Japanese culture in built form." Kikutake Kiyonori, *Edo-Tōkyō hakubutsukan* (Tokyo: Kajima shuppankai, 1989), 185, 191. For further discussion of Kikutake's design and of individual exhibits, see Iwatake, "The Tokyo Renaissance," 176–193; Jordan Sand, "Monumentalizing the Everyday: The Edo-Tokyo Museum," *Critical Asian Studies* 33, no. 3 (2001): 359–363.

43. On the lost decade, see Harry D. Harootunian and Tomiko Yoda, "Introduction," and Tomiko Yoda, "A Roadmap to Millennial Japan," in *Japan after Japan: Social and Cultural Life from the Recessionary 1990s to the Present,* edited by Harry D. Harootunian and Tomiko Yoda (Durham, NC: Duke University Press, 2006), 1–53.

44. On the end of Shōwa, historical reflection, and nostalgia, see Carol Gluck, "The Idea of Showa," in *Showa: The Japan of Hirohito,* edited by Carol Gluck and Stephen Graubard (New York: W.W. Norton, 1993), 1–26.

45. Laura Neitzel, "Living Modern: *Danchi* Housing and Postwar Japan" (PhD dissertation, Columbia University, 2003), 174.

46. Kawamura Saburō, *Shōwa 30 nen Tōkyō beru epokku* (Tokyo: Iwanami shoten, 1992).

47. Interview with Adachi Tsuneo, Takatsu Decorative Art, January 23, 2007.

48. For further discussion of ideological investments in the *chabudai* and the fate of a particular example at the Edo-Tokyo Museum, see Jordan Sand, "The Kodera Family Folding Table," *Impressions* 30 (2009): 98–105.

49. Early examples include the Katsushika-ku kyōdo to tenmon no hakubutsukan, opened in 1991, the Shōwa Everyday Museum in Nagoya (discussed in this chapter), opened in 1993, and the indoor theme park Namuko Namja Town, opened in Ikebukuro in 1996. Since the turn of the millennium, similar exhibits and "Shōwa museums" have appeared throughout the country.

50. "Shōwa sanjū nendai o saigen shite mite" (Yamazaki Takashi interview), *Sumairon* 81 (Winter 2007): 11. On this image of television and other

appliances "arriving," see also Yoshimi Shun'ya, *Shinbei to hanbei: Sengo Nihon no seijiteki muishiki* (Tokyo: Iwanami shoten, 2007), 183–186.

51. Kerry Smith, "The Showa Hall: Memorializing Japan's War at Home," *Public Historian* 24, no. 4 (Fall 2002): 35–64.

52. *Hong Kong Museum of History Brief Guide*, rev. ed. (Hong Kong: Leisure and Cultural Services Department, 2006), 26–27; on the Hong Kong Museum, see also Emily Stokes-Rees, "Recounting History: Constructing a National Narrative in the Hong Kong Museum of History, " in *National Museums: New Studies from Around the World*, edited by Simon J. Knell et al. (London: Routledge, 2011), 339–354.

53. Interview with Kaneko Atsushi, Tama Parthenon, July 6, 2006.

54. Kaneko Atsushi, "Sensō shiryō no riaritii: Mono o baikai to shita sensō taiken no keishō o megutte," in *Iwanami kōza Ajia Taiheiyō sensō 6: Nichijō seikatsu no naka no sōryokusen,* edited by Kurasawa Aiko et al. (Iwanami shoten, 2006), 344–345.

55. Aoki Toshiya, "Gendai seikatsu o tenji suru: Danchi 2DK seikatsu saigen tenji no sono go," in *Rekishi tenji to wa nani ka,* edited by Kokuritsu rekishi minzoku hakubutsukan (Tokyo: Amu puromōshon, 2003), 81–95.

56. Interview with Abe Yukihiro, curator at the Edo-Tokyo Open Air Architectural Museum, July 7, 2006. On the phenomenon of visitors "talking back" to exhibits, see Arjun Appadurai and Carol Breckenridge, "Museums Are Good to Think: Heritage on View in India," in *Museums and Communities: The Politics of Public Culture,* edited by Ivan Karp, Christine Mullen Kreamer, and Steven D. Lavine (Washington, DC: Smithsonian Institution Press, 1992), 50–51.

57. "Shōwa sanjū nendai o saigen shite mite," 22–23. Shōwa nostalgia was often tinged with irony, too. The Shōwa everyday was reconstructed to be enjoyed as camp at the Shin-Yokohama Ramen Museum, opened in 1994, and in several subsequent theme parks. See Jordan Sand, "Ambivalence of the New Breed," in *The Ambivalent Consumer: Questioning Consumption in East Asia and the West,* edited by Sheldon Garon and Patricia L. Maclachlan (Ithaca, NY: Cornell University Press, 2006), 104–107; Kitada Akihiro, *Kōkoku toshi Tōkyō: Sono tanjō to shi* (Tokyo: Kōsaidō shuppan, 2002), 111–116.

58. Yamazaki nevertheless expressed satisfaction that people were "watching so seriously." "Shōwa sanjū nendai o saigen shite mite," 17.

59. Ichihashi Yoshinori, " 'Shōwa nichijō hakubutsukan no kokoromi' no keizoku to 'kaisōhō, kōreisha kea no furukute atarashii tsūru' ni tsuite," *Shikatsu-chō rekishi minzoku shiryōkan kenkyū kiyō 14: Hakubutsukan to kaisōhō* (2004): 2.

60. Interview with Ichihashi Yoshinori, November 28, 2008.

61. Ibid. At the time, they had twenty sewing machines. Ichihashi commented that "it would be interesting to see a collection of five hundred sewing machines."

62. Ibid. Ichihashi refused the requests from film companies.

63. Ichihashi Yoshinori, *Shikatsu-chō rekishi minzoku shiryōkan kenkyū kiyō 15: Shōwa nichijō hakubutsukan no kokoromi* (2005): 10.

64. Interview with Ichihashi Yoshinori, November 28, 2008.

65. A similar example of a museum exhibit built of objects collected from patrons and showing recent history may be seen in the Vietnam Museum of Ethnology's popular "Hanoi under the Subsidy Economy, 1975–1986" exhibit, held in 2006–2007. Nguyen Van Huy, ed., *Hanoi under the Subsidy Economy, 1975–1986* (Hanoi: Vietnam Museum of Ethnology and The Gioi Publishers, 2007). Both the display of everyday life in the recent past and the participatory approach to museum collection attract audiences. This may be particularly the case in Asia, where people have seen rapid social change accompanying economic growth. It bears noting, however, that the idea of the museum as repository of collective memory is old and widely shared: the Smithsonian Institution was nicknamed the "nation's attic" some time in the first half of the twentieth century.

66. For a review of the psychological literature on reminiscence therapy in English, see Barbara K. Haight and Jeffrey Dean Webster, *Critical Advances in Reminiscence Work: From Theory to Application* (New York: Springer Publishing, 2002), 3–30.

67. Ichihashi Yoshinori, " 'Shōwa nichijō hakubutsukan no kokoromi' no keizoku to 'kaisōhō, kōreisha kea no furukute atarashii tsūru' ni tsuite," 12.

68. Takeuchi Makoto, personal communication, July 6, 2006.

69. Interview with Abe Yukihiro, curator at the Edo-Tokyo Open Air Museum, July 7, 2006.

70. "Edo-Tokyo hakubutsukan news," vol. 48 (December 20, 2004), unpaginated; on open lots in cartoons, see Yomota Inuhiko, "Shaauddo wa doko e itta ka: Shōnen manga ni okeru 'harappa,' " in *Rojō kansatsugaku nyūmon,* edited by Akasegawa Genpei et al. (Tokyo: Chikuma shobō, 1986), 291–292. *Doraemon* was serialized in comic books from 1969 to 1996 and on television in 1973, then again starting in 1979. In 2006, the Edo-Tokyo Open Air Architectural Museum also mounted an exhibit on the Tokyo of 1958, the year that Tokyo Tower was built, explicitly referencing the popular film *Always.*

71. "Edo Tōkyō hakubutsukan ni kansuru seimei," *Rekishi hyōron* 477 (January 1990): 123.

72. Quoted in Koizumi Yumiko, "Naze Edo-Tōkyō hakubutsukan nanoka," *Rekishi hyōron* 490 (February 1991): 62. Koizumi provides an account of the debates between participating scholars and critics surrounding the exhibit planning.

73. Yoshimi Shun'ya, *Posuto sengo shakai* (Tokyo: Iwanami shoten, 2009), 219–222.

CONCLUSION

1. John Ruskin, *The Seven Lamps of Architecture,* 6th ed. (Sunnyside, UK: George Allen, 1889), 197. Indeed, Ruskin goes on to qualify the problem as one of what might be called lebensraum, writing: "A fair building is necessarily worth the ground it stands upon, and will be so until Central Africa and America shall have become as populous as Middlesex." Thus, at least hypothetically, he presents his preservation ideals as possible only within the context of a stable national population or of imperial expansion.

2. On the expansion of the category of historical monuments in Europe from the Renaissance through the nineteenth century, see Françoise Choay, *The Invention of the Historic Monument,* translated by Lauren M. O'Donnell (1992; Cambridge: Cambridge University Press, 2001).

3. For the celebration of ruin and renewal in Japanese monster films, see William Tsutsui, "Oh No, There Goes Tokyo: Recreational Apocalypse and the City in Postwar Japanese Popular Culture," in *Noir Urbanisms: Dystopic Images of the Modern City,* edited by Gyan Prakash (Princeton, NJ: Princeton University Press, 2010), 104–126.

4. Henri LeFebvre, "The Everyday and Everydayness," in *Architecture of the Everyday,* edited by Steven Harris and Deborah Burke (New York: Princeton Architectural Press, 1997), 32–37. See also Ben Highmore, *Everyday Life and Cultural Theory: An Introduction* (London: Routledge, 2002), 118–127; Stephen Johnstone, "Introduction: Recent Art and the Everyday," in *The Everyday,* edited by Stephen Johnstone (London: Whitechapel Gallery; Cambridge, MA: MIT Press, 2008), 12–13; Mary McCleod, "Henri LeFebvre's Critique of Everyday Life," in *Architecture of the Everyday,* 28.

5. Michael Taussig, "Tactility and Distraction," in *Beyond the Body Proper: Reading the Anthropology of Material Life,* edited by Margaret Lock and Judith Farquhar (Durham, NC: Duke University Press, 2007), 259.

6. On the longer history of thinkers seeking a politics of the everyday to cope with modernity and the problem of conservative reification of local traditions, see Harry D. Harootunian, *History's Disquiet: Modernity, Cultural Practice, and the Question of Everyday Life* (New York: Columbia University Press, 2000).

7. "Nihonbashi," *Edogaku jiten,* edited by Nishiyama Matsunosuke et al. (Tokyo: Kōbundō, 1984), 28. See also Marcia Yonemoto, "Nihonbashi: Edo's Contested Center," *East Asian History* 17/18 (1999): 49–70.

8. Hasegawa Takashi, *Toshi kairō, aruiwa kenchiku no chūseishugi* (Tokyo: Sagami shobō, 1975), 65.

9. "'Nihonbashi' no ue o wataru hashi: Kōsoku dōro ga hashiru," *Asahi shinbun,* December 24, 1962, Tokyo edition, 12.

10. "Omona katsudō naiyō," Meikyō Nihonbashi Hozonkai official website, www.nihonbashi-meikyou.jp/main_act.html.

11. Hasegawa, *Toshi kairō,* 82–83.

12. Itō Shūichirō, *Jichitai hatsu no seisaku kakushin: Keikan jōrei kara keikan hō e* (Tokyo: Bokutakusha, 2006), 44–45. Based on broader criteria, the Ministry of Land, Infrastructure, Transport and Tourism counted 470 municipalities in 2004.

13. See the Ministry of Land, Infrastructure, Transport and Tourism publications at "Keikan pōtaru saito," www.mlit.go.jp/toshi/townscape/toshi_townscape_mn_000003.html.

14. Utsukushii keikan o tsukuru kai, eds., *Utsukushii Nihon o tsukuru: Ibun'ya 12 mei no toppu riidaa ni yoru rentai kōdō sengen* (Tokyo: Shōkokusha, 2006); Igarashi Tarō, "Minikui keikan gari," *10+1* 42 (March 2006): 22–24. The list, which received wide attention in the press and on blogs, featured seventy "bad" examples and thirty that had been improved. Igarashi notes that much of the response to the group online was negative.

15. The bridge structure had been designated an important cultural property by the national Agency for Cultural Affairs in 1999. Designation was the result of architectural historians' advocacy of more designations for Meiji-period structures rather than of campaigning on the part of the Nihonbashi Preservation Society.

16. Igarashi Tarō, *Utsukushii toshi, minikui toshi: Gendai keikanron* (Tokyo: Chūō kōron shinsha, 2006), 55–86.

17. Ōta Hiroshi, "Keikan no saki o miyo," *10+1* 43 (July 2006): 162–172.

18. This is a point made in general terms by David Harvey in "Heritage Pasts and Heritage Presents: Temporality, Meaning, and the Scope of Heritage Studies," *International Journal of Heritage Studies* 7 (2001): 319–338.

19. See the website of the "Return the Sky" group, www.nihonbashi-michikaigi.jp/index.html. For remarks on Nihonbashi and local *seikatsu bunka*, see "Dai 19 kai zadankai: Yomigaere Nihonbashi," *Tōkyō shinbun: Tokyo Web,* April 25, 2005, www.tokyo-np.co.jp/hold/2007/welove/CK2007031602102341. html.

20. Kobayashi Shin'ya, "O-Edo Nihonbashi to toshi keikan," *Edo o yomu, Tōkyō o aruku* (blog), November 11, 2005, http://skumbro.cocolog-nifty.com /edo/2005/11/post_3541.html; Kobayashi Shin'ya, "O-Edo Nihonbashi to toshi keikan, sono 2," *Edo o yomu, Tōkyō o aruku* (blog), November 19, 2005, http://skumbro.cocolog-nifty.com/edo/2005/11/post_e40a.html.

21. The critical literature on heritage is large. In specific connection to architecture and historic sites, one of the standard works is Robert Hewison, *The Heritage Industry* (London: Methuen, 1987). Along similar lines, although broader and less polemical, is David Lowenthal, *The Heritage Crusade and the Spoils of History* (Cambridge: Cambridge University Press, 1998); on the commodification of space in the postmodern city, see, for example, the essays in *Variations on a Theme Park: The New American City and the End of Public Space,* edited by Michael Sorkin (New York: Noonday Press, 1992). For a critical reevaluation of the assumptions underlying critiques of late twentieth-century museification, see Andreas Huyssen, *Twilight Memories: Marking Time in a Culture of Amnesia* (New York: Routledge, 1995), 13–36.

22. For examples of some of the extravagances of the bubble years, see Tsuzuki Kyōichi, *Baburu no shōzō* (Tokyo: Kabushiki gaisha Asupekuto, 2006).

23. Lowenthal, *The Heritage Crusade and the Spoils of History,* 249.

24. Miguel Tamen, *Friends of Interpretable Objects* (Cambridge, MA: Harvard University Press, 2001).

25. Frederic Jameson, *Postmodernism, or, the Cultural Logic of Late Capitalism* (Durham, NC: Duke University Press, 1991), 18–19.

26. Marilyn Ivy, *Discourses of the Vanishing: Modernity, Phantasm, Japan* (Chicago: University of Chicago Press, 1995), 241–242.

27. Marilyn Ivy, "Formations of Mass Culture," in *Postwar Japan as History,* edited by Andrew Gordon (Berkeley: University of California Press, 1993), 239–258.

28. I use the word *compose* here to contrast the preservationist relation to the past with a stance of reflection or critique, drawing on Bruno Latour's concept of "composition" as a form of engagement "searching for universality but

without believing that this universality is already there, waiting to be unveiled and discovered." Bruno Latour, "An Attempt at a 'Compositionist Manifesto,'" *New Literary History* 41, no. 3 (Summer 2010): 474.

29. Stephen Bann, *The Clothing of Clio: A Study of the Representation of History in Nineteenth-Century Britain and France* (Cambridge: Cambridge University Press, 1984), 30.

30. Fujimori Terunobu, "Kōkyo ga mitsukatta," in *Kenchiku tantei no bōken* (Tokyo: Chikuma shobō, 1986).

31. Matsuura Sōzō, *Tennō Hirohito to Tōkyō daikūshū* (Tokyo: Ōtsuki shoten, 1994), 57–78.

32. Cary Lee Karacas, "Tokyo from the Fire: War, Occupation, and the Remaking of a Metropolis" (PhD dissertation, University of Calfornia, Berkeley, 2006), 264–324. Karacas notes that focus on the firebombings would have relativized Japan's unique status as victim of the atomic bombings and might have complicated the narrative of Japan's suffering in the war since Japanese forces used incendiary bombs in China. See Karacas, 282.

33. Saotome Katsumoto, *Gomame no hagishiri* (Tokyo: Kawade shobō shinsha, 2004), 208–215.

34. These two examples are sample questions 2 and 6 for the level 2 test, included on the association website for the 2011 test, http://edoken.shopro.co.jp/test/index.html.

35. Yoshiharu Tsukamoto, "Architectural Behaviorology," translated by Steven Chodoriwsky, in *Behaviorology: Atelier Bow-Wow,* by Atelier Bow-Wow, Yoshiharu Tsukamoto, and Momoyo Kaijima (New York: Rizzoli, 2010), 11, 14.

36. Fujimori himself became a prize-winning designer in the 1990s. His signature buildings were low-tech and eccentric, accenting handcraftedness and incorporating natural accident. They reflected the same ideal of the self-built city that had motivated street observation. He served as commissioner for the Japanese pavilion at the Venice Biennale of 2006, where the theme was his own architectural work and street observation studies.

37. Kitayama Kō, "Dai 12 kai Benezia Bienaare kokusai kenchikuten kikaku gaiyō" (press release), Japan Foundation, www.jpf.go.jp/j/about/press/dl/0494.pdf.

38. See the Chiiki Bosai Machizukuri Sentaa website, www.tokyo-machidukuri.or.jp/.

39. Koizumi Hideki, "Roji o ikashita machizukuri ni mukete," in *Roji kara no machizukuri,* edited by Nishimura Yukio (Tokyo: Gakugei shuppan, 2006), 206–207.

40. Kibe Shigeru, "Tsukishima chiiki ni okeru machinami yūdō gata chiiki keikaku: Roji kūkan, Tsukishima rashisa o ikashita machizukuri," *Machinami* 31, www.tokyo-machidukuri.or.jp/machi/vol_31/m31_06.html.

41. For a review of these elements of Tokyo's bubble-era restructuring, see Machimura Takashi, *"Sekai toshi" Tōkyō no kōzō tenkan: Toshi risutorakuchuaringu no shakaigaku* (Tokyo: Tōkyō daigaku shuppankai, 1994).

42. Igarashi Takayoshi and Ogawa Akio, *"Toshi saisei hō"o tou: Kenchiku museigen jidai no tōrai* (Tokyo: Iwanami shoten, 2003); Hirayama Yō, "The

Governance of Urban Renaissance in Tokyo: Post-urbanization and Enhanced Competitiveness," in *Changing Governance and Public Policy in East Asia,* edited by Ka Ho Mok and Ray Forrest (London: Routledge, 2009), 303–325.

43. The notion of collective memory built over generations is developed in Maurice Halbwachs, *On Collective Memory,* translated by Lewis A. Coser (Chicago: University of Chicago Press, 1992).

44. J.B. Jackson, *The Necessity for Ruins* (Amherst: University of Massachusetts Press, 1980), 101–102.

Index

CPSIA information can be obtained
at www.ICGtesting.com
Printed in the USA
JSHW032125081220
10123JS00001B/17